PERFORMANCE OF HIGH SCHOOL CHILDREN IN PHYSICAL SCIENCE

PERFORMANCE OF HIGH SCHOOL CHILDREN IN PHYSICAL SCIENCE

By

Dr. S. Siddi Raju

Principal

K.K.C. College of Education, Puttur

Chittoor District

Andhra Pradesh

(India)

DISCOVERY PUBLISHING HOUSE PVT. LTD.

NEW DELHI-110 002

Published by:
Tilak Wasan

DISCOVERY PUBLISHING HOUSE PVT. LTD.
4383/4B, Ansari Road, Darya Ganj
New Delhi-110 002 (India)
Phone : +91-11-23279245, 43596064-65
Fax : +91-11-23253475
E-mail : parul.wasan@gmail.com
discoverypublishinghouse@gmail.com
web : www.discoverypublishinggroup.com

***First Edition:* 2012**

ISBN: 978-93-5056-112-6

Performance of High School Children in Physical Science

Printed at:
Shree Balaji Art Press
Delhi

Foreword

Education is one of the potent instruments in the development process. It is properly geared for that purpose. A man without education is like a flower without fragrance. Education strengthens the powers of body and mind. It is a life-long process. It is the most powerful and effective instrument for inducing radical changes in the behaviour of students. It plays a significant role in the development of human resources. In a democratic country, education can be used for giving training in a good citizenship.

Education is found to be an effective tool to bring the required changes in the society. The National Education Commission (1964-66) has emphasized that education is the one and only instrument that can be used to bring about a change towards the social and economic betterment of India. Further the Commission quoted: "India is now being shaped in her class rooms". It is not only a saying but also a reality. In the world, based on Science and Technology, it is the education that determines the level of prosperity, welfare and security of the people.

Scholastic/ academic achievement is of paramount importance, particularly in the present socio-economic and cultural contexts. Great emphasis is placed on achievement right from the beginning of formal education. A considerable number of students from schools go to the colleges and institutions of higher learning. It is very important to ensure that such students acquire the requisite competence so as to benefit more out of higher education. Setting the stage for achievement of youth is thus a fundamental obligation of the educational system.

Scholastic/Academic achievement has raised several important questions for educational researchers. What factors promote achievement in students? How far do the different factors contribute towards academic achievement? Many factors have been hypothesized and researched upon.

Though there are considerable number of studies on scholastic achievement related to sociological and psychological factors at primary and secondary/high school level, very few studies were found particularly at school level in Physical sciences. The present investigation entitled, "*Performance of High School Children in Physical Science*", undertaken by Dr. S. Siddi Raju is a presage - product study in the area of scholastic achievement. It is considered to strike at the combination of both psychosociological factors in the prediction of scholastic/academic achievement of IXth class students in Physical sciences.

I am confident that the findings of this study are of great relevance to the pre-service teachers, in-service teachers and teacher educators. I have no hesitation to say that the book will be useful in enhancing the quality of the teachers.

Dr. B. Ramachandra Reddy
Professor (Retd.)
Department of Education
Sri Venkateswara University
Tirupati-517 502. A.P., India

Preface

Scholastic achievement continues to be one of the most important variables held in high esteem in all cultures, countries and times. Hence, the research related to the area of academic achievement is an ever growing concern of the researchers, educationalists and administrators.

Scholastic/Academic achievement is a multi-dimensional phenomenon and may be effected by three main types of factors viz. subjective, objective and personality factors. Subjective factors are related to the individual himself, his intelligence, learning ability, aptitude, self-concept, perception of school, study habits and level of aspiration; Objective factors lie with in the environment, socio-economic status, family traits, education system, system of evaluation, school situation, type of the school, number of students in the class etc. Personality factors are related to the individuals' adjustment with the school environment, his attitude towards the subject, attitude towards the teachers, adjustment with his peers and emotional adjustment.

Though there are considerable number of studies on scholastic achievement related to sociological and psychological factors at primary and secondary/ high school level, very few studies were found particularly at school level in Physical sciences. The present investigation is considered to strike at the combination of both psycho-sociological factors in the prediction of scholastic/ academic achievement of IXth class students in Physical sciences.

Another interesting feature observed was that majority of the studies in the areas of scholastic / academic achievement confined to simple correlation analysis between predictor and criterion variables. Individual and cumulative effects of several independent factors on scholastic achievement could be assessed more accurately by employing regression analysis. Therefore, the main aim of the study was to predict the multiple effect of the independent factors on scholastic achievement of IXth class students in Physical Sciences and further to suggest suitable regression equations in the prediction of scholastic achievement of IXth class students in Physical Sciences.

Several psycho-sociological factors may contribute to the scholastic achievement. The present book is aimed to identify the influence of certain psycho - sociological factors on scholastic achievement of IX class students. The relevant data from 1800 IXth class students were collected.

The book is presented in six chapters. In Chapter 1 , brief introduction of the topic is given. Chapter 2 deals with a brief review of related literature. Chapter 3 deals with the present study. Chapter 4 gives an account of methods employed in the investigation. Chapter 5 consists of analysis of data, results and discussion. The last one forms the summary, major findings, conclusions, educational implications, recommendations and suggestions for further research.

It is just fitness of things to state that this book is prepared to meet the requirements of pre-service teachers and in-service teachers. I do not know to what extent I have succeeded in my attempt, but I will feel amply rewarded if this book can further the understanding of the concept 'scholastic achievement'. Any constructive suggestions for the betterment of this book will be greatly acknowledged.

Dr. S. Siddi Raju

Acknowledgements

I am deeply beholden to *Dr. B. Ramachandra Reddy*, M.A; M.Sc; M.Ed; M.Phil; Ph.D; B.L; Dip in Adult Education, Dip in Statistics, Professor (Retd), Dept. of Education, Sri Venkateswara University, Tirupati, who as guide and supervisor of my work warmly encouraged me and gave me excellent guidance and sustained my morale. In preparing my book, I had the privilege of being instructed by him in the essentials pertaining to my work with his invaluable suggestions throughout the course of my studies.

I would like to express my hearty thanks to *Dr. Dayakar Reddy*, M.A; M.Ed, Ph.D, Professor and Head of the Department of Education and Principal IASE, Sri Venkateswara University, Tirupati for his unending encouragement and valuable suggestions throughout the study.

I wish to express my deep sense of gratitude to *Dr. Y. Sudhakara Reddy* M.A; M.Ed; Ph.D, Professor, Directorate of Distance Education, and Dean, faculty of education Sri Venkateswara University, Tirupati, for his constant encouragement and good wishes to complete this work.

I owe a lot to the generosity and kindness of Prof. *V. Kodanda Rami Reddy* Department of Econometrics Sri Venkateswara University, Tirupati, for his timely help in statistical analysis of the data.

I wish to express my deep sense of appreciation to all the research scholars and non-teaching staff the Department of Education, Sri Venkateswara University, Tirupati, for giving me the source of strength and moral support, throughout the course of my study.

I wish to express my heartfelt thanks to all the Teaching and non Teaching staff of IASE, S.V. University, Tirupati for their kind co-operation throughout this investigation.

I place on record my special thanks to the principal and staff of the office of the Principal, SVU College of Arts and Education and Extension Studies, SVU, Tirupati.

I am thankful to the Authorities of Sri Venkateswara University, Tirupati for providing and extending the facilities to complete my research work.

I am thankful to *Sri C.S. Dinakar*, Proprietor and Sri *M.Ramesh*, Computer Operator, Students Xerox, Prakasam Road, Tirupati, for his timely computer typing, xeroxing and binding.

I wish to express my thankfulness to all the Headmasters, teachers and students of the selected schools for their kind co-operation and help in colleting the required data for my work.

I am highly indebted to my wife, children and relatives for their constant support and help in carrying out this work, without which, it would not have been possible for me to complete the work.

I have pleasure to express my thanks to my colleagues, friends and well wishers for their co-operation in completing this work.

I am highly thankful to *Sri Kuppaiah Chetty*, correspondent, K.K.C. College of Education, Puttur, for his encouragement and help in carrying forward this research work.

Finally I am thankful to one and all who have helped me in completing my investigation.

S. Siddi Raju

Contents

CHAPTER

1

Introduction

The word "Science" has its origin from a Latin word "*scientia*" meaning to "know". Science is both a body of knowledge and the process of accruing and refining the knowledge. The science education programme in secondary schools based on a sound pedagogical basis should be directed towards achieving awareness, knowledge, attitude, skills and participation. The science education keeps the students in programming learning experiences from simple to complex; to proceed from indefinite ideas to definite ones; ordering of learning experiences from the empirical to the rational; and to proceed from the concrete to the abstract. Science education being an important component of the educational system should contribute for the solution of the problems of the country by developing desirable understandings, skills, abilities, and attitudes among every one. The greatest challenge is to humanize science that is to make it relevant to human needs and aspirations.

Science Education is to a nation what protein is to a young organism. As a vital tool for the understanding and application of science and technology, the discipline plays the vital role of a precursor and harbinger to the much needed technological and of course national development, which has become an imperative in the developing nations of the world. Former President of India A.P.J.Abdul Kalam called upon the universities to turnout a global cadre of skilled professionals in science and technology to make India to realize its dreams of a developed Nation by 2020.

The huge potential of science to alter the very life style of an individual is gaining ground in these days. The utilization of science and technology can easily be visualized because science has made its supreme power felt in every field of life. Science teaching is mainly intended to provide the student with the right kind of education that will provide an understanding not only about the existing problem, but also to develop the ability to recognize and interpret signals for the future. No society can progress if it neglects the growth in the quality and content of education and research in science and technology. The knowledge of scientific approach and method is vital for coping with the day-to-day needs of life. Science has no doubt helped in eradicating the regional, religious and caste prejudices and also in building up correct values and appreciation of scholastic and democratic institutions. Owing to this huge potential of science, the status enjoyed by science in school curriculum is also high. Educators every where have always been trying their level best to instill in the children such qualities like scientific attitude and a spirit of scientific enquiry.

Physical sciences play a very important role in the life of human beings. In the modern scientific world physical sciences occupies important place in the school curriculum. Hence the achievement in physical sciences is crucial for every pupil, studying in the schools. If the teacher teaches in a planned and methodological way it is expected that achievement of children is certainly going to be satisfactory.

One cannot deny the importance of intelligence in predicting scholastic achievement yet, intelligence is not the sole determinant of academic achievement. Now a-days education is taken as the awakening of curiosity, development of interests, attitudes and values and building capacity to think and judge for one self. There is a need and accountability on the part of the teacher to this in the interest of the pupils.

Meaning and Definitions of Education

Education is the most important invention of mankind. Man without education would still be living just like an animal. It is education, which transformed man from a mere 'two-legged animal' into human. It helps him to behave like a man and prevents him from behaving like an animal.

The word 'education' is a diamond which appears to be of a different colour when seen from different angles. It is as basic to civilization, to social survival, as reproduction and nutrition are essential to biological evolution. Education of man does not begin at school, it begins at birth. It ends not when he graduates from the university but at his death. Hence education is a life long process. Education is the most powerful and effective instrument for inducing radical changes in the behaviour of students.

There have been a lot of controversial statements about the meaning of education, beginning from Socrates and Plato to Dewey and Gandhi. If it is not completely impossible, it is rather very difficult to assess the real value of the term 'Education'

Hereunder, we analyze the various view points of various thinkers about the word 'Education':

Education is a process through which a child makes its internal, external.

– Frobel

The development of all those capacities in the individual which will enable him to control his environment and fulfill his possibilities. By capacities is meant physical, mental and moral capacities. *– John Dewey*

Education means bringing out the ideas of universal validity which are latent in every human being. *– Socrates*

By Education, I mean an all round drawing out of the best in child and man-body, mind and spirit. *– Mahatma Gandhi*

Education is defined as natural, harmonious and progressive development of one's innate powers. *– Pestalazzi*

Education is the creation of a sound mind in a sound body. *– Aristotle*

Education is not a preparation for life ; Education is life itself.

– John Dewex

Education is the manifestation of divine perfection already in man.

– Swami Vivekananda

In a world based on science and Technology, it is the Education that determines the level of prosperity, welfare and security of people.

– Kothari Commission (1964-66)

Importance of Education in Human Life

In scaling the top pinnacles of education the expedition can be successfully accomplished by one who has the necessary physical, psychological and intellectual equipments. Education strengthens the powers of body and mind. It fits a man to perform Justly, skilfully and magnanimously all the offices private and public of peace and war. A man without education is like a flower without fragrance. Thus we can conclude that education is not only ambrosia for a novice or a neophyte but also a panacea for the ignorant and non-chalant.

The overall development of a nation depends on the proper utilization of its natural as well as human resources. The opinion of the planning commission in the 7th Five Year Plan (1985-90) may be mentioned in this context. "Human resources development has necessarily to be assigned a key role in any development strategy particularly, in a country with a large population. Trained and educated on sound lines, a large population can itself become an asset in accelerating economic growth and in ensuring social change in designed directions. Education develops basic skills and abilities and fosters a value system conducive to and in support of national development goals, both long-term and immediate".

Hence the development of human resource is a must for any modern society. As Swami Nathan remarks "Human resource is the most valuable global resource and any short or long term development strategy should be oriented towards the continued well being of human race".

Education plays a significant role in the development of human resources. If this change on a grand scale is to be achieved without violent revolution, there is one instrument only that is education.

Other agencies may help and indeed some times have a more apparent impact. But the national system of education is the only instrument that can reach all the people.

The school can help in manpower planning; though it has no direct role in the matter. It is a social agency and it has social accountability. Education is a social process and so it has a significant role in manpower planning in the light of individual as well as social needs.

In all the countries of the world, it may be seen that high per-capita incomes are associated with high rates of literacy. Education is valued because; it contributes to a better life. Alfred Marshall emphasized the importance of education as a national investment - it is the most valuable of all capital, invested in human beings. Economic growth in any society is dependent on education.

In a democratic country, education can be used for giving training in a good citizenship. It can produce leaders who are capable of independent thought, judgement, self-expression, originality and initiative emphasizing the importance of education. The Kothari Commission's report on Indian Education (1964-66) says, "In a world based on science and technology, it is the education that determines the level of prosperity, welfare and security of the people and the quality and number of persons coming out of our schools and colleges, will depend on our success in a great enterprise of national reconstruction, whose principal objective is to raise the standards of living of our people."

The development of a country is primarily determined by the quality of its human resources, which depend on the level of knowledge, skills, attitudes etc. Therefore, creating the right minds through the right process of education requires the top-most priority.

From the above discussion, it is clear that Education leads to the overall personality development (spiritual, moral, social, cultural, mental and economic etc). Therefore 'Education' is a must for any individual and for the development of one's country. The education is the key which allows people to move up in the world, seek better jobs and ultimately succeed in their lives. So, education is very important and no one should be deprived of it.

Need for Science Education

In the daily life of a person from the womb to the tomb science plays a vital role in all aspects such as food, clothing, shelter, social movability etc. Hence there is a need for each and every person to have a scientific knowledge which can be attained only through science education. Modern society is basically rooted in science. According to Jawaharlal Nehru, "Science education has developed at an ever increasing pace since the beginning of the twentieth century, so that the gap between the advanced and backward countries has widened more and more. It is only by adopting the most vigorous measures and by putting forward our at most effort into the development of science that we can bridge the gap. It is an inherent obligation of a great country like India, with its tradition of scholarship and original thinking and its great cultural heritage to participate fully in the march of science which is probably mankind's greatest enterprise today."

The Secondary Education Commission (1952-53) states that the science syllabus in the secondary schools is not directed to the production of scientists. Its aim is to give basic understanding and appreciation of scientific phenomena biological and physical which may prepare the non-scientist for a fuller and more complete life. At the same time, the courses should give fundamental principles to those relatively few who will latter specialize in science.

The Indian Parliamentary and Scientific Committee (1962) recommended that at the high school stage science should be compulsory for all the students, but it has to take the form of separate subject as mathematics, physics, chemistry, biological science etc., along with the other humanistic subjects. General science, should be made compulsory for all at the lower stage to enable every citizen to understand the modern world.

The Education Commission (1964-66) took a pivotal stand on science education. It saw science as a basic component of education and culture. It was not only necessary to take science as an integral part of our education but also urgent to raise the quality of science teaching to promote an ever deepening understanding of basic principles, to develop problem solving and analytical skills and to foster the sprit of enquiry and experimentation. The scientific outlook has to become a part and parcel of our daily living. India should strive to bring science and the values of the sprit together and in harmony.

Historical Development of Science Education

India is not a science-oriented nation. Its signal contributions in the realms of philosophy, ethics and religion have obscured its scientific aura. Certain sections in the *Vedas* and the *Upanishads* are replete with scientific information. There are references to the origin of the universe, the concept of atom, medicinal herbs and so on. The ancient Indians were experts in military science. Indian scientists and scholars did a great deal of pioneering work in the field of mathematics, medicine, astronomy, agriculture and architecture till about A.D. 600. The oldest Indian scripture, *Rig-Veda* which was written about 4000 years ago, refers to physicians and speaks of the healing powers of medicinal herbs. The concept of atom and the formation of the world were discussed in the *vaiseshika*, one of the *Upanishads*. The *upavedas* or secondary *Vedas* discuss various sciences. *Ayurveda* consists of six books, deals with surgery, nasology, anatomy, therapeutics, toxicology and a supplementary section of it deals with various local diseases.

From the point of view of methods and techniques of acquiring scientific knowledge there had been in our land, considerable development and refinement of observation. The early universities of Taxsilla and Nalanda could be taken as a first giant steps towards institutionalization of teaching and acquiring knowledge.

Buddhism, in its normal cause and as a part of its tenets (before AD 750 to AD 1000) discouraged further development of life sciences. Rules of caste became stricter and Brahmins, for fear that their blood would be contaminated withdraw from all practices of medicine. They even shrank from touching dead bodies and as a result the number of good physicians dwindled and public hospitals had to be closed. Later on the gradual conquest of the country by invaders from West Asia and Central Asia also brought an element of discontinuity in the ancient Indian tradition. There is however, some evidence to suggest that many of the scientific ideas brought to India by foreigners during the medieval period.

The modern period represents another sharp break in the traditions of scientific thought and practices in India which arose with the conquest of the country by the British. Modern science was introduced in India with the coming of the British rule and it stood in some opposition to the earlier two traditions especially because the new system was to be learnt in a foreign language i.e., English. Modern science came to India at a stage of its development which marks a radical change from the medieval and ancient sciences. Till the end of 18th century the universities sadly neglected the teaching of science and it had no place in the school curriculum.

In the early part of the nineteenth century a number of philosophical societies were at work for the spread of education. By the middle of nineteenth century however there were very few schools which were imparting instructions in science.

The most outstanding contributions to the history of teaching science are in the last quarter of nineteenth century. Since the beginning of the twentieth century there has been a substantial increase in the availability of equipments and facilities for teaching science in schools. In the year 1916 Sir J.J. Thomson had a committee which examined the position of natural science in the educational system.

As a consequence of the findings of this committee known as a Thomson report many advanced courses in science were added in many schools. As a consequence of all this, the Education Act of 1944 came into force in April 1945 which has meant an increase in the amount of science taught though not to the extent to which it should have been.

Radhakrishnan Commission (1949) made recommendations for improving laboratories and libraries. It was against narrow specialization in science and technology. The Commission opined that the curriculum of general education should have relevance to the student's physical and social environment and have sciences, language and literature at various levels upto the end of the secondary stage. The three-year degree course for science students should have two optionals like Mathematics, Physics and Chemistry and so on. Admission to P.G. course should be made on merit preferably on All-India basis.

The report of Secondary Education Commission (1953) recommended the teaching of general science as a compulsory subject in the higher secondary schools. In the year 1956 the all India seminar on the teaching of science in secondary schools held at Taradevi dealt with almost all the problems facing the inclusion of general science as a core subject for higher secondary classes. It was the first of its kind which touched almost all the aspects concerning the teaching of science in schools. It suggested a unique and uniform system of science teaching for the entire country, suited to its needs and resources. The Indian Parliamentary and Scientific Committee was set up in August, 1961 under the chairmanship of late Sri Lal Bahadur Shastri to study the problems of "Science education in schools" with a view to finding out the relation between the policies and decisions of the centre and the states in the matter of science courses attended in the schools.

In 1963 the USSR experts of the UNESCO planning mission visited India to study the implementation of technical assistance projects in the country.

In the year 1964-66 the Indian Education Commission was set up under the chairmanship of Dr. Kothari for upgrading school curriculum which recommends curriculum development, the revision of text books and teaching and learning material. The commission recommended that "Science teaching should be linked to agriculture in rural areas and to technology in urban areas.

The methods of teaching science should be modernized, stressing the investigatory approach and the understanding of the basic principles.

The State Institute of Science Education (SISE) have been set up in all states to effect improvement of science education in schools. The following are the main functions of the SISE.

1. In-service training to science teachers with a view to make them aware of the developments in science education.
2. Preparation of Instructional Material in Science.
3. Research on science education in the region.
4. Arrange for guidance service in science education.
5. Find out and introduce innovations in science education.
6. To actively take part in the national science programmes.

Today science is regarded with due admiration and respect. Learning science by doing is stressed and liberal grants are given to schools to built up laboratories and buy equipment. Mobile science laboratories supplement built in school laboratories. In-service training is provided to teachers teaching science at various levels. The importance of organizing science clubs in schools has been recognized. The science talent search scheme is being put into practice and aids are available to make teaching and learning effective.

According to National Policy on Education (1986) (NPE – 1986) Secondary Education begins to expose students to the differentiated roles of science, the humanities and social studies. Science programme will be designed to enable the learners to acquire problem solving and the decision making skills and to discover the relationship of science with health, agriculture, industry and other aspects of daily life.

National Policy on Education 1992, has laid great stress on the development of scientific temper among the students of all the classes. It has stated specially that Science Education will be strengthened to develop in the children the following:

1. The sprit of Enquiry 2. Creativity 3. Objectivity 4. The courage to question 5. Aesthetic sensibility 6. Problem solving and decision making skills and 7. Relationship of science with health, agriculture, industry and other aspects of daily life.

Importance of the Science in the Present-day Society

We are now in an age of rapid changes and science has been playing a dominant part in bringing about these changes. Science has provided the spring board for all the progress in our world and man has been able to conquer time and distance with its help. It has enabled man to probe into the vast space beyond the sky. It is no exaggeration to say that at present, science dominates every field of our activities. Science has improved the conditions and quality of living and has saved mankind from excessive toil and boredom. The technological advances have sought to explore and multiply the possibilities of affording more effective and responsible methods of providing sustenance and comforts to living creatures. Thus, from birth to the death, scientific discoveries and inventions have inextricably woven themselves into the febric of human existence.

According to Ross and Stanley (1955) our environment to a great degree is influenced by science. The clothing we wear, the houses in which we live, the agricultural methods which produce our food and necessities, our automobiles, our telephones, radios, TV, cell phones, the electrical appliances, are based on scientific information.

Science has specific applications in many of our activities. It is in operation in the application of the statistical methods. Psychology is a science applied for securing information regarding the working of the mind and without advancement of technology we would not be, at present, having any industry worth the name. When one postulates into the contributions of science to the various branches of human progress one can only marvel at the advances made in medicine, astronomy, agriculture, engineering, oceanography, mountaineering, aeronautics, space travel, microbiology, nuclear biology and innumerable other branches of scientific study.

The explosion of scientific knowledge has been so rapid in our age, that in every decade, our stock of knowledge on any subject has tended to become double or more.

In such an age of rapid scientific advancement every body must have some knowledge of science. We require trained minds, capable of coping with more and more problems relating to basic and applied sciences. For ensuring welfare of the people, the country has to undertake many programmes for achieving increased agricultural production, industrialization, community development, including various social services, providing people with better nutrition, better houses, proper clothing and improve health. For implementation of these programmes a very large number of scientists and technicians are required.

Finally, a scientific literacy is needed. First of all, be each member of a culture such as ours that is so thoroughly based upon technology and scientific endeavour. We believe that in order to make effective decisions in personal, civic and national affairs, the citizens must have some knowledge of processes and products by which he is fed and clothed, entertained and inspired and defended from enemies, foreign and domestic.

The Place of Science in School Curriculum

At the high school level, the beginning made at the earlier stage to introduce science as a discipline is to be further strengthened without emphasis on formal rigor. Concepts, principles and laws of science may now appear in the curriculum appropriately, but stress should be on comprehension and not on mere formal definitions. The organization of science content around different themes, as being practiced seems appropriate at the secondary stage, but the curricular load needs to be substantially reduced to make room for the additional elements of design and technology, and other co-curricular and extra-curricular activities.

At the secondary school stage, concepts that are beyond direct experience may come to occupy an important place in the science curriculum. Since not all phenomena are directly observable, science also relies on inference and interpretation. For example, we use inference to establish the existence and properties of atoms, or the mechanism of evolution. By this time, the student should have developed the critical ability to evaluate the epistemological status of facts that encounter in science.

Experimentation, often involving quantitative measurements as a tool to discover verify theoretical principles should be an important part of the curriculum at this stage.

Participation in co-curricular activities must be regarded as equally important at this stage. These may involve taking up projects (in consultation with teachers) that bear on logical issue and involve the problem solving approach using science and technology.

The various components of science curriculum indicated above should be integrated imaginatively. The entire upper primary and secondary should have horizontal integration and vertical continuity.

Science has now become a compulsory subject in the school curriculum because of its multifarious value to the individual as well as the society.

Science education in schools is more so emphasized as it improves concept development, fosters higher cognitive abilities and skills besides promoting the spirit of enquiry and experimentation.

In the past decades science lessons were mainly reading text books and hearing the teachers talk. There was practically no seeing and doing. We never saw the various articles of science apparatus, except in the pictures given in the text books or the drawing on the black boards. But now conditions have greatly changed. The pupils have more things to do and learn and to hear with the help of more number of audio-visual aids.

With respect to science and mathematics in past days it is observed that the time provided in the time table is not quite adequate, more number of periods were allotted to languages especially English language. But now the trend is changed. More number of periods were allotted to science and mathematics in the school time table with the other subjects.

The science courses in the past were mostly based on foreign books having no relevance or little relevance to the Indian science. But now the science courses were designed with the relevance of Indian conditions. It must address to the problems of Indian masses for example, energy, health, hygiene, disease, nutrition, conservation, pollutions etc.

The science courses of the past could not be very functional, because of lack of equipment, lack of teachers with proper attitudes, abilities and skills and the approach. But now most of the schools have well equipped laboratories and necessary science kits. These are helpful to teachers for demonstration as well as experimentation and give the first hand experience to the students. The method of teaching is also changed from teacher centered to activity centered.

It is time that the countries intelligentsia, educational planners, educational administrators, educationists, politicians, teachers and parents should give some serious thought to what direction the countries educational system should go and what should be the place of science in the curriculum. To quote this, the late Prime Minister of India, Morarji Desai, while addressing the members of the review committee on the curriculum for the ten-year school at New Delhi stated "The books that I did carry in college are being carried by school students today. The knowledge of science almost doubles every decade. We are to keep pace with this new development. Then the problem is how much knowledge in science should be given to a child at a particular level, so that he is not burdened." National Policy on Education (1968) also recommended that "Science and mathematics should be an integral part of general education till the end of class X. The quality of science teaching should be improved at all stages and scientific research should be promoted. Thus science has now become a compulsory subject in the school curriculum because of its multifarious value to the individual as well as the society.

The main features of the *National curriculum Framework for School Education – 2000* pertaining to Science education have been:

1. Teaching of environmental studies as a single subject of study at the primary stage instead of environmental studies (Science) and environmental studies (Social studies),

2. Teaching of 'science and Technology' in place of 'science' at the upper primary and secondary stages, so as to familiarize the learner with various dimensions of scientific and technological literacy, and
3. To continue the practice of teaching science at the higher secondary stage as separate disciplines: Physics, Chemistry and Biology.

Academic Achievement

Scholastic/Academic achievement has been playing an important role, since formal education decides the level of learning of different students in different subjects in all classes. Achievement can be defined as total marks or score obtained by a student in a particular subject. Achievement differs from student to student and from subject to subject. Factors for this difference also vary from person to person. Various factors play their role for this difference in the achievement. It has been observed that in subjects like mathematics, science and English, the achievement is considerably low; when compared to the other subjects, in the case of majority of students at secondary level, due to various factors.

Scholastic/Academic achievement is a multi-dimensional phenomenon and may be effected by three main types of factors viz. Subjective, objective and personality factors. Subjective factors are related to the individual himself, his intelligence, learning ability, aptitude, self-concept, perception of school, study habits and level of aspiration; Objective factors lie with in the environment, socio-economic status, family traits, education system, system of evaluation, school situation, type of the school, number of students in the class etc. Personality Factors are related to the individuals' adjustment with the school environment, his attitude towards the subject, attitude towards the teachers, adjustment with his peers and emotional adjustment.

Scholastic/Academic achievement has raised several important questions for educational researchers. What factors promote achievement in students? How far do the different factors contribute towards academic achievement? Many factors have been hypothesized and researched upon.

Scholastic/ academic achievement is of paramount importance, particularly in the present socio-economic and cultural contexts. Great emphasis is placed on achievement right from the beginning of formal education. A considerable number of students from schools go to the colleges and institutions of higher learning. It is very important to ensure that such students acquire the requisite competence so as to benefit more out of higher education. Setting the stage for achievement of youth is thus a fundamental obligation of the educational system.

In schools/colleges, great emphasis is placed on the achievement right from the beginning of the formal education. The school has its own systematic hierarchy, which is largely based on achievement and performance rather than ascription. The school/college performs the function of selection and differentiation among students on the basis of their scholastic and other attainments and open out avenues for advancement, primarily in terms of achievement.

The central aim of all formal educational efforts is academic achievement, on the part of the students. Even though, it is desirable to have all-round development as a goal of educational process, where academic achievement would be just one of the dimensions; but in most of the educational institutions, academic achievement continues to be the exclusive concern, narrowing down the very concept of educational process. Nevertheless it is important to note that achievement in curricular subjects is not an independent phenomenon. Rather, it is directly influenced by a number of factors, some of which are personal to the individual while many others are located in the environment in which learning process takes place. Thus in order to fully understand the concept, as well as, the process of academic achievement, it is imperative to identify and explore various factors related to the academic achievement

Need for the Present Study

Scholastic achievement continues to be one of the most important variables held in high esteem, in all cultures, countries and times. Hence the research related to the area of academic achievement is an ever growing concern of the researchers, educationists and administrators. Any enquiry into the previous works suggested that studies related to this area may be broadly classified into three categories. 1. Studies with sociological base.2.Studies with psychological base.3.Studies relating to both sociological and psychological areas.

Some outstanding studies conducted by Curry (1962), Chopra (1966, 1967, 1982), Gupta (1968, 1982) and Raymond (1977) have focused their attention mainly on sociological factors related to the academic achievement. The main emphasis on those studies, were on the variables, like socio-economic status, parental aspirations, family environment and so on.

In contrast, some of the prominent researches by Entwistle Kundu and Chakravarthy (1997) and Panda (1978) have in their own right, laid emphasis on psychological factors like personality, intelligence, adjustment, anxiety, self concept, motivation and so on in relation to the academic achievement.

"The destiny of India is being shaped is her class rooms" (Education Commission 1964-66). So there is a dire need for teachers to reflect, visualize, plan and act accordingly, so that the children of today can become world class citizens of tomorrow. The cognitive growth and academic development of the individual has become a matter of concern for the psychologists, sociologists and educationists. Day-by-day achievement related problems are increasing. There is growing awareness of developing ways and approaches for improving children's scholastic achievement (Pathak 2007).

Though there is considerable number of studies related to the sociological and psychological factors at primary and secondary levels, very few studies were found, particularly at high school level in science. The present investigation considered to strike at the combination of both socio-psychological factors in the prediction of academic achievement in physical sciences.

Another interesting feature observed was that majority of the studies in the area of academic achievement confined to simple correlation analysis between predictors and the criterion variables. Individual and cumulative effects of several independent factors on academic achievement could be assessed more accurately by employing regression analysis. Therefore, the main aim of the study was to predict the multiple effects of the independent factors on academic achievement and further to suggest a suitable regression equation in the prediction of academic achievement in physical sciences.

The achievement in physical sciences, particularly at IXth class level has been chosen, keeping in view the fact that physical sciences is a compulsory subject of study up to Xth class only and after Xth class, it is an optional subject. Those who develop interest and aptitude for physical sciences will only opt for physical sciences after Xth class. Since the students of Xth class are busy with the public examination at the end of the academic year, hence it is felt that there is a need for research study to find out the influence of various Psycho- Sociological and personal factors on the achievement in physical sciences, at IXth class level.

It is observed that the study of physical sciences and its importance is very much felt in engineering and technical fields. Today it is observed that there are innumerable polytechnic and engineering colleges and technical institutions. Without the sound knowledge in physical sciences at secondary school level, the students may not shine in their future studies in engineering and technological courses. Hence the investigator felt that there is a need to know various psycho-sociological and personal factors contributing for physical sciences achievement at IXth class level, so that proper and suitable suggestions and recommendations can be offered for physical sciences teachers, working in secondary schools.

Resume of Succeeding Chapters

Chapter 2 deals with an analytical presentation of research work conducted so far in the area, in which the investigator is interested to investigate further.

Chapter 3 deals with present study, which includes: Statement of the problem, Need for the present study, Operational Definitions of various terms, Objectives of Study, Hypotheses to be tested, Variables included and delimitations of the present study.

Chapter 4 deals with tools employed, methods of collecting data, and statistical techniques employed in the analysis of data.

Chapter 5 deals with analysis of data, and a detailed discussion of results of the present study.

Chapter 6 deals with summary of investigation, major findings, conclusions, Educational implications, recommendations and suggestions for further research.

CHAPTER

2

Review of Related Literature

This chapter deals with the internal review of the literature. It is an attempt to discover relevant material published in the problem area under study. This covers the empirical research studies done previously in the problem area. The studies conducted during the last few decades in the field of achievement that are more relevant and pertinent to the present investigation are discussed in this chapter.

Purpose of Related Literature

Review of related literature, provides a comprehensive understanding about what has already been known about a topic. It forms the basis for subscribing rationale for having chosen the problem for the study. Review of related literature allows the researcher to acquaint himself with the current knowledge in the field or area in which, he is going to conduct his research. It enables the researcher to define the limits of his study. It also helps the researcher to delimit and define his problem. The knowledge of the related literature brings the researcher up to date on the work, which others have done and thus state the objectives clearly and concisely.

By reviewing the related literature the researcher can avoid unfruitful and useless problem areas. He can select those areas in which positive findings are very likely to result and his endeavors would be likely to add to the knowledge in a meaningful way. Through the review of related literature, the researcher can avoid unintentional duplication of well-established findings.

It is no use to replicate a study, when the stability and validity of it's results have been clearly established.

The review of related literature gives the researcher an understanding of the research methodology, which refers to the way, the study is to be conducted. It helps the researcher to know about the tools and instruments, which proved to be useful and promising in the previous studies. It also provides an insight into the statistical methods, through which the validity of the results is to be established.

The important specific reason for reviewing the related literature is to know about the recommendations of the previous researchers, listed in their studies for further research.

Good, *et al.* (1941) analysed the purposes of review of related literature as given under:

- To show whether the available evidence material solves the problem adequately without further investigation.
- To provide ideas, theories, explanations or hypotheses valuable in formulating the present study
- To suggest the research methods to the problems
- To locate comparative data useful in interpretation of the results
- To contribute to the general scholarship of the investigator

Need to Know About Related Literature

For any worthwhile study in any field of knowledge the research worker needs an adequate familiarity with the library and its many sources. Only then will an effective search for specialized knowledge be possible. The search for reference material is a time consuming but very fruitful phase of research programme. Every investigator must know what sources were available in his field of enquiry, which of them, he is likely to use and where and how to find them. (Sukia et al, 1980)

According to Best (1959), Practically all human knowledge can be found in books and libraries. Unlike other animals that must start a new life with each generation, man builds up accumulated and recorded knowledge of the past.

Availability of adequate information about educational thought and research does not by itself result in possession of its knowledge by investigator. The investigator may be very keen to possess up to date information regarding his field, and may try hard to be posted up to date, and yet fails to get enough information due to non-existence of source of such information (Sukhia, 1980).

In the field of education, as in the other fields too, the research worker needs to acquire up to date information about what has been thought and done in the particular area from which, he intends to select a problem for research. But it is found that generally the extent of important, up to date information regarding educational research and ideas possessed by educational workers, is very limited (Sukhia, 1980).

The investigator should strive hard to be posted with necessary information, relating to his field of enquiry, basing on which, he has to build up his findings.

Academic Achievement in General

Academic achievement is of paramount importance, particularly, in the present socio-economic and cultural contexts. Obviously in the school/college level, great emphasis is placed on the achievement, right from the beginning of formal education. The school performs the function of selection and differentiation among pupils on the basis of their scholastic achievement and other attainments, which open out avenues for advancement in life.

The central aim of all formal educational efforts is academic achievement on the part of the students. Even though, it is desirable to have all-round development, as the goal of educational process, where academic achievement would be just one of the dimensions; but in most of the educational institutions, academic achievement continues to be the exclusive concern, narrowing down the very concept of educational process. Nevertheless, it is important to note that achievement in curricular subjects is not an independent phenomenon; rather it is influenced by a number of factors, some of which are personal to the individual, while many others are located in the environment, in which learning takes place.

Physical sciences is one of the subjects included in the school curriculum. The main concern of the investigator is to know various socio-demographic and Psychological factors which influence the achievement in physical sciences, which is considered to be one of the most important subjects in the school study. In this context, the investigator has presented some of earlier studies made in this direction.

There are number of studies relating to the scholastic/academic achievement done in the past. However only the literature pertaining to the independent variables used in the present study is referred in the succeeding pages.

In general terms, achievement refers to the scholastic achievement of the student, at the end of an educational programme. It is to this concept that the term achievement is referred here. To maximize the achievement within a given set up, therefore is the goal of every educationist, a teacher or an educational administrator. Research has been to our aid, looking into what variables - personal, home, school etc. promote achievement and what are the determinants to it.

A glance at the related literature reveals that a number of variables have their impact on the academic achievement or in particular achievement in physical sciences.

The present investigation took note of the above facts and attempted to treat some of the prominent intellectual and non intellectual factors as Psychological and sociological factors and coined it as Psycho-sociological factors. The influence of certain Psycho-sociological factors on the scholastic achievement in physical sciences of IXth class students is investigated.

Under Achievement in Physical Sciences

"Human talent is our greatest national resource. Its conservation and development should, therefore, be a primary concern of every one. When human talent is wasted, every one is deprived. When it is rightly developed, every one is benefited" Harriot (1963)

The wastage of talent is mainly observed in under achievers. In fact, under achievement is a crucial problem that needs urgent solution, so as to enable the society, to derive optimum benefits from the system of education. Though it is necessary to identify under achievement at different stages, during the course of the students educational career, there is a strong view that it is unfair to label a youngster as under-achiever. For once he is labelled so, he remains such for ever and very often the label is erroneous in many respects. This is a misconception in students, where they are backward or dull. A child, who is lagging behind in class, is considered backward. On the other hand, a child who does not fair well in class, even though his level of intelligence is normal or even above normal, is also considered to be backward, only because his educational achievements are not satisfactory. In many cases the teachers are not able to distinguish one from the other, and label both these types of children under the category of "Dull children". Under such circumstances, even the child of normal intelligence becomes unable to exert himself, as he is made to believe that he is dull.

The under-achievers have restricted themselves opportunity for higher education. At the same time, they have difficulties in obtaining a job. Many times these under-achievers who could have been of great use to the society, misuse their potentialities and become a nuisance to the others. They can create tension in the society by their violent behavior

The studies have proved that the large number of drop-outs at school level is because of under-achievement, especially in physical sciences is a single subject which has caused maximum wastage. Kothari Commission (1966)

while contemplating on the problem of underachievement has observed: "The group of under-achievers who are not intellectually dull but are not at least of average and may even be superior ability. The failure of such children should be of great concern to developing country like India which can not remain indifferent to this loss of potential man power within the higher ability range. Several factors like physical, intellectual, emotional and environmental contribute to the failure of under achievers to come up to the level of their talent abilities."

Dr. Akre pointed out that there are 18.46 per cent of under-achievers in mathematics at secondary school level. It is a very serious problem, because of importance of mathematics in daily life. Especially in new vista of 21st century, mathematics is one of the important subjects to enable to fit oneself into a changing world and make one ready to adopt one self to new circumstances. Right from human civilization, use of mathematics is very close for development of man. At the present 'competitive era', mathematics may be offered in various competitive examinations. It gets witnessed for 'all-rounder personality' of the child, one who knows mathematics. Physical sciences are closely related to mathematics.

Under achievers are the lots of large students population of our country, who are just neglected and left unmotivated, thus causing a great loss to the society, collectively and individually. Hence it is our duty to attend these under achievers and challenge to our educators, psychologists and national leaders. Hence necessary steps are to be undertaken to find the root causes for this under-achievement so as to eliminate the problem of under-achievement, thus reducing the wastage of talent.

Some of the earlier studies conducted on the impact of various Psycho-sociological variables on the achievement are presented in the following pages.

Earlier Studies Relevant to the Present Study

There are a number of studies relating to the scholastic/academic achievement done in the past. However only the literature pertaining to the independent variables, used in the present study, is presented here under.

Achievement and Educational Divisions

Educational divisions may have influence on scholastic achievement of the students. On the review of literature, the investigator has not found relevant studies with respect to the educational division and scholastic achievement.

Achievement and Age

Age of the students may have some relationship with their scholastic achievement. Some of the related studies are presented here.

Srivastava (1967) found that the relationship between the age and academic achievement is insignificant.

Har Govinda Gupta (1968) reported that no significant relationship existed between the age of the pupils and their academic achievement.

Asud Ulla, Prakasham et al. (1982) revealed that the age of the pupils was found to be not effective in bringing any variation in scholastic achievement.

Vyas (1982) reported that age of B.Ed students was significantly related to the total marks.

Quraishi and Bhat (1986) found that there is no significant relationship between the age and academic achievement.

Dowson *et al* (1999) observed that age is strongly related to the academic motivation and achievement.

Biswas (2001) investigated into the relationship between the age and academic achievement of distance education learners and found that age has no effect on their performance.

Govinda Reddy (2002) found that there is no significant relationship between the age and total marks of D.Ed students.

Suneetha and Mayuri (2002) found that age has significant influence on academic achievement.

Manchala (2007) found that age has significant influence on the academic achievement of B.Ed students.

Krishna Reddy(2008) investigated that age has no significant influence on the scholastic achievement of Xth class pupils in mathematics.

Banarugn (2009) showed that age has significant relationship with academic achievement. Age ($r = 0.33, P<.01$) was inversely related with respondents academic achievement.

Fayegh , Yousefi & Rumaya Juhari (2010) Studied that Age and academic achievement were significantly correlated.

Junani & Redzuan (2010) studied that age and academic achievement were significantly correlated ($r = 0.23, p< 0.000$).

It is observed from the above studies that there is controversial results showing the relation between the age and academic achievement of the students. Hence age is taken as one of the variables in the present study.

Achievement and Annual Income

Annual income of the family may have some impact on the scholastic achievement of students. Studies related to annual income and achievement, conducted earlier, are presented here under:

Fraser (1959) found higher correlation between income and scholastic achievement (r = 0.44), than between income and IQ (r =0.35)

Wiseman (1964) did not find any significant influence of father's income on the brightness of the child in the school.

Gopal Rao (1965) found a significant and positive correlation between economic status and scholastic achievement (r = 0.39)

Har Govinda Gupta (1968) found that except in the high intelligent group a significant relationship between academic achievement and their father's income, seems to exist, than in the moderate and low income groups.

Jagannadhan (1986) conducted a study on high school pupils and found that father's income had much impact on the academic performance.

Vijayakumar Sethi (1990) observed that the parents of high achievers of all four courses engineering, medicine, law and teaching were generally had better income than those of low achievers.

Bujendra Nath Panda (1991) found that IX and X class students with high income parents were better in their academic achievement, than those of students with low income parents. The studies of chopra (1964) and Khanna (1980) strengthened the above findings.

Jayachandrama Nadiu (1998) found that the influence of father's income is not significant on the academic achievement of learners from formal education (N=300); where as mother's income has significant influence on the academic achievement of learners of non-formal education (N =300) and total sample (N =600).

Krishnamoorthy (1999) observed that the economic conditions of the family has caused no significant differences in respect of academic achievement in History of the second year higher secondary students.

Govinda Reddy (2002) found that the family income has significant influence on academic achievement of DIET Students (N = 600).

Selvam and Sundaravalli (2002) conducted a study on 300 higher secondary students and found that the academic achievement has significant relationship with their economical, educational and vocational problems.

Thomas (2005) : Indicated that family income affects academic achievement. He indicated that students with low family income had low academic achievement

Manchala (2007) found that 'Annual income' of the family has significant influence on the scholastic achievement of B.Ed.students.

Krishna Reddy (2008) found that 'Annual income' of the family has significant influence on the scholastic achievement of X class pupils in mathematics.

Ekber Tomul and Kzim Celik (2009) investigated the effects of familial variables (education of the parents and family income) on the academic achievement (in mathematics, reading skills and science) of 15 years old students in Turkey with respect to regional diversity. The study was carriedout based on the data obtained from the PISA 2006 research in Turkey. The independent variables of the research are education level of the parents, and average annual income; the dependent variables the students proficiency levels in science, mathematics and learning skills. Familial variables affect students academic achievement in mathematics most and their reading skills least. As regional developmental levels decreases, effects of familial variables on academic achievement decreases as well.

Sanadaj & Junani (2010) showed that family income significantly affected academic achievement [(F(2) = 19.17; p = 0.000)].

From the above observations, it is clear that there is a difference in results with respect to the variable income of the family. Hence 'income of the family' has been included as one of the variables in the present study.

Achievement and Father's Education

Education of the father may have some influence in the academic achievement of the pupils. General assumption is that educated fathers would assist their children in their studies in the form of counseling and guidance. Hence there may be some relationship between the scholastic achievement and father's education. Some of the studies reviewed in this regard are given below.

Fraser (1959) found that there exists significant relationship between academic achievement and father's education.

Pavithran and Feroze (1965) found that there is no significant relationship between the scholastic achievement of X class pupils and the education level of the fathers or other members of the family.

Har Govinda Gupta (1968) observed that in the case of all the three (i.e.) high, moderate and low intelligence groups of VIII class pupils, no significant relationship seem to exist between subjects academic progress and their father's education.

Sarma (1984) found that father's and mother's education is highly associated with the scholastic achievement.

Jagannadhan (1986) found that high school pupils academic performance and father's education are significantly related.

Vijaya Kumar Sethi (1990) found that father's education has got much impact on the academic achievement of their sons and daughters studying in professional course (or) engineering, law, medicine and teaching.

Shamsuddin (1996) found that most of the secondary school male teachers were from families where fathers were not highly qualified, whereas most of the female teachers were from families with highly qualified fathers.

Krishnamurthy (1999) found that there is significant relationship between father's education and the academic achievement in history of second year higher secondary students. This gets support from earlier studies : Chatterjee et al. (1971), Khanna (1980) and Rajput (1985).

Grouws, Douglas and CebullaKristis (2000) stated that there is a positive relationship between educational level of the parents and students' performance in mathematics. But there is a considerable overlap in the performance of students from different educational background. Infact many students whose parents had a high school education or less scored higher than students whose parents had a university degree. Students whose parents were university educated, performed about two-thirds of a proficiency level higher than those whose parents had no more than high school education. However there is one important nuance to add to this finding. Students whose parents worked in an occupation that required advance mathematics skill, infact, performed almost one proficiency level higher than students whose parents had similar education levels and income but whose occupation did not require advanced mathematics.

Barbara and Rupa Das (2002) reported that:

1. Backward caste children of literate parents scored higher than the children of illiterate parents.
2. The academic achievement of first generation learners (i.e.) children of illiterate parents was found to be the lowest.
3. The achievement of girls was found to be comparatively better than that of boys.

Chakrabarthi and Sharmista (2002) observed that the education level of the family influenced female learners(N=320) literacy achievemnt attending to literacy centres.

Gnanasundaratharasu and Vincent De Paul (2002) found that due to video assisted instruction, there is no significant difference in mean achievement scores in social science among the primary school pupils of parents with below metric and those of above metric.

Govinda Reddy (2002) investigated that

1. Father's education and mother's education have significant influence on the academic achievement of DIET students.
2. Brother's education has significant impact on the total academic achievement of DIET students.

Panda (2002) revealed that V class pupils of college educated fathers had shown better achievement in mathematics.

Manchala (2007) found that, there would be no significant influence of 'Father's education' on scholastic achievement of B.Ed students.

Krishna Reddy (2008) found that, father's education has significant influence on the scholastic achievement of X class students in mathematics.

Muola (2010) studied relationship between academic achievement motivation and home environment among standard eight pupils. He found that there is significant relationship (r = 0.15) between father's education and academic achievement motivation.

It is noticed from the above studies that very few studies are found showing relationship between the scholastic achievement of students and education of father. Hence father's education is included as one of the variable in the present study.

Achievement and Father's Occupation

Scholastic achievement of the students may vary according to the occupational status of father. Some of the studies reviewed are presented here under

Pavithran and Feroze (1965) found that the occupational status of the parents highly accelerates the scholastic achievement of X class students.

Har Govinda Gupta (1968) found no significant relationship between academic achievement and occupation of the father in the case of VIII class students, except in the case of moderate intelligent group. Other research studies namely Fraser (1959), Alexander (1965) and Smith (1966) corroborate these results.

Rangaswamy and Visvesvaran (1977) reported that no definite pattern of correlation could be noticed between the academic achievement and occupational status of the family of XI class students.

Jagannadhan (1986) found much impact of father's occupation on the achievement of students

Bhujendranath Panda (1991) observed that IX and X class pupils (N=280) with skilled professional parents were found to be better in their academic achievement when compared with their counterparts. This finding is in agreement with the findings of Jammar (1964).

Jayachandrama Naidu (1998) found that the influence of father's occupation is not significant on the academic achievement of learners from formal education (N=300); whereas father's occupation has significant influence on the academic achievement of learners from non-formal education (N=300).

Govinda Reddy (2002) reported that the employment of father, brothers and sisters have significant effect on the academic achievement of DIET students in practical work and practical examination (N=600).

Panda (2002) investigated that father's occupation did not have any significant impact on the learning achievement of V class pupils (N=882) in rural, urban and tribal primary schools.

Manchala (2007) found that father's occupation has significant influence on the scholastic achievement of B.Ed students.

Krishna Reddy (2008) found that father's occupation has significant influence on the scholastic achievement of X class students in mathematics.

Muola(2010) found significant relationship (r = 0.22) between father's occupation and academic achievement motivation of standard eight pupils.

Achievement and Mother's Education

Educational status of the mother may have influence on the scholastic achievement of the students. If mother is educated, it would have an impact on the child's performance. Some of the studies reviewed are presented hereunder.

Pavithran and Feroze (1965) found that there is no significant relationship between scholastic achievement and educational status of the mother in the case of X class students.

Har Govinda Gupta (1968) found that there is no significant relationship between academic achievement of pupils and their mother's education.

Ranga Swamy and Visveswaran (1977) reported that no definite pattern of relationship between the academic achievement of pupils and educational status of parents, is noticed.

Sarma (1984) showed that mother's education is highly associated with the academic achievement of their sons and daughters.

Jagannadhan (1986) conducted a study on high school pupils and found that mother's education is not associated with the achievement of the pupils whereas father's education has impact on the scholastic achievement.

Vijaya Kumar Sethi (1990) revealed that the parents of high achieving students of all the four professional groups i.e., engineering, law, medicine and teaching are better qualified than those of low achieving students.

Bhujendranath Panda (1991) concluded that IX and X class pupils with college educated mothers are having better academic performance than illiterate or elementary class educated mother's.

Krishnamurthy (1999) revealed that there is significant relationship between academic achievement and education of mother.

Borbora and Rupa Das (2002) reported that backward classes children of literate mothers showed better academic achievement, than the children of illiterate mothers.

Chakrabarthi and Sharmistha (2002) observed that educational level of the mothers influenced female learners' literacy achievement attending the literacy centres.

Gnanasundaratharasu and Vincent Depaul (2002) inferred that due to video assisted instruction, there is no significant difference in mean achievement scores among the primary school pupils whose mother's qualification is below metric and those above metric.

Govinda Reddy (2002) investigated that mother's education has significant effect on the academic achievement of DIET students both in theory and total achievement.

Hijazi and Naqvi (2006) conducted a study on the student performance by selecting a sample of 300 students (225 - males, 75 - females) from a group of colleges affiliated to Punjab University of Pakistan. It was found that factors like Mother's education and Students family income are highly correlated with the student academic performance.

Manchala (2007) found that, mother's education has significant influence on the scholastic achievement of B.Ed students.

Krishna Reddy (2008) found that, mother's education has significant influence on the scholastic achievement of X class students in mathematics.

Muola (2010) found that there is significant relationship ($r = 0.14$) between mother's education and academic achievement motivation of standard eight pupils

It is noticed from the above studies that very few studies are found showing the relation between scholastic achievement of the students and mother's education. Hence mother's education is included as one of the variables in the present study.

Achievement and Mother's Occupation

Scholastic achievement of students may vary depending upon the occupation of mother. Some of the earlier studies are shown hereunder.

Pavithran and Feroze (1965) found that the occupational status of the parents highly accelerates the scholastic achievement of X class students.

Ford Dawson (1970) found that the employment of mother had no effect on the achievement of children either in a positive or negative direction.

Rangaswamy and Visvesvaran (1977) reported that no definite pattern of correlation could be noticed between the academic achievement and occupational status of the family of XI class students.

Bhujendranath Panda (1991) observed that IX and X class pupils (N=280) with skilled professional parents were found to be better in their academic achievement when compared with their counterparts. This finding is in agreement with the findings of Jammar (1964).

Ayishabi and Moly Kuruvalla (1998) found that there is no significant difference between mean scores of achievement motivation of pupils of IX standard of working and non-working mothers, for the total sample (N=871). The findings are congruent with the findings of Stein (1973) and Bal (1988) who found a positive effect of maternal employment on the achievement motivation of adolescent and college going children.

Goswami and Meenakshi (2002) found that children studying IX class with working mothers were more achievement oriented than the children of non-working mothers. Boys with working mothers were most achievement oriented than girls with working mothers.

Manchala (2007) found that mother's occupation has significant influence on the scholastic achievement of B.Ed students.

Krishna Reddy (2008) found that, mother's occupation has significant influence on the scholastic achievement of X class students in mathematics.

Muola(2010) found significant relationship (r = 0.26) between mothers occupation and academic achievement motivation of standard eight pupils

Achievement and Number of the Children in the Family

It is assumed that number of children in the family may have relation with scholastic achievement of students. Some of the earlier studies are presented hereunder.

Bhujendranath Panda (1991) observed that IX and X class pupils coming from small families were better in their academic achievement, when compared to that coming from big families.

Jayachandrama Naidu (1998) reported that family size has no significant influence on the academic achievement of learners from formal education centres (N = 300); whereas family size has significant influence on the academic achievement of total sample i.e. formal and non-formal education learners (N = 600).

Manchala (2007) found that there would be no significant influence of total children to the parents on the scholastic achievement of B,Ed. Students.

Krishna Reddy (2008) found that there would be no significant influence of total children to the parents on the scholastic achievement of X class students in mathematics.

From the above, it is clear that there were limited studies on the effect of family size on the academic achievement. Hence size of the family is included as one of the variables of the present study.

Achievement and Birth Order

Birth order means, the child born first, second, third and so on. Birth order may have some relationship with the academic achievement of the students. The investigator included Birth order as one of the variables in the present study. Some of the earlier studies are presented hereunder.

Jagannadhan (1983) found that the birth order of V, VI and VII class pupils did not have any significant influence on their academic achievement.

Bhujendranath Panda (1991) found that birth order of IX and X class students did not have any significant influence on their academic achievement.

Govinda Reddy (2002) revealed that the birth order of DIET students have significant influence on the academic achievement in practical and in total achievement.

Manchala (2007) found that birth order did not have significant influence on scholastic achievement of B.Ed students.

Krishna Reddy (2008) found that birth order did not have significant influence on scholastic achievement of X class students in mathematics.

Tenibiaje Joseph (2009) found that family size and birth order have no significant influence on academic performance of pre degree students of the University of Ado-Ekiti, Nigeria.

Achievement and Total Members in the Family

It is assumed that total members in the family may have some impact on the studies of the children and hence on the academic achievement. Some of the earlier studies are presented hereunder.

Bhujendranath Panda (1991) observed that IX and X class pupils coming from small families were better in their academic achievement, when compared to that coming from big families.

Jayachandrama Naidu (1998) reported that family size has no significant influence on the academic achievement of learners from formal education centres (N = 300); whereas family size has significant influence on the academic achievement of total sample i.e.formal and non-formal education learners (N = 600).

Manchala (2007) found that, family size did not have significant influence on the scholastic achievement of B.Ed. Students.

Krishna Reddy (2008) found that, family size did not have significant influence on the scholastic achievement of X class students in mathematics.

Tenibiaje Joseph (2009) found that there is no significant difference between family size and academic achievement of students in higher institution.

Muola (2010) found significant relationship (r = 0.26) between family size and academic achievement motivation of standard eight pupils

From the above it is clear that there were limited studies on the effect of family size on the academic achievement. Hence size of the family is included as one of the variables of the present study

Achievement and Sex

In a male dominated society, girls are deprived in all aspects in the society. Pre-determined notion of Parents, Partiality in treatment, restrictions in their mobility, lack of freedom, Social evils like dowry system, have been the biggest impediments in the progress of the girls in the field of education. Sex is one of the important variables in the academic achievement.

The following are some of the studies reviewed on this aspect:

Farquhan (1963) observed no significant relationship between academic achievement and sex of XI grade High School students.

Pavithran and Feroze (1965) found that there is no marked difference between boys and girls in the scholastic achievement of X class pupils. Both are more or less on the same levels of achievement.

Padmanabhan Nayar and Visweswaran (1966) found that there was significant difference between the achievements of urban boys and girls of X class. But however, they found that there existed a marked difference in the achievement of rural boys and girls.

Balasubramanian and Feroze (1966) found that there existed no significant difference in the achievement of boys and girls of urban locality, while there was some marked difference in the achievement in mathematics between boys and girls of rural areas of X class.

Gupta (1968) observed no significant differences between boys and girls of IX class in three variables (ie) academic achievement, intelligence and economic status.

Hargovinda Gupta (1968) observed that except, in the high intelligence group of VIII class Pupils, a significant relationship between academic achievement and sex appears to exist in both the moderate and low intelligence groups.

Vasantha Ramkumar (1969) found that there existed significant differences in the achievement of boys and girls.

Aggarwal (1974), Sharma (1976), Tiwari (1980) and Dubey (1982) have found that girls performed better than boys in all the school subjects.

Rangaswamy and Visveswaran (1977) found that there was no significant difference in the achievement of sports men and non sports men in SSLC (XI class) Pupils examination. However they said that girls who participate in sports are better achievers than boys. Sex difference is however not significant in case of non sports boys and girls.

Roach (1979) conducted a study on 206 boys and 212 girls from 5(five) urban elementary schools in Jamaica and found that the girls scored significantly higher than boys on a mathematics achievement test.

Dhalakia (1980) found no significant difference in the achievement of male and female teacher trainees.

Aruna (1981), and Chanda and Sunanda Chandira (1985) have reported that boys had better achievement than girls.

Asudullakhan et al. (1982) showed that sex of Pre-university students (XII class) was found to be not effective in bringing about any variation in the scholastic achievement.

Gupta (1983) found that girls on the whole, had better achievement motivation than boys and had higher academic achievement than boys. The relationship between achievement motivation and academic achievement is positive and significant.

Jagannadhan (1983) reported that sex does not have any significant influence on the academic achievement of V, VI and VII class pupils.

Gopalacharyulu (1984) found no difference in the achievement levels between male and female teacher Trainees (TTIs).

Watkins, Hattie and Astilla (1984) showed that there existed significant influence of sex, self-concept and intelligence on academic achievement of pupils.

Quraishi and Bhat (1986) conducted a study on 200 undergraduate students of M.S. University of Baroda and found that sex has a significant effect on academic achievement.

Ramaswamy (1990) observed no significant difference between boys and girls of high and low achievers.

Verma and Gupta (1990) revealed that VIII class boys belonging to the high environment group achieved significantly greater mean than boys belonging to the low environment group. However no significant differences were found in the case of girls of high, medium and low environment groups.

Bujendranath Panda (1991) observed that IX and X class boys of rural areas and urban girls were better in academic achievement than their counter parts.

Vijayalakshmi and Hemalatha Natesan (1992) found that XI class girls (N=50), have better mean academic achievement than boys (N=50) which is significant at 0.01 level.

Rama Rao and Sinha (1993) reported that the performance of girls in examinations at all levels of higher education was much better than that of boys.

Gilson and Judith (1999) observed that large differences were not found in mathematics achievement, quantitative ability of VIIIth grade girls from single sex schools or girls from Co-educational schools.

Sood (1999) in her study found that although girls achieved somewhat higher than boys, yet insignificant differences exist in their mathematical achievement.

Natesan and Susila (2000) reported that there is a significant difference at 0.01 level in the scholastic achievement of V standard boys (N=300) and girls (N=300) in Environmental Science.

Erllekka Kumar (2001) found that there was no significant deference in achievement in Physics between boys and girls: 1. The mean scores of achievement related motivation was higher for Girls than boys. 2. The positive correlations were found between the achievement related motivation and achievement marks in physics in respect of girls students studying in Tamil medium.

Govinda Reddy (2002) found that sex does not have any significant influence on the academic achievement of DIET students (N=600).

Panda (2002) observed that V class boys (N=478) and girls (N=404) studying in Urban, Rural and Tribal areas did not differ in their achievement in all the school subjects.

Suneetha and Mayuri (2002) reported that gender was found to be more important variable than IQ in deciding the high academic performance, as more girls were found among top ranking students of classes IX and X.

Gakhar and Aseema (2004) found no significant difference in the academic achievement of boys and girls of X class, in their Previous annual examination (Class IX)

Mohammad Khayyer and Philip Delaccy (2005) found that girls academic achievement was higher than boys academic achievement.

Abiam and Odok (2006) found that there is no significant relationship between gender and achievement in number and numeration, algebraic process and statistics.

Manchala (2007) found that 'Sex' has significant influence on the scholastic achievement of B.Ed students.

Krishna Reddy (2008) found that 'Sex' does not have significant influence on the scholastic achievement of X class students in mathematics.

Paavola Sapiyonja (2008) stated that a research group from Kellago school of management of North Western University headed by professor Paavola Sapiyonja conducted a study on the Proficiency in mathematics of boys and girls below the age of 15 years over 40 countries. The research group made a study on 2.70 lakhs students. The details of the study were given, by *Daily Telegraph*. As per the details given; in the worldwide average rate of efficiency in mathematics, girls average rate is 2% higher than boys. In Britan girls, average rate of scoring is 0.7% less than boys. Where there is no much encouragement for girls education, like in Tourkey, the girls average performance is 4% less than boys. If equal opportunities are given, the difference in scoring between boys and girls can be reduced.

Pondey and Faiz Ahmad (2008) conducted a study on a sample of 621 students of XI standard (Male adolescents = 417 and Female adolescents = 204) from, Azamgarh (Dt), Bihar (State) and found that there is no significant difference between male and female adolescents on the measures of academic performance.

Subramanyam and Srinivasa Rao (2008) revealed that boys and girls do not differ significantly in academic achievement.

Mohmood Alam (2009) revealed that a significant positive relationship between: 1. Creativity and academic achievement, 2. Achievement motivation and academic achievement.

Sam Willam Bassey and Joshua (2009) concluded that there is a significant gender differences in rural students of mathematics achievement in cross river state Nigeria.

Noorjehan & Wajiha (2009) concluded that many factors like mathematical creativity , attitude towards Mathematics and achievement motivation and low level of anxiety, influence the academic achievement in mathematics at secondary stage and recommend the inclusion of curricular and co - curricular programs to improve performance in mathematics.

Umadevi (2009) concluded that there is a positive relationship between emotional Intelligence and academic achievement. Male and female, arts and science students do not differ in emotional intelligence and academic achievement.

Chandran & Lim (2010) concluded that cognitive ability, gender, pre - maturity and social factors contribute to poor academic achievement during the early school years.

From the above observations, it is clear that there is a difference in the results with respect to sex and academic achievement and hence sex has been included as one of the variables in the present study.

Achievement and Religion

Cultural background of the students may have some influence on the academic achievement of the students. Community / religion may also have some impact on the scholastic achievement. With this view, studies related to community/ religion and achievement are presented hereunder.

Nair (1974) and Asudullakhan et al. (1982) found that religion of pre-university students (XII class) was found not to be effective in bringing any variation in the scholastic achievement.

Radhamohan (1998) reported that there is significant difference in the high school students academic achievement belonging to different religions viz.,Hindu, Muslim and Christian.

Kobal-Palcic *et al* (1999) showed that French pupils scholastic achievement was more, when compared to that of Slovenian pupils.

Regnerus Mark's (2000), study indicates that respondents' participation in church activities is related to heightened educational expectations and those more intensely religious students score higher on standardized Maths/ reading tests.

Haynie's (2004) study on the association between parent/child religious homogamy and delinquency by examining how adolescent academic achievement relates to intergenerational religious dynamics between parents and children.

Manchala (2007) found that religion does not have significant influence on the scholastic achievement of B.Ed. Students.

Krishna Reddy (2008) found that 'Religion' has significant influence on the scholastic achievement of X class students in mathematics.

Benjamin Mckune and Hoffmann (2009) indicate that the association between adolescents, religiousity and academic achievement is largely due to family, social capital, but the association between academic achievement and religious homogamy between parents and adolescents is largely independent of family and community social capital. In particular the highest achievement is predicted when parents and adolescents report similar levels of religiosity. The lowest achievement is predicted when parents report high religiosity and adolescents report low religiosity.

Rohani & Ahmad Tormizi (2010) : Studied that illustrated and identified significant relationship between students beliefs about importance of mathematics and beliefs on one's ability in mathematics with mathematics achievement.

Form the above shown studies, it is clear that there were limited studies showing the relationship between achievement and Religion. Hence Religion is included as one of the variables in the present study.

Achievement and Caste

In Indian societies caste system is special social evil. There are reservations in the name of the caste in educational institutions for making admissions and in the recruitment to the various posts in the government service. There are many associations in our societies in the name of the castes, for their upliftment.

Hence the investigator is interested in knowing the effect of caste on the achievement of marks in various subjects and particularly in physical sciences at secondary level. Hence caste is included, as one of the variables in the present study.

Some of the earlier studies made in this direction are presented here under:

Dubey and Mishra (1977) have reported that the school environment was significant predictor of academic achievement among upper caste, backward caste, the S.C and Muslim girls.

Jagannadhan (1983) observed that the academic achievement of forward caste pupils of V, VI and VII classes is significantly better than that of backward caste pupils.

Gopalacharyulu (1984) found that different castes of student teachers of TTIs had, same achievement of three variables: Theory, Practical and total achievement.

Kumaraswamy (1992) found that caste of the adult learners did not have any influence on their academic achievement in the case of reading, writing, arithmetic (3Rs) as well as total achievement.

Lidhoo and Khan (1990) Mehata (1992) and Singh (1993), have found that the academic performance of upper castes was significantly higher than that of scheduled castes, scheduled Tribes and Back ward castes.

Jayachandrama Naidu (1998) observed that the influence of caste is not significant on the academic achievement of learners (N=300) of formal education; where as caste has significant influence on the academic achievement of learners (N=300) of non-formal education and the total sample (N=600).

Dubey and Mishra (1999) made a study to find the determinants of academic success of scheduled caste (SC). Backward castes (BC), Muslims (MS) and upper castes (UC) of rural high school boys (N=400). Results suggest that there was no consistency in the prediction of academic success across the four groups.

Dash (2002) reported that ST students had the lowest percentage of passes in Higher Secondary Certificate (HSC) examinations in the state of Orissa. A considerable number of X class students of high schools, managed by Tribal welfare Department, Government of Orissa were detained and were not allowed to take H.S.C. examination.

Govinda Reddy (2002) found that caste does not have significant influence on the achievement in Theory and total (Theory and practical) achievement of DIET students (N=600)

Manjula (2002) revealed that the achievement of Tribal students was low, except in language and mathematics, which was only on border line of average performance.

Manchala(2007) found that caste has significant influence on the scholastic achievement of B.Ed students.

Krishna Reddy (2008) found that caste has significant influence on the scholastic achievement of 10 th class students in mathematics.

Achievement and Nativity/Locality

This variable is a neglected one in educational research, particularly the influence of nativity on achievement in physical sciences. As the investigator is interested in physical sciences, nativity is included as one of the variables in the present study to examine it's impact on the achievement in physical sciences. Some of the earlier studies in this direction are presented below.

Pavithan and Feroze (1965) observed that, the scholastic achievement of urban students of X class is significantly better than rural students in all the subjects.

Jagannadhan (1983) concluded that the Pupils of V, VI and VII classes from urban areas had better achievements than rural pupils.

Narayana Koteswara and Ramachandra Reddy (1998) showed that there is significant influence of locality on the reading achievement of high school pupils. Pupils in residential schools performed better than pupils in rural and urban. Among the three groups, pupils from rural areas were the lowest in their achievement.

Salinm Kumar (1998) reported that locality has significant influence on the achievement in biology of secondary schools pupils (N=700) at 0.01 level.

Krishna Moorthy (1999) found that locality has caused no significant difference in respect of academic achievement in History.

Prakash (2000) in his study concluded that urban students were better in their mathematical achievement when compared to the rural students.

Naresh Kumar Gupta (2002) reported that the achievement of majority of V class pupils (N=946) in slum area schools has been observed to be unsatisfactory, not only in mathematics but also in all other subjects.

Ponda (2002) revealed that V class rural students had shown better performance in all the school subjects, when compared to their urban and tribal classmates. (N=887)

Anice James and Marice (2004) studied the academic achievement in science among XI standard students (N=470). Students hailing from rural (N=199) and urban (N=271) areas have the same type of academic achievement in Science.

Gakhar and Aseema (2004) found that X class rural students significantly achieved better in their annual previous examination (IX class), than the urban students.

Panchalingappa (2004) concluded that there is no significant difference between rural and urban high school pupils of Devadasis in respect of their academic achievement.

Manchala (2007) found that nativity has significant influence on the scholastic achievement of B.Ed students.

Krishna Reddy (2008) found that nativity has significant influence on the scholastic achievement of X class students in mathematics.

Prabhu Swamy (2010) revealed that Government D.Ed College trainees have scored that better marks in fill up the blanks type , classification type and true / false type. Also they have scored better in total performance. Rural area D.Ed trainees scored better marks in multiple choice type-Match the following type and over performance. Urban area students have scored better marks in classification type and true/ False. So Locality has significant influence on the marks scored.

Achievement and Economic Position

Economic position of a family plays an important role in different aspects of an individual's life. There may be some significant relationship between the economic position and academic achievement of an individual. Some of the earlier studies made, on the relationship between Economic position and academic achievement of the students are presented here with

Rossi (1950), Gopal Rao (1956), Washburne (1959), Saini (1968), Lincoln (1969) and Srivastava et al (1980) found significant relationship between academic achievement and socio economic status.

Thorndike (1952), Cattell *et al* (1966), Meller (1970), Ahuwalia and Deo (1978), and Venkaiah (1980) found either negative or very low correlation between academic achievement and SES.

Pavithran and Feroze (1965) found that the relationship between economic status of the family and scholastic achievement of X class students is extremely low and almost negligible. There is no any conclusive evidence of either favourable or unfavourable influence of economic status of the family on the academic achievement

Rao (1965), Srivastava (1967), Bernstein (1968), Sudamma (1973), Ahuliwalia and Shyam (1975) and Sharma and Bhargava (1980) found very little and negligible impact of SES on the academic achievement.

Gupta (1968) revealed that the students of IX class with higher economic status and mental ability were better in their scholastic achievement, compared to those with lower SES

Anand (1973) observed the relationship of SES and academic achievement. He found that the relationship between the two existed even when the influence of intelligence of non-verbal as well as verbal types were partilled out. He revealed that there was some impact of socio-economic status of family on the mental abilities as well as academic achievement of students of classes VIII, IX and X.

Mennon (1973) in his study revealed that overachievement and under achievement were influenced by socio-economic and demographic variables.

Rangaswamy and Visvesvara (1977) claimed that no definite pattern of correlation could be found between socio-economic status and academic achievement.

Asud Ullakhan *et al.* (1982) showed that SES of pre-university students (XII class) was found to be not effective in bringing about any variation in the scholastic achievement

Shakiba-Nejad *et al.* (1983) observed a strong positive correlation between SES and academic achievement of the students.

Lal Singh (1984) found that there is no effect of socio-economic status on the academic achievements of XIth class students (N =200), when the students have intellectual ability.

Jagannadhan (1986) conducted a study on V, VI and VII class students and found that SES had got much impact on the academic performance.

Quaraishi and Bhat (1986) conducted a study on 200 undergraduate students of M.S University, Baroda and found that socio-economic status has a significant effect on academic achievement.

Ramana Sood (1990) found that there is no significant effect on academic achievement of Pre-Engineering students (N = 120) and their socio economic status.

Vijayalakshmi and Hemalatha Natesan (1992) found a positive relationship (r =0.46) between academic achievement and SES of IX class students (N =100) which is significant at 0.01 level.

Marcon and Rebecea (1999) observed that SES was found to be an important factor in the academic performance, with poorer performance noted for lower income students

Young and Deindra (1999) revealed that SES had certainly some impact on the overall performance of students. They found the effect of other variables like self-concept, class-room environment also, when they conducted a survey on 3397 covering 28 rural and urban schools in Australia.

Alam (2001) found that there is significant positive relationship between socio-economic status and academic achievement.

Saxena (2001) revealed that the students who secured first division in High school examination, belong to the middle socio-economic status, indicating that the SES had only a little effect on the academic achievement.

Karla and Pyari (2004) investigated into the relationship between family climate and income and academic achievement. The study finds in congruence with many research findings (Hari Krishnan 1992; Garg, 1992) that student achievement is found to be affected by the income status of the family.

Khan (2005) conducted a performance study on 400 students comprising 200 boys and 200 girls selected from the senior secondary school of Aligarh Muslim University, Aligarh. India. It was found that girls with high socio-economic status had relatively higher academic achievement in science stream and boys with low economic status had relatively higher academic achievement in general.

Manchala (2007) found that economic position has significant influence on the scholastic achievement of B.Ed students.

Krishna Reddy (2008) found that economic position has significant influence on the scholastic achievement of X class students in mathematics.

Achievement and Separate room for Study

Scholastic achievement of the students may vary according to the separate room for study. Some of the studies reviewed are presented here under

Krishna Reddy (2008) found that separate room for study has significant influence on the scholastic achievement of X class students in mathematics.

Achievement and Study Hours at Home

Scholastic achievement of the students may vary according to the study hours at home. Some of the studies reviewed are presented here under

Krishna Reddy (2008) found that study hours at home has significant influence on the scholastic achievement of X class students in mathematics.

Muola (2010) found significant relationship (r = 0.23) between learning facilities at home and academic achievement motivation of standard eight pupils.

Achievement and Works at Home

Scholastic achievement of the students may vary according to the works at home. Some of the studies reviewed are presented here under.

Krishna Reddy (2008) found that works at home has significant influence on the scholastic achievement of X class students in mathematics.

Meena Siwath (2008) revealed that boys of high home environment group achieved significantly greater mean score than the boys falling in the group of low home environment. The impact of home environment has also been observed in the mean value of scholastic achievement of girls belonging to high, medium and low home environment groups. Good quality of home environment had significant positive correlation with 'high' level of scholastic achievement.

Achievement and Study Habits

Individual study habits play an important role in determining the academic achievement of pupils in different subjects. The students performance in the class room depends upon several factors namely, the interest in the subject, study facilities, own study habits etc.

Most of the previous investigators pointed out that there is much impact of study habits on the academic achievement.

In this connection, it is worth mentioning the former president A.P. J. Abdul Kalam's views, on inculcating good reading habits in children and youth of the country. He inaugurated a book fair held in Delhi and told the people to encourage their children and students with the advice that if they give one hour a day exclusively to book reading, they will become a knowledge centre in a few years. To acquire the habit of reading is to construct for yourself a refuge from almost all of the miseries of life. Reading is certainly one of the best experiences, a child can have and habits developed at a young age stay with a person for the rest of his life. What a gift for a child! There is more treasure in books than in all the pirated loot of Treasure Island. The more that you read, the more things you will know. The more that you learn, the more places you'll go. Students who score higher on tests, tend to come from schools which have more library resources, staff and more books, periodicals and videos.

A wonderful thing about a book, in contrast to a computer screen, is that you can take it to bed with you. Reading is to the mind, what exercise is to the body. The brains of the next generation need to be sharpened so that we can make our dream to be one of the best in world come true.

Some of the studies already made previously on the relation between the academic achievement and study habits of the individuals are presented here under.

Woodruff (1940) found that study habits failed to show some definite relationship with academic achievement.

Gordon (1941) found that the coefficient of correlation between scores on study habits and course grades was higher when students were tested late in the semester than when tested at its beginning.

Wrenn and Humber (1941) found that there existed relationship between the study habits and academic achievement in general.

Mary Esther (1945) found that there existed statistically significant differences in the achievement of most successful students with good study habits and least successful students with poor study habits.

Burnett (1951) reported that the student who has taken the course "How to study" increased their scores, as compared with those who had not taken the course.

Corter (1955) found a moderate positive linear relationship between the study habits and academic achievement.

Brown and Holtman (1955), Patel (1981), and Chauhan and Singh (1982) found that there exists significant relationship between study habits and academic scores among school going children.

Noltan (1959) conducted an investigation into the relationship between study habits and achievement in general science and found that there existed no relationship between them.

Diener (1960) obtained the similarities and differences between over achieving and underachieving students and observed that the two groups differed significantly in their study habits, indicating a positive relationship between them.

Sinha (1960) found significant relationship between study habits and scholastic achievement.

Brown and Dubois (1964) revealed that there existed a moderate positive relationship between the study habits and academic scores.

Richard and verginia (1967) found a positive relationship between good study habits and achievement.

Samuel and Rao (1967) conducted a study on a sample of 500 pre-university course (P.U.C) students and showed that there is a significant positive relationship between the study habits and academic achievement.

Agarwal and Saini (1969) found that the coefficient of correlation between the study habits score and scores on achievement in mathematics of VIII and IX class students came to be +0.014. Although this index seems to be quite poor, it was found significant at 0.05 level of confidence.

Krishna Murthy and Rao (1969) conducted a study on 300 students. They observed that there existed significant correlation between study habits and academic achievement of urban students.

Sinha (1972) found that there is significant relationship between study habits and scholastic achievement.

Marentic-Pozaranik (1974) found positive relationship between study habits and scholastic achievement of IX Class pupils.

Girija, Bhadra and Ameen Jan (1975) made a study on the relationship between the study habits and academic achievement of first and final year students of under graduates of university of Agricultural sciences, Bangalore. They found the two groups differed significantly with regard to their study skills and achievement.

Asha Bhatnagar (1980) made a study on 600 students of X class of Delhi and found that there existed a positive relationship between the study habits and academic achievement.

Tuli (1980), Patel (1981), Chopra (1982) found that there was a positive relationship between study habits and academic achievement.

Premalatha Sharma (1986) reported that the underachieving rural girls significantly differ in their study habits from high achieving rural girls of IX and X class students.

Harbans Singh (1989) showed no significant differences in the study habits at different levels of achievement of X class scheduled caste pupils (N= 300). But boys were found to have significantly better study habits than girls.

Deb and Gravel (1990) reported that the study habits and the academic achievement of B.Sc., final year students are positively related.

Ruth Leef (1992) revealed that the development of study skills in IX and X class students resulted in improvement of grades.

Stella and purushothaman (1993) showed that there is no significant difference between study habits of under achieving boys and Girls.

Chitra, Thiagarajan and Santhana Krishnan (1993) found that the academic habits and achievement were positively related to intelligence of higher secondary students.

Ramamurthi (1993) found that despite the students possessing good intelligence, their academic achievement hampers due to the absence of good study skills.

Aruna (1994) found that study habits of X class Pupils have significant influence on their scholastic achievement in all the subjects.

OnTseka and Watkins (1994) found that the study habits are significantly correlated with school grades of first year school students in Hong Kong.

Rawat and Leela (1995) found that there was no significant difference between the study habits of boys and girls and their academic achievement.

Patel (1996) revealed that : 1. The achievement scores of the pupils having high and low general ability were significantly different. 2.Those pupils who had good study habits did get significantly more achievement scores than those who had poor study habits. 3. It was,found that sex and study habits interacted significantly in explaining achievement scores.

Varma (1996) found that the academic achievement in mathematics and general science is more or less same in the case of students with good study habits and students with poor study habits.

Kumar (1998) reported that there existed a significant positive correlation between academic achievement and study habits.

Gordan Darlene (1998) found that the students having good study habits possessed good achievement. Venden Hurl et al., (1998) showed that the study habits of medical students were correlated with their academic achievement.

Verma and Kumar (1999) found that : 1.The achievement in mathematics was positively and significantly correlated with the study habits of the Students.

Overall achievements were significantly and positively related to the study habits of students.

Sam Sanada Raj and Sreethi (2000) found that study habits and academic achievement of students are positively and significantly related.

Nagaraju (2001) concluded that the academic achievement in all the school subjects has positive significant influence at 0.01 levels on the Study habits of the pupils (N=1800).

Govinda Reddy (2002) found that study habits of a DIET students have significant influence on achievement.

Vamadevappa (2002) found that there existed positive and significant relationship between study habits and achievement of pre University students in Biology subject.

Archana and Mona Sharma (2002) conducted a study on 26 Grade-1 children in Indoor. The results found that the instructional material could positively influence the achievement of students.

Naveen Kumar Reddy (2003) reported that study habits and academic achievement are positively and significantly related.

Guravaiah (2004) investigated into the academic achievement of X class students in all the school subjects and found that study habits of pupils do not have any significant influence on the scoring.

Rajani (2004) observed that the academic achievement of Intermediate students (N=1200) in all the subjects including group subjects is positively related to their study habits.

Lakshmi (2004) identified positive relationship between study habits and achievements of DIET students.

Bhaskara Rao, Somasurya Prakash Rao and Bhuvaneswara Lakshmi (2004) have identified a positive relationship between study habits and academic achievement.

Ramana Sood and Dalcinder Kumar (2007) found that learners having good study habits have better academic achievement.

Manchala (2007) showed that all the ten areas of study habits inventory have significant influence on scholastic achievement of B.Ed students. Better study habits is associated with better scholastic achievement.

Krishna Reddy (2008) showed that all the seven areas of the study habits inventory have significant influence on the scholastic achievement of X class students in Mathematics. Better study habits is associated with better scholastic achievement.

Nalini and Ganesh Bhatta (2009) found significant relationship between study habits and academic achievement.

Achievement and Self-concepts

Self-concepts play an important role in the life of pupils. Muktha Rani Rasthogi's (1974) self-concept scale is adopted in this study to examine the impact of self-concepts on the achievement of IX class students in physical sciences. Some of the earlier studies showing the relationship between scholastic achievement and self-concepts are presented hereunder.

Manger and Eikeland (2006) studied that the effect of mathematics self concept on girls and boys mathematical achievement found that Norwegian elementary school boys showed significantly higher mathematics , self concept than girls. Boys also had a significantly higher mathematical achievement score than girls.

Thomas and Robert (2006) found that self concept of academic ability and to lessor extent, students study activity were positively associated with student achievement. Students self concept of academic ability ratings were also linked to students engagement in generative, proactive study activities.

Krishna Reddy (2008) found that self concepts have significant influence on the scholastic achievement of X class students in Mathematics.

Corlos and Rodrgvez (2009): Found that high students academic self - concept and unambiguous out come expectations encourage critical thinking, reflective approaches and academic performance.

Philias Qulatunde (2010) showed that students of secondary schools have good self - concept of themselves in performing well in mathematics.

Achievement and Personality

Personality of a student plays an important role in his/her scholastic achievement. Some Indian researchers have attempted to isolate the personality structure of good and poor students. A few studies are comprehensive, while a few others, have concentrated on specific aspects and dimensions of personality assessment. Some of the studies showing the relationship between personality and scholastic achievement are given below.

Cattell, Sealey and Sweeney (1966) claimed that High School Personality Questionnaire (HSPQ) was predicting the school achievement of the students.

Vyas (1982) observed that personality adjustment was significantly related to university practical marks.

Anuradha Joshi (1990) reported that the personality of class IX students, effected the academic achievement. The extroverts were found to benefit significantly more through the developed instructional strategy, as compared to the intraverts.

Vijaya Kumar Sethi (1990) studied the personality patterns of high achieving and low achieving students in professional courses (Engineering, Medicine and Teaching)

The major findings are:

1. High and low achieving students taken together differed significantly from each other on personality factors of Lower-higher scholastic mental capacity (Factor-B); emotional instability (Factor-C); experience conscientiourness (factor G); shyness-venture some ness (H); placidity apprehensiveness (factor O) and Low-High ergictension (Factor-Q1).
2. High achieving students were found to differ significantly from each other, on personality factors of Lower-higher scholastic mental capacity (Factor-B); desurgency-surgancy (Factor-F) and tough mindedness-tender mindedness (Factor-I).
3. Low achieving students were found to differ significantly from each-other on factors of reservedness-out goingness (Factor-A), Low - Higher scholastic mental capacity (Factor-B) tough mindedness-tender mindedness (Factor-I); trust placement suspiciousness (Factor-L) and Lower-higher ergictension (Factor Q4).

Mavi and Iswar Patel (1997) explored the relationship between academic achievement and selected personality variables of IX grade students. The personality variables are Personality adjustment, intelligence, self-concept and level of aspirtation. It was found that there was a weak relationship between the personality variable and academic achievement, in the case of tribal students. The non-tribal students, scored higher than the tribal.

Koteswara and Ramachandra Reddy (1998) reported that :

(1) All the 14 factors of HSPQ have significant influence on reading achievement of high school students in Telugu Language.

(2) Students whose personality characteristics were observed as outgoing, more intelligent, emotionally stable, excitable, assertive, happy-go lucky, superego strength, venturesome, tense minded, doubting, apprehensive, self-sufficiency, controlled and tense, performed significantly better on reading achievement in Telugu language, than the students, whose personality characteristics were observed as less intelligent, emotionally less stable, phlegmatic, obedient, sober, moral standards, shy, tough minded, vigourous, placid, group dependent, undisciplined and relaxed.

Panchanadhan (1999) found that maintaining emotional balance, among students, through a psychologist by using auto counselling increased their academic performance.

Nateson and Susila (2000) indicated that the choosen personality factors (cattell's children personality questionnaire) are not significantly influencing the achievement of V standard boys (N = 300) and girls (N =300) in the age group of 9 to 10 years studying in the schools.

Govinda Reddy (2002) investigated that, factors B, E,F,M,Q2 and Q4 of 16 PF have significant influence on the total scholastic achievement of DIET students

Kagade (2002) observed that 1) There was no significant relationship between educational adjustment, home adjustment and educational achievement of pupils (N=1941) studying classes VIII and IX. 2) There was a significant relationship between social adjustment and educational achievement.

Ayodya (2007) while studying the emotional problems of school children and their relation to life events and school achievement found that :

1. Boys out numbered girls in decreased scholastic achievement
2. Emotional problems did not have influence on scholastic achievement in the present study
3. Life events too did not have influence on scholastic achievement

4. No difference was found with regard to socio-demo-graphic factors and emotional disorders, scholastic achievement
5. No association was found between scholastic achievement and intelligence

Subramanyam and Sreenivasa Rao (2008) while studying to assess the impact of gender on emotional intelligence and academic achievement of secondary school pupils, concluded that :

1. There is no significant difference between boys and girls with regard to their academic achievement
2. There is no relation between academic achievement and emotional intelligence

Martinsen and Swanberg (2010) showed that conscientiousness and openness were mediated by the strategic and an indirect effect on achievement through the surface approach".

Anca Munteanu and Iuliana Costea (2010) showed that psychological personality type does not significantly influence school performance, meaning that students, even if have or not these personality features can have similar school achievements. Energetic pattern of personality and emotional pattern are not conditions for school performance in adolescents.

It is observed that few studies are found establishing the relationship between, scholastic achievement and personality of the students. Hence personality is taken as one of the variables in the present study.

Miscellaneous Studies and Achievement

Misra *et al* (1960) found that children coming from high home environment achieve better in schools than their counter parts coming from low family environment.

Morrow and Willianson (1961) while analyzing the back ground of the family factors responsible for higher achievement of physically challenged group children, concluded that more congenial home environment, less parent domination and sympathetic parental encouragement, have been found to be responsible for achievement of children.

Husen (1967) in his study "International study of achievement in mathematics; A comparison of twelve countries" found that boys were on the whole superior to girls in mathematics.

Husten (1967); Dave and Dave (1971) found that poor academic achievement was due the low educational standards of their parents

Lalithamma (1975) conducted a study on "some factors affecting achievement of secondary school pupils in mathematics". It revealed that

1. The average performance of pupils in mathematics was 23.14 with S.D. of 8.20 and the distribution was negatively skewed
2. There was significant difference in the performance of boys and girls in mathematics, the difference being in favour of boys.
3. The urban pupils were superior to rural pupils in mathematics.
4. Intelligence and interest in mathematics were higher in boys and urban pupils than in their respective counter parts.
5. The achievement in mathematics is positively related to intelligence, interest in mathematics, study habits and socio-economic status.
6. Studying lessons daily, studying mathematics by writing, repetition in learning spaced learning, over learning etc. influenced the achievement in mathematics positively.
7. Private tuition, electric light facilities, radio equipment for study etc influenced the achievement in mathematics.
8. Achievement of the first born was better than that of the last born, and
9. Achievement of the students of scheduled castes and tribals was lower than that of the total sample

Sharma (1977) made an attempt to examine the achievement of children in relation to the school system. He found that children of the recognized private schools achieved higher scores in Arithmetic than those of the corporation schools.

Desai (1979) found that low achievers of high school had high ability in mathematics and less favourable attitude to the subject ; they came from families with very strict standards or discipline, they were kept very busy in domestic work and did not receive any out side help for the study.

Sudha R Sinha (1980) in the study "Effect of school system on the competence of secondary school students", investigated into the difference between the system of private and government schools and how it influenced the competence of its students. Three aspects of the system were, examined-the material, organizational and human relations. The findings revealed that despite less physical facilities and higher workload, the private schools had better organizational structure and more competent students than the government schools.

Head (1981) found that extraverted boys and introverted girls did well within their own sex group, when they were given mathematics activities.

Gakhar (1982) in his article "A study of acquisition of mathematical concepts among VIII graders of different types of schools", clearly demonstrates the differential effects of the type of the school on the acquisition of the mathematical concepts by the students on the whole. He found that the students studying in private schools better achievement than those studying in government schools.

This achievement was due to the strict supervision by the principal and managements of private schools, better teacher- pupil interaction, good educational environment, teachers special care of the weak students, teachers interest in the study of the children and sense of security and guidance and counseling in private schools.

Chopra (1982) found that students achievement was not significantly different in different organizational climate of schools even at 0.05 level. There was no significant relationship between students' achievement and teachers' job satisfaction.

Lalithanhawla (1983) studied the causes of failures in science and mathematics among high school students of the Mizoram state and found that general standard of achievement in science was 33.24% as compared to 27.86% in mathematics. Students from urban areas and from privately managed schools and older schools did better than those in rural areas and government schools and newly established schools. The provision of good library, laboratory and special coaching classes are not related to the students achievement in these subjects.

Pattison and Grive (1984) studied whether sex differences contribute to special skills to tackle different types of mathematical problems. They found that boys excelled in problems related to measurement and proportion and in special problems, where as girls performed better in more abstract and deductive problems.

Davidson (1985) reviewed studies that compared students achievement in small group settings with traditional whole class instruction. He found that using small groups of students to work on activities, problems and assignments can increase student's mathematics achievement.

Chada and Sunanda Chandna (1990) observed that : 1. There is a positive and significant correlation at 0.01 level between creativity and intelligence of XI grade students', when the effect of scholastic achievement is partialed out.

There is a positive and significant correlation at 0.01 level between intelligence and scholastic achievement when the effect of creativity is partialed out.

There is negative and significant correlation at 0.01 between creativity and scholastic achievement when intelligence is partialed out

Venkataiah and Jayachandrarama Naidu (1990) reported that there is significant difference between academic achievement of dropouts (N=39) and

Non- Starters (N=261) at Non Formal Education Centres (NFE). The dropouts from formal primary schools are superior to non starters in their academic achievement at NFE centres.

Mac Aculay (1990) reported that there is a positive significant relation between academic achievement and home environment.

Yeh-Hsiang-Yeng (1991) reported that weak but positive correlation existed between achievement motivation and academic achievement.

Sundararajan and Dhandapani (1991) conducted a study on the achievement in mathematics of higher secondary students of Pondicherry. The important findings of the study reveal the following:

- There is no significant difference in the achievement of boys and girls in the case of Government and private schools.
- Urban students are better than rural students in respect of their achievement in mathematics.

Cobb (1991) and his colleagues found that students number sense was improved by a problem centered curriculum that emphasized students interaction and self generated solution methods. Students also demonstrated increased persistence in solving problems.

Kumar Swamy (1992) investigated that variations in the amount of General Ability possessed by the adult learners significantly effects their achievement.

Vyas (1993) found that academic failure was associated with lower affiliation, teacher control, rule clarity and teacher support variables.

Nwankwo and Kemjika (2003) found that the relationship between test anxiety and academic achievement were inversely proportional at secondary levels.

Varghese (1995) found that the achievement scores showed a systematic improvement with improvement in facilities of school and that the difference in the mean achievement scores between the learners in the last facility schools and the best facility schools was very large in both in Hindi and Mathematics.

Martin (1995) concluded that there was a significant relationship between academic achievement and home environment.

Slemmer (1997) found that required tutoring seemed to be an effective way of improving the academic achievement of marginal students of X, XI and XII grades.

Walberg and Paik (1997), Marjoribanks (1996), Walf Richard (1996), Martins (1995), Mc Robbie and Fraser (1993) and Mac Aculay (1990) reported that there is a positive significant relation between academic achievement of students and their home environment.

Khalid (1997) focused his research on factors affecting mathematics achievement and found that confidence, socio-economic status, gender, location of the school and school environment contributed significantly for the achievement in mathematics.

Shui Feng (1997) conducted a study on family influences and disadvantaged children's academic achievement. The study revealed that the academic achievement has been shown to be influenced by many family factors. It indicates that the authoritative parenting and children's academic achievement were significantly correlated

Sumangala (1998) in her article "Effect of tutoring on achievement in mathematics of Secondary School Pupils", found that home-tutoring in Mathematics, whether by parents or by sibling has significant positive effect on achievement in mathematics.

Wood (1999) found that discussion following individual and group work improves students achievement.

Molia (1999) showed that the use of inductive thinking models improved the achievement of the students in mathematics.

Panda (2000) found that

1. Rural students exhibited better performance in all the school subjects as compared to their urban and tribal class mates
2. Boys and girls studying in different areas did not differ in their performance in all the school subjects.
3. Non-SC/ST students performed better in mathematics as compared to their counter parts in rural areas
4. Children of college educated father had shown better achievement in mathematics, general science and language subjects in rural areas, where as children of middle income group had shown better performance in science achievement in urban areas.
5. Father's occupation and tuition did not have any significant impact on the learning achievement in all the three areas.
6. Students studying in urban schools had shown better performance in mathematics where P.G. trained mathematics teachers taught the subject.
7. Rural students performed better in all the school subjects where infrastructure facilities were available in the schools compared to the schools with less facility.

Dhall, Gautam, Autar, Ram and Sankar (2000) revealed that the teaching of students with low achievement with remedial materials prepared after diagnostic test increased their achievement.

Alam (2001) showed that:

1. The academic achievement of normal children was found to be significantly higher than that of learning impaired children in both boys and girls when taken together and when taken separately
2. The normal students were found to be higher in academic achievement.

Basantia and Mukhopadyaya (2001) indicated that academic achievement of secondary school rural students (N=320) was significantly related to their home environment, but the school environment was not significantly related to academic achievement, where as both school environment and home environment were significantly correlated to each other.

Christman *et al.* (2001) reported that a cost effective analysis was performed to determine the relationship between district expenditure and XI grade mathematics and reading achievement during 4-year period from 1995 to 1999. The study indicates that the increases on expenditures were accompanied by decreases in academic achievement.

Elegbelye and Akoda (2001) investigated that there existed a significant difference between the academic performance of pupils (N=150) of secondary schools from single and double parenting background. A significant difference was observed between the performances of father present, absent children in mathematics. Academic performance of children of mother present was significantly better than children of mother absent.

Rose and Elizebath (2001) examined the patterns of academic progress and outcome in different inner city school settings for African American and White, lower, middle and upper socio-economic strata students. They revealed that the overall academic out comes were higher for gifted students enrolled in the programme sometime during their school career than for general education students.

Soundaravalli (2001) found that the academic achievement of standard XII students (N=300) had significant relationship with physical problems and family problems scores.

Anuradha and Bharati (2002) found that a trend of negative association was observed between III, IV and V classes children (N=300) academic achievement and their amount of T.V watching. Watching only a selected programmes improved children's academic achievement significantly rather than watching all the programmes.

Basantia, Jaga Mohan and Mukhopadyaya Dulal (2002) revealed that Psycho-social constraints and academic achievement of high school students are negatively correlated with each other.

Panda (2002) observed that V class pupils (N=882), who were taking midday meal, free uniform, scholarships and free textbooks as incentives performed well when compared to that of not receiving any incentives.

Chakraborthi, Bhupal Prasad (2002) found that the urban and semi-urban students performed better when they were provided with multiple choice items and that the urban students performed better both in multiple choice items and non multiple choice items than semi urban students in mathematics.

Agrawal, Archana (2002) found that :

1. Significant positive relationship was found between academic achievement and intelligence.
2. Academic achievement was found to be positively related with their socio-economic status.
3. There was significant negative relationship between the academic achievement and size of the family.
4. Significant negative relationship was found between academic achievement and birth order.

Goel Swami Pyari (2002) in their study on the relationship of achievement and feeling of security, family attachment found that

1. Low achievement had a positive relationship with the feelings of security, where as the average and high achievement had a negative relationship with the feeling of security.
2. Family attachment and achievement scores were negatively related. A related factor responsible for higher educational achievement was parental attitude.
3. Feelings of security- insecurity were significantly and positively related to the family attachment.
4. Theoretical, aesthetic and religious values were positively related with achievement score, but economic and political values were negatively related with achievement score. Social value had a positive relationship with the average achievements but the low and high achievements were negatively correlated.
5. There was no difference in value pattern of low and average achievers where as high achievers gave the first preference to theoretical, value, than to social, political, economic, aesthetic and religious value.

Sharmaj Nidhi (2002) in their study examined the effect of parental involvement and aspirations on academic achievement of +2 students found that:

1. Parents of high and low achieving students exhibited differentiated behavioral profiles with regard to some dimensions of parental

involvement. Parents of high achieving students often provided academic guidance to them and also planned various cultural activities such as arranging picnics, dance show and other festivals.

2. Achievement scores of children belonging to high, average and low groups of parental educational aspirations were not equal.
3. The academic achievement scores were different for children belonging to different parental involvement groups.
4. High parental involvement group, scores higher on educational aspirations as compared to their counter parts in the low parental involvement group.
5. Higher parental involvement resulted in higher occupational aspirations of students.
6. High, average and low parental occupational aspirations groups yielded unequal levels of learning styles.

Mohanty (2002) conducted a survey to see whether components of family environment bear any relationship with academic achievement of gifted, underachievers and his findings were:

1. The mean score of boys was higher than that of girls.
2. The boys scored higher on cohesion, intellectual cultural organization, Moral and Religious emphasis, while the girls scored higher on conflict, achievement orientation and organization of components of family environment scale (FES).
3. Underachievers' academic achievement was significantly related with all components of FES except active recreational organization.
4. For underachieving boys no correlation between a component of FES and academic achievement was found to be significant. However in the case of underachieving girl's cohesion, independence and control components of FES were found to be correlated significantly with academic achievement.

Devi and Mayuri (2003) revealed that :

1. Family factors were not found to be critically important for the achievement of residential school children.
2. School factors like, qualified teachers, good physical facilities and classroom organization, checking of the curriculum and subject matter, time maintenance, impressive method of teaching and teacher student interaction contributed significantly to the academic achievement.

Rahman (2003) in his comparison of achievement in mathematics of eighth grade students of different ethnic groups of Nepal found that

1. There was significant difference among the four ethnic groups with regard to the over all achievement in mathematics.
2. Tamang students were found to be the best among the four groups in over all achievement in mathematics
3. The four ethnic groups differed significantly from each other with respect to the achievement, on knowledge in arithmetic
4. Ethnic groups significantly differed from each other with respect to the achievement on knowledge, skill, comprehension and application levels.
5. No significant difference was found between Tamang and Magar groups in knowledge
6. Sarkari children were found to be the lowest achievers on knowledge among all ethnic groups. Prakash (2003) found that :
   1. The ascendance, vigorous and persistent temperaments were significantly related with mathematics achievement in girls and total sample
   2. Among boys, the ascendance, accepting, vigorous, cooperative and tough-minded temperaments were significantly and positively correlated with mathematics achievement.
   3. The memory of the subjects was significantly and positively correlated to their mathematics achievement.
   4. Girls with low sociability appeared significantly higher in mathematics achievement than girls with higher sociability at high memory level only.

Suneel Kumar Singh, Saheen Malik and Singh (2003) in the article "Achievement difference of class II students in mathematics with regard to the area, Gender and social groups, reveal that locality affects the achievement in mathematics. Urban students were found better than rural students where as sex would not affect the achievement in mathematics.

Newankwo and Kemjika (2003) found that the relationship between test anxiety and academic achievement were inversely proportional at secondary levels.

Shukla (1981), Rao (1983), Bhattacharya (1986), Patadia (1987), Bharadwaj (1987), Deshmukh (1988), Doshi (1989), Duitta (1990), Mishra (1991), Vasanthi (1991), Bhatia (1992), Dandapani (1992), Prabha (1992), Rosali (1992), Srivatsava (1992), Hazelfaker and Deforah Jean (1997), Jackson and Jeanetha Williams (1997), and Sumangala (1998) conducted research on the improvcement of learning and teaching of school mathematics and found that :

1. It is generally seen that less importance has been paid to students attitude by the classroom teachers or researchers in comparison with considerable amount of attention, given to the cognitive achievement.
2. Mathematics, specially, can be quoted as an example in which very few attempts at measuring attitudes towards it's study have been made.
3. Mathematics is generally regarded as a difficult subject for study.
4. It is not so popular even at the college level where less number of students offer it for their studies. Even now models of teaching, innovations and modern techniques of teaching the subject, have not changed the situation.

Shahpur Nagappa and Panchalingappa (2004) while investigating the influence of the study habits, family climate adjustment and academic achievement of Devadasi, children of Karnataka State, found that:

1. There is no significant difference between boys and girls children of Devadasi in respect of their academic achievement.
2. There is no significant difference between rural and urban children of Devadasi in respect of their academic achievement.
3. There is no significant difference in interaction effects of sex and location in terms of academic achievement of Devadasi children.

Mehera (2004) found that :

1. Achievement in mathematics was significantly related to major learning environment, attitude towards the subject, mathematics.
2. Urban students showed significantly higher achievement in mathematics, better learning environment and better attitude towards mathematics than their rural counter parts
3. No sex-wise difference was found in achievement of students in mathematics.

Sensarma (2004) while attempting to determine the relationship between class-room interaction variables of different branches of mathematics and mathematics achievement and attempting to predict the achievement from interaction variables concluded that :

1. Higher values of Praise, acceptance of pupil's ideas, asking questions by teacher, pupil's response and the rate of class-room transaction are associated with higher pupil's achievements in mathematics.

2. Higher values of lecturing, criticizing and Justifying authority and silence and confusion are instrumental in lowering pupil's achievement in mathematics.
3. Teacher's tendency to react to the ideas and feelings of pupil's is positively and significantly related to the better achievements in algebra, arithmetic, and geometry.
4. Velocity of class-room transition is positively and significantly related to the achievement in algebra, arithmetic and geometry separately.
5. The pupil's initiation is negatively associated with mathematics achievement in all the branches, algebra, arithmetic and geometry.

Uma (2004) on studying the role of computers in the performance found that:

1. The achievement scores improved in the test conducted after the revision of the lesson by 'teacher'.
2. Thoroughly revising the lesson through computers has increased their performance, the best scores are when the revision is by the Teacher and when computers are not used.
3. Some of the interesting points observed by her are :
   (i) Learning through computers was high with below average students than with good students.
   (ii) The attention span and interest duration of the slow learners is comparatively, less than that of very good students.
   (iii) Very good and good students have better reading and comprehension skills. Thus they were fast on the computers. The below average students took time to read and comprehend. Thus they usually took more time to complete the work on computers.

Kumar and Anita (2004) from their findings revealed that :

1. Both the variables self-learning module and classroom environment can not be ignored in respect of their effect on achievement.
2. There was no interaction between mode of teaching and classroom environment.

Bose and Joshi (2004) studied the effect of parents involvement in the achievement of students and found that:

1. Children whose parents were involved in their education led a disciplined life at home and had better academic achievement at school.
2. Involvement of parents was also reflected in the activities that a child pursued in his leisure time.

3. It was found that parents could not reinforce the things, the children learnt at school and some children attended tutorials.
4. Tutorials did not help the children in performing better, rather the children who attended school regularly and received proper care at home, fare better.
5. The study also found that home environment that indoctrinates children into a disciplined life and healthy life style ensures better academic achievement.

Madankar (2004) observed that: 1. Residence, 2. Peer group, 3. Curriculum, 4. Classroom teaching and, 5. Evaluations have negative and significant relationship with academic achievement, where as 'food' and 'co-curricular activities' have negative and not significant relationship with academic achievement of school subjects.

Peria Swamy (2005) showed that the teaching and learning of addition and subtraction through activity based learning materials (TLM) improves academic achievement of IV standard pupils (N=30). 1. A significant relationship was found between student's perception of teacher's attitudes towards them and their academic achievement. 2. A significant relationship was found between the academic achievement of students and their self-perception.

Vamadevappa (2005) conducted a study to find out the relationship between parental involvement and academic achievement. His findings were :

1. There was positive and significant relationship between parental involvement and academic achievement.
2. There was a significant difference in the achievement scores of boys and girls of high parental involvement group.
3. There was no significant difference in the achievements of boys and girls of high parental involvement group.
4. There was significant difference between high achievers and low achievers with respect to the parental involvement.
5. There was no significant difference between boys and girls in their academic achievement.

Satya Prakash and Patnaik (2005) made a study to find out the effect of cooperative learning and found the following:

1. There was positive effect of cooperative learning on achievement motivation.
2. Cooperative learning has a positive effect on achievement in biology in terms of understanding, Knowledge and application of objectives as well as total achievement.

Dwivedi (2005) conducted a study to compare the educational achievements of students belonging to different categories of schools, according to their environment and found the following:

1. The students from schools with enriched environment had significantly better academic achievement than students from poor school environment.
2. The students who were high approval seekers had significantly greater achievement than the students who were low approval seekers.
3. Academic achievement of students of the urban schools was significantly higher than that of the schools of the rural schools.

Neetha George and Anitha Ravindan (2005) revealed that there is a linear relationship among accuracy in time perception, coping styles and level of academic achievement. In other words time consciousness or punctuality is a quality that would enhance the academic achievement. They suggested that these results can be considered in helping low achievers.

Manas Ranjan Panigrahi (2005) while studying the influence of intelligence and socio-economic status on academic achievement of high school students concluded that :

1. There exists a significant and positive correlation between academic achievement and intelligence. It is also found that high intelligence leads to better academic success.
2. There exists a low positive correlation between academic achievement and socio-economic status. It is observed that high socio-economic back-ground might not always facilitate high academic success.
3. It is found that there is no significant difference between boys and girls with respect to academic achievement.
4. The students having higher intelligence are high achievers in academic performance than students having low intelligence.
5. High socio-economic status has effected the girls greatly to be very conducive to high achievement and *vice versa* is the case with boys.
6. The girls of high socio-economic status are high achievers in academic performance than boys of high socio-economic status, boys of low socio-economic status and girls of low economic status.

Manoranjan Panda (2005) in his study on correlation between academic achievement and intelligence of class IX students concluded that :

1. There is significant difference in academic achievement of students studying in different categories of schools.

2. There is no significant difference in intelligence of students studying in different categories of schools.
3. There is low relationship between academic achievement and intelligence in different categories of schools.

Arockiadoss (2005) studied the correlation between study habits and academic performance of college students (N=025) He reported that the academic performance of college students is influenced by study habits.

Malvinder Ahuja (2006) studied the impact of parental involvement and socio-economic status of the family on academic achievement of IX class students. Their findings indicated that 1. Socio-economic status of the family and parental involvement were associated with each other 2. Socio-economic status and academic achievement of students were independent of each other 3. Academic achievement of high and low parental involvement group were not significantly different and 4. There was an interaction effect of socio-economic status and parental involvement on academic achievement of IX class students.

Annakkodi (2008) in her study entitled "study of scientific attitude of pupils of class XI and their achievement in Science, concluded that there was positive significant difference in the scientific attitude of students in relation to their achievement in Science.

The N.C.E.R.T. (2008): Conducted a mid-term national survey to gauge the learning achievement of class V children. The survey covered Eighty four thousand, three hundred and twenty two (84322) students, fourteen thousand, eight hundred and ten (14810) teachers and six thousand, eight hundred and twenty eight (6828) schools across. two hundred and sixty six (266) districts, in the country. The survey tested the learning achievement of class V level students in mathematical, environmental studies and languages. It concluded that 1. Mother's education is important than father's education. 2. The schools that enjoyed better infrastructure and facilities like T.V, computer, more number of teachers and community participation contributed ten Percent (10%) more in (E.V.S) Environmental studies, eight point four (8.4%) percent better in mathematics and Nineteen point six (19.6%) percent better in languages.

Appraisal

From the brief review presented in the foregoing pages it may be seen that a few studies have been carried on, in the area of academic achievement at secondary level and more particularly the achievement in physical sciences. Again by and large, except on a few variables the results obtained are not coinciding, which necessitates further exploration in this area. Further, studies on the relative impact of each of the several independent variables that effect academic achievement are rare to find.

Selection of some important demographic variables, sociological and psychological variables are supported by many other studies, even though, they are not exhaustive for obvious reasons.

It is an attempt to see the relationship between the academic achievement and various psycho-sociological variables. The area under investigation is novel and unexplored with respect to the IX class students and their achievement levels in physical sciences.

Further the study aims at providing some mathematical models with which it can be possible to estimate the academic achievement of IX class students in physical sciences. The need for research on the area of scholastic achievement in physical sciences of IX class students, is rather warranting.

The above crucial conditions lead the investigator to make an attempt in this area of scholastic achievement of IX class students in physical sciences in relation to certain psycho-sociological factors. Keeping all these observations in view the problem is stated clearly with its objectives and suitable hypotheses are formulated in the succeeding chapters.

Chapter 3

The Present Study

This chapter deals with the statement of the problem, title of the problem, need for the present study, purpose of the study, scope of the study, definitions of various terms, objectives of the study, hypotheses formulated, variables included and delimitations of the present study.

Introduction

Education plays a very prominent role in the life of human beings. The development of a country is primarily determined by the quality of it's human resources. India today needs effective and productive citizens with scientific and constructive thinking and positive attitudes. This need can be met by well-planned educational curricula, including a systematic Physical sciences at the school level.

At present in our country, there are five levels of education. Pre-Primary, Primary, Secondary, Intermediate and Higher education levels. Primary and secondary levels are considered very important, as they lay proper foundation in the life of the students.

Physical sciences forms part of the subjects of study at secondary level of education. Different education commissions set up by the government of India have stressed the need for strengthening the teaching of Physical sciences at school level. National policy of education 1986, made a mention about Physical sciences education as "Physical sciences should be visualized as the vehicle to train a child to think, reason, analyse and articulate logically. Apart from being a specific subject, it should be treated as a concomitant to any subject, involving analysis and reasoning"

The achievement in Physical sciences of IX class students is the primary concern of the investigator, in the present study. Physical sciences have been considered a difficult subject by majority of students at secondary level. Is it due to lack of proper teaching of the subject? or due to lack of proper attitude towards the subject or lack of proper encouragement or lack of proper study habits. One should ponder over it. But research in psychology has shown that "almost every subject can be taught in some intellectually honest form to any child at any stage of development, if it is properly taught". No system of education, no methodology and no text book, can rise above the level of it's teachers. If a country wants to have quality of education, it must have quality teachers. Hence the Physical sciences teacher plays a pivotal role in making the students to develop positive attitude towards the subject and to remove the fear of the subject.

At present, the state of teaching Physical sciences, in the majority of our schools is far from satisfactory. The rate of failures is considerably high when compared with other subjects. The Physical sciences teachers have to think over this problem of failures in Physical sciences or under achievement in Physical sciences and try to change the situation, by suitably finding ways and means of improving the achievement in Physical sciences. The investigator wants to find out the effect of various psycho-sociological and demographical variables on the achievement in Physical sciences at secondary level. It is against this backdrop that a comprehensive and constructive research work is felt necessary, relating to the achievements in Physical sciences, to suggest various ways and means of improving the achievement in Physical sciences of IX class students.

After reviewing the related literature in the area of academic achievement particularly the scholastic achievement in Physical sciences, the investigator observed that there were no studies on the effect of variables like 'number of study hours', 'time spent daily for Physical sciences and 'separate study room' etc. on the scholastic achievement. Hence the investigator has shown some interest to know the effect of these variables on the achievement of IX class students in Physical sciences.

Statement of the Problem

The present study is concerned with the finding out the effect of various psycho-sociological and demographic variables on the scholastic achievement in Physical sciences of IX class students of chittoor district, belonging to the different educational divisions (i.e) the four educational divisions of chittoor district. It examines the achievement in Physical sciences IX class students of the schools belonging to the above divisions. It establishes the relationship between the various psycho-sociological and demo-graphical variables and other variables namely study habits, self-concepts, personality factors, and socio-economic conditions of the students and achievement in Physical sciences of IX class students of chittoor district. It also predicts scholastic achievement with the help of different sets of psycho-sociological variables / independent variables.

Title of the Problem

The title of the present study is stated as "Scholastic Achievement of IX class Pupils in Physical sciences in relation to certain Psycho-Sociological Variables"

Need for the Present Study

In olden days, the system of education was totally different from that of the present day system. The teacher and the taught lived together and they had devoted their entire time for studies exclusively. Now things have changed, as civilization improved and with the explosion of knowledge, the life style of people is changed beyond imagination.

The societies have come under the impact of science and technology and as a result of which, there are many means and sources of learning. Various psychological theories came into existence, which have their impact on methods of teaching. Both the teachers and students have to adopt new methods of teaching and efficient procedures of learning.

Everybody needs some knowledge of Physical sciences in one way or other. It is felt that for an ordinary man, the knowledge acquired during primary and secondary level is sufficient. It is believed that Physical sciences is exceptionally a difficult subject. Its study requires some special ability and intelligence and hence everybody should not be burdened with the study of this subject. But the other view is that Physical sciences does not require special ability for its successful performance but it needs general intelligence. A dedicated and honest teacher of Physical sciences can make the learning very interesting and exciting, thus changing the attitude and outlook of Physical sciences. However it has been widely accepted for its inclusion in the school curriculum as a compulsory subject up to X class level on the recommendations of various Education Commissions appointed by government of India. It is clear that at the secondary level Physical sciences functions as a strong foundation for those who want to pursue Physical sciences at higher level. At the same time it functions as a tool to provide necessary Physical sciences skills for those who want to opt for arts, commerce, or humanities at higher level. Hence the role of physical sciences at the secondary level is very significant as it safeguards the interests of both types of students. Accordingly physical sciences teachers at secondary level have to realize the role of physical sciences and teach the fundamental concepts in the subject, thus creating interest for the subject among the pupils.

Syllabus in various subjects has been constantly under revision and so also in physical sciences. Various factors will have their effect on the achievement in various subjects and so in physical sciences. Having accepted the influence of various factors on achievement in physical sciences, the investigator desires to establish a relationship between achievement in physical sciences and various psycho-sociological factors and demographic variables. Scholastic achievement continues to be one of the most important variables held in high esteem in all cultures, countries and times. Hence the research related to the area of academic achievement is an ever growing concern of the researchers, educationists and administrators.

Academic achievement is of paramount importance, particularly in the present socio-economic and cultural contexts. There is a need to identify the psycho-sociological factors, which influence the scholastic achievement in physical sciences of IX class students, in order to draw conclusions and suggest, remedial measures, if any. It is rather interesting to know which of the variables of personality, study habits, Self-concepts, socio-demographic etc contribute to the scholastic achievement in physical sciences. There is a need to develop Mathematical models to explain the relationship between scholastic achievements in physical sciences of IX class students and psycho-sociological variables.

Though there are considerable studies on the scholastic achievement in relation to sociological and psychological factors at primary and secondary level school subjects, very few studies are found particularly in physical sciences of IX class students. The present investigation is to find the relationship between achievement in physical sciences and socio-psychological, and demographical factors and also to predict the achievements in physical sciences with the help of various independent variables. Further there is no much research studies showing the relationship of scholastic achievement of IX class students in physical sciences with sociological variables like caste, birth order, age, sex, and personal factors like time spent for physical sciences daily, total number of hours of study and separate room for study. Hence there is a need of research study to know the influence of the above factors on the achievement in physical sciences. The main aim of present study is to predict the multiple effects of independent variables on the scholastic achievement and further to suggest suitable regression equations in the prediction of scholastic achievement of IX class students in physical sciences.

The above crucial conditions lead the investigator to make an attempt in this area of scholastic achievement of IX class students in physical sciences in relation to various psycho-sociological factors.

Purpose of Present Study

In view of the important role of physical sciences in the modern world, it has been imperative for any nation or the world to promote physical sciences education in their respective countries. But physical sciences have been considered by majority of students as a difficult subject. Hence it is necessary for a physical sciences teacher, to know the factors influencing achievement in physical sciences. Learners motives, emotions, needs, attitudes, outlook and interests play a very important role in learning the subject. Certain factors like, parents' educational background, home environment, study habits, educational divisions, environment in the school, abilities, self-confidence, general habits, social environment and emotional feelings etc. may have some impact on the achievement of physical sciences. Hence every physical sciences teacher has to evince a keen interest in knowing the effect of these factors and act accordingly so as to make the students learn the subject effectively.

Physical sciences education provides a good Physical sciences background with the knowledge of concepts and theories. It also provides ability to apply Physical sciences concepts and knowledge of theorems to new situations. Sufficient Scientific skills are needed to meet the demands of the daily life. The fundamentals in physical sciences have got an immense practical value in life. The knowledge and skills in these processes can be provided in an effective and systematic manner, only by teaching physical sciences in schools.

The teachers of physical sciences are now required to up-date their knowledge in the subject. The physical sciences teacher will have to be essentially a learner. He must also have the knowledge of the factors which influence the achievement in physical sciences. Sound knowledge of the effect of these factors enable the physical sciences teachers to discharge their duties effectively. The variations in the performance of the pupil in physical sciences may probably be due to some personal, socio-demographic, psychological factors, which the physical sciences teachers are expected to know and hence the present study.

If physical sciences teachers are aware of factors influencing the achievement in the subject, they can accordingly choose the methods of teaching, use of teaching-learning materials and there by creating interest in physical sciences among the students.

In general, the examination results of IX class reveal that more percentage of students fail in physical sciences, as compared with other school subjects. Hence it is necessary for physical sciences teachers to know which of the personal, socio-demographic, psychological etc variables influence the learning and achievement of physical sciences. Hence the present investigation is taken up for the purpose of knowing the influence of various variables on the achievement of IX class students in physical sciences. The present study attempts to answer the following questions :

1. Whether there is any significant influence of demographic factors on the achievement in physical sciences of IX class students ?
2. Whether there is any significant influence of study habits of IX class students on their academic achievement in physical sciences ?
3. Whether there is any significant influence of self-concepts of the students on the achievement of IX class students in physical sciences?
4. Whether there is any influence of 14 personality factors on the achievement in physical sciences of IX class students ?
5. Whether there is any impact of socio-economic factors on the achievement in physical sciences of IXclass students ?
6. Whether there is any influence of personal factors like sex, Locality, Age, caste, birth order, number of members in the family, number of children's in the family, Mother's Education, Mother's Occupation, Father's Education, Father's Occupation, Religion, Income of the family, Economic position, Separate room for study, Study hours at home, Works at home , etc on the achievement in physical sciences ?
7. Whether it is possible to predict the achievement in physical sciences with the help of various psycho-socio-logical factors.

Scope of the Study

The main intention of the present study is to find out the relationship between scholastic achievement in physical sciences of IX class students and psycho-sociological factors, and demographic variables. The study habits, self concepts and personality factors are measured by using relevant tools. An achievement test is constructed with the help of senior physical sciences teachers and experts in the subject and standardized by the investigator, following the procedure described by Garrett in the text book "statistics in psychology and education." The score obtained in the test is taken as achievement in physical sciences (Dependent Variable).

Academic achievement depends on a number of factors. It is not possible to include each and every factor in this study. Only a few variables like, age, sex, locality, caste, educational and occupational level of parents, religion, economic position of the family, size of the family, Educational divisions etc. have been included in this study. Attitude of pupils towards physical sciences, intelligence of pupils, teachers' commitment and so many other variables having impact on achievement are beyond the scope of this study.

The study attempts to identify the type of relationship between dependent variable (scholastic achievement) and independent variables (psycho-sociological variables).

The study also attempts to predict the scholastic achievement in physical sciences with the help of different sets of independent variables.

The study also attempts to suggest suitable regression equations in the prediction of scholastic achievement of IX class students in physical sciences.

Operational Definitions of the Terms

The definitions of some of the important terms used in this study are given below:

1. Academic Achievement

(i) Knowledge attained or skills developed in the school subjects, usually designated by test scores or by marks assigned by teachers or by both.

(Good, 1973)

(ii) Accomplishment or proficiency, performance in a given skill or body of knowledge, progress in school theoretically different from intelligence but overlaps with it to a great degree.

(Good, 1973)

Measured ability and achievement level of a learner in school subjects or particular skills.

(Derek Rowntree, 1981)

Refers to performance in school or college in a standard series of educational testing.

(Teneja, 1991)

Accomplishment of specified objectives, past performance and what an individual or organization has accomplished in the past, in contrast with ability which refers to what an individual or organization can do now (in the present) or in future (Madhu Raj, 1996 and Singh, 2002).

Successful accomplishment or performance in particular subjects, areas, or courses, usually by reasons of skills, hard work and interest. Typically summarized in various types of grades, marks, scores or descriptive commentary (John Bellingham, 2004).

A measure of knowledge gained in formal education usually indicated by test scores, grade points, averages, and degrees (Madhu Raj, 1996; John Bellingham, 2004).

2. Scholastic

Used to denote relationship with school, for example, scholastic average. Relating to school or school men, pendantic (Webster's New Dictionary and Tresaurus,1975).

Of or concerning Universities, schools, education teachers etc (Della Thompson, 1996)

Pertaining to or characteristic of scholar's education or schools (Britannica Word Language Dictionary, 1961)

3. Achievement

(i) Accomplishment or proficiency of performance in a given skill orbody of knowledge. ii) Progress in school, theoretically different from intelligence but overlaps with it to a great degree (Good, 1973)

Refers to the performance in school or college in a standardized series of educational tests (Taneja, 1991)

4. Academic

Pertaining to the fields of English, Foreign language, History, Economics, Physical sciences and Science. (Good, 1973)

(i) A scholarly teacher and / or researcher in higher education. ii) Relating to the school activities especially when concerning a discipline or a subject, not necessarily at higher educational level. **(Derek Rowntree, 1981)**

5. Achievement Test

A test designed to measure a person's knowledge, skills, understandings etc in a given field, taught in school, for example a physical sciences test or an English test etc (Good, 1973)

Refers to a test designed to measure the effects of specific teaching or training in an area of the curriculum. (Taneja, 1991)

A standardized test designed to measure and compare levels of knowledge and understanding, in a given subject already learned (John Bellingham, 2004)

In the present contest, achievement test means, an Objective Achievement Test (OAT) constructed and standardized by the investigator.

6. Objective Test

Any examining device, whose scoring is not dependent upon the discretion of the examiners. In a psychological testing, any test for which the use of subjective judgement, by test scores is virtually eliminated, so that, qualified educators, scoring the test independently, would derive essentially the same scores (John Bellingham, 2004)

7. Personality

A psychological term that refers to the predictable and unique indicators of the way, an individual might respond to the environment. A personal reference that usually Connotes acceptance ability and likeability. (Madhu Raj, 1996; John Bellingham, 2004).

Personality is that which permits a prediction of what a person will do in a given situation.

(Cattell, 1970)

The total psychological and social reactions of an individual, the synthesis of his subjective, emotional and mental life, his behaviour, and his reactions to the environment; the unique or individual traits of a person are connoted to a seller degree by "personality" than by the term "character".

(Good, 1973)

For individual all the aspects of behaviour, thought and feeling that make the person unique. For psychologists a major area of theory and research.

(Derek Rowntree, 1981)

8. Personality Trait

A general aspect of a person that may pre-dispose how he or she reacts to particular situations (Madhu Raj, 1996; John Bellingham, 2004)

9. Socio-Economic-Status

The background or standing of one or more persons in the society on the basis of both social class and financial situation. (John Bellingham, 2004)

The level indicative of both economic positions of an individual or group (Good, 1973).

A person's status or position within the society (or any smaller social group) as determined by social class and wealth or income (Derek Rowntree, 1981).

An indicator of an individual or family's social ranking, based on such factors as level of education, income, neighborhood of residence or type of occupation (Madhu Raj, 1996; Ring, 2002).

The background or standing of one or more persons in the society on the basis of both of social class and financial situation (John Bellingham, 2004).

10. Factor

(i) An element in the composition of any thing or in bringing about a certain result. ii) A fact, which has to be taken into account or which affects the course of events. (Davidson *et al*, 1998)

11. Teacher

A person employed in an official capacity for the purpose of guiding and directing the learning experiences of pupils or students in an educational situation, whether public or private (Good, 1973).

12. Study Habits

(i) The basic features involved in the application of mind to a problem or subject. (ii) The academic pattern which an individual follows in learning about things and people (Good, 1973).

The evaluation of pupils behavior in terms of attitudes, appreciation and habits of work is fundamental to a well-rounded study of out comes of the teaching (NSSE, 1935).

Study habits include student's habits of concentration, note taking, time budgeting and study methods (Smith, 1951).

13. Self Concept

An individuals perception of himself, as a person, which includes his abilities, appearance, performance in his job, and phases of daily living (Good, 1973).

How a person sees himself (e.g competent, amusing, homely etc). This may differ from other people's views of him, though they will have influenced it. (Derek Rowntree, 1981).

Self-concept refers to the picture or image, a person has of himself (Taneja, 1991; A group of Experts 2003).

(i) An individual's perception of self. (ii) A psychological contact that is more complex, than implied or assumed by most educators. (Madhu Raj, 1996).

14. Class

A group of pupils or students scheduled to report regularly at a particular time to a particular teacher (Good, 1973).

(i) A group of students assigned to one or more teachers or other staff members for a given period of time for instruction or other activity in a situation where the teacher(s) and students are in presence of each other. (ii) All students in the same grade level such as fifth grade class or tenth grade class. (iii)The group of students who graduate at the same time. (Madhu Raj, 1996 and Singh, 2002).

15. Secondary School

Schools with classes VI to X are called high schools or secondary schools in the state of Andhra Pradesh in India. There will be a public examination at the end of VII and X classes in these schools in Andhra Pradesh.

16. Physical Sciences

One of the compulsory subjects of study from VIII class to X class in schools of Andhra Pradesh.

Physical sciences is the science dealing physical and chemical properties of materials. which draws necessary conclusions after experimentation.

Physical sciences is a way to settle in the mind a habit of reasoning.

17. Educational Divisions

For the present study, the investigator has taken the four existing educational divisions in Chittoor District, namely, Chittoor Division, Tirupathi Division, Madanapalle Division and Puttur Division. In this study, schools under the authority of Zilla Parishad, Government, municipalities, Private unaided have been considered for present investigation.

18. Nativity/Locality

The scholastic achievements of students coming from rural areas (villages), semi Urban areas (small towns) and Urban Areas (municipal areas) may differ. Hence students are divided into three groups namely rural, semi urban and urban students and scholastic achievements have been studied. In this investigation locality means rural, semi-urban and urban.

19. Caste

In the present educational system, which is in vogue, in Andhra Pradesh, students are categorized into scheduled castes and scheduled tribes, back ward castes and other castes not covered under the above two types. In the present investigation the students are divided into three categories basing on their caste, namely SC/ST, BC and OC students.

20. Sex

Male (Boys) and Female (Girls) students are considered as sub samples to carry the differential analysis.

21. Age

The chronological age of the students as reported by them through the personal data sheet is considered to study the variations in their achievements.

22. Size of the family

It refers to the number of total living members of the family.

23. Sample

(i) A sample possessing the same characteristics as the population with reference to some variables other than, but thought of to be related to, the one under investigation. (ii) Some times used to refer to a stratified sample, in which the sub sample numbers are proportional to the size of the strata (Good, 1973).

A sample drawn from a population in such a way that it should (or does) contain members of various categories and classification in the same proportions as they appear in the population (Derek Rowntree, 1981).

Sample refers to a group that is selected from a large group or population for examination with a view to making generalizations about the population, as a whole (Taneja, 1991).

Sample that corresponds to or matches the population of which it is a part with respect to characteristics important for the purpose under investigation. (Madhu Raj 1996, Singh, 2002 and John Bellingham 2004).

24. Variable

Any trait that changes from one case or condition to another, more strictly, the representation of the trait, usually in quantitative form, such as a measurement or an enumeration (Good, 1973).

Refers to a factor in educational research that influences the observation or management of an educational phenomenon (Taneja, 1991 and a group of experts, 2003).

In educational research, an entity that can vary.

25. Independent Variable

(i) A variable to which values may be assigned at will. (ii) The variable on which an estimation or prediction is based in a regression problem. (iii) In the plural, often used to refer to variables that are unconnected, when presented graphically, the x-axis or horizontal axis is conveniently used for the independent variable. (Good 1973).

In a statistical study, the variable whose values are deliberately changed (or natural difference observed) in order to see how this influences the values of another variable (the dependent variable). (Derek Rowntree, 1981).

Refers to variable whose changes are considered as not dependent upon transformations in other specific variables (Taneja ,1991).

In experimental research, the aspects of the study that the investigator manipulates or controls in order to observe the effect on the dependent variable (Madhu Raj, 1996).

An independent variable is one that the researcher manipulates; e.g, a type of instructional programme (John Bellingham, 2004).

26. Dependent Variable

A dependent variable is one that changes in consequence with changes in the independent variable (John Bellingham, 2004).

A variable whose magnitude depends on or is a function of, the value of the another variable (or other variables); a variable whose value is being estimated (for example by regression techniques) from that of one or more independent variables to which it is related; when represented graphically, the y-axis or vertical line is conveniently used for the dependent variable. (Good, 1973).

In a statistical study, the variable in whose values, we are expecting to see changes as a result of changes, we have made or observed in the values of some other variable (the independent variable) (Derek Rowntree, 1981).

Refers to a variable that is the presumed effect of a presumed cause of an event (Taneja, 1991 and Group of Experts, 2003).

A factor in an experimental relationship which has or shows variation that is hypothesized to be caused by another independent factor or variable (Madhu Raj, 1996 and Singh, 2002) .

27. Demographics

(i) Statistics showing an area's population characteristics such as age, race, income and education.

(ii) Basic information about an individual including such characteristics as age, place of residence and marital status. (Singh, 2002; John Bellinghom, 2004)

28. Regression

(i) The tendency for observations that show a high deviation from the mean and a low degree of variability among themselves in regard to one trait to display wider variability and markedly less deviation (on the average) from the mean in a second trait; (ii) The psychological mechanism of retreat from difficulties of adult world of reality to an imaginary world patterned on an earlier, more comfortable mode of life, as in childhood; normally seen in adults as play and make believe; (iii) A movement of the eyes, backward from right to left along the line of type being read; (iv) An error in silent or oral reading in which the reader retracts or goes back over what he has seen reading – (Good,. 1973).

The term relates to the techniques of analyzing relationships between two or more variables with a view to prediction (or estimating) values of one from values of other(s). (Derek Rowntree, 1981).

(i) In the context of child development, the temporary lapses or set backs that occur in the other wise smooth course of normal development (ii) In the context of learned behavior or skills, the loss or forgetting of previously learned skills in the absence of opportunities for continued practice. (iii) A psychological withdrawal to an earlier period of life, which may be manifested by infinite or immature behavior (Madhu Raj, 1996; Singh, 2002).

In the context of child development, the temporary lapses or set backs that occur in the otherwise smooth course of normal development. (John Bellinghom, 2004).

A method which makes use of a correlation in order to predict probable relationships. (Taneja 1991 & A group of Experts, 2003).

A method for describing the nature of relationship between two variables, so that the value of one can be predicted if the value of the other is known. Multiple regression analysis involves more than two variables.

(Madhu Raj, 1996; Singh, 2002).

Objectives of the Study

The present study has the following objectives:

1. To understand the present status of IX class students with regard to their achievement in Physical sciences.
2. To study the influence of the variables, Educational Division, Sex, Caste and their interaction on scholastic achievement in physical sciences.
3. To study the influence of the variables Age, Religion, Nativity and their interaction on scholastic achievement in Physical sciences.
4. To establish a relationship of scholastic achievement with Socio-demographic variables like, Income of the family, Father's Education, Father's Occupation, Mother's Education, Mother's Occupation, Numbers of children, Birth order, Number of members in the family, Economic position, Separate room for studies, Study hours at the Home and works at Home.
5. To study the impact of Study habits on scholastic achievement of IX class students in physical sciences.
6. To study the influence of self-concepts on scholastic achievement of IX class students in Physical sciences.
7. To study the impact of personality factors on scholastic achievement of IX class students in Physical sciences.

8. To predict the scholastic achievement of IX class students in Physical sciences with the help of socio-demographic variables, Study – habits, Self-Concepts and personality factors.
9. To predict the scholastic achievement of IX class students in Physical Sciences with the help of all the 51 independent variables in the investigation.
10. To develop mathematical equations for predicting the scholastic achievement of IX class students in Physical sciences.
11. To summarize the findings of present investigation
12. To make appropriate recommendations on the basis of findings of the present investigation.
13. To provide suggestions for further investigation.

Hypotheses Formulated

On the basis of the above objectives the following major Hypotheses, in the null form are formulated for testing:

1. All the IX class students would not have the same scholastic achievement abilities in physical sciences.
2. Educational Division, Sex, Caste, and their interactions would not have any significant influence on scholastic achievement of IX class students in physical sciences.
3. Age, Religion, Nativity and their interactions would not have any significant influence on scholastic achievement of IX class students in physical sciences.
4. Socio-Demographic variables would not have any significant influence on scholastic achievement of IX class students in physical sciences.
5. Study habits would not have any significant impact on scholastic achievement of IX class students in physical sciences.
6. Self-concepts would not have any significant impact on scholastic achievement of IX class students in physical sciences.
7. Personality factors would not have significant influence on scholastic achievement of IX class students in physical sciences.
8. It would not be possible to predict scholastic achievement with the help of socio-demographic variables, study habits self-concepts and personality factors.
9. It would not be possible to predict scholastic achievement with the help of all the 51 independent variables.

10. It would not be possible to develop mathematical equations for predicting scholastic achievement in physical sciences with the help of different sets of independent variables.
11. None of the independent variables in this investigation turns out to be a significant predictor of scholastic achievement of IX class students in physical sciences.

Variables Included in the Present Study

On basis of study of literature, it has been found that the achievement of students in all classes in physical sciences in general and IX class in particular, it depends on several factors. The investigator has selected the following Psycho-Sociological variables for the present study.

A. Dependent Variable

The scores obtained in the scholastic achievement test, in Physical sciences, constructed and standardized by the investigator has been taken as dependent variable.

B. Independent Variables

The independent variables studied in this investigation are given below:

1. Socio-Demographic variables

The socio-demographic variables included in the present investigation are:

1. Educational Divisions
2. Age
3. Income of the Family
4. Father's Education
5. Father's Occupation
6. Mother's Education
7. Mother's Occupation
8. Number of Children
9. Birth Order
10. Number of members in the family
11. Sex
12. Religion
13. Caste
14. Nativity/Locality
15. Economic position

16. Separate room for study
17. Study Hours at Home
18. Works at Home

2. *Psychological Variables*

The following psychological variables are included in the present investigation:

(i) Study Habits questionnaire consisting of seven areas,
(ii) Self-Concepts questionnaire consisting of 10 areas and
(iii) High School Students Personality Questionnaire (HSPQ) consisting of 14 personality factors

Method of Study

The investigator following the scientific principles and procedures of test construction,developed a preliminary objective scholastic achievement test in physical sciences for IX class students with 150 multiple choice questions with the help of senior Physical sciences teachers for the use of pilot study. The preliminary form is standardized following the method described by Garrette (1973) from pages 365-368 and after deleting fifty questions, a final objective Scholastic achievement test paper is prepared with 100 (one hundred) multiple choice questions with four alternatives carrying one mark each. A personal data sheet is prepared to collect the people's data on Socio – Demographic variables. Study habits Inventory of Dr. B.V. Patel is adopted to measured the Study Habits of the students. Dr. (Miss). Muktha Rani Rasthogi's Self-Concepts Scale is adopted to measure the self-concepts of pupils. Cattel's High School Students Personality Questionnaire (H.S.P.Q) is used to collect the information regarding the personality characteristics of the students.

A sample of 1800 IX class students representing four Educational Divisions of Chittoor District are selected by following standard procedures. The necessary data is collected in a planned way and are analyzed using appropriate statistical techniques and the results are interpreted accordingly.

Delimitations of Present Study

The following are the delimitations of the present study:

1. The study is confined to only chittoor district of Andhra Pradesh
2. The study is confined 36 schools in the four Educational divisions of Chittoor District.
3. The study confined to the IX class students.
4. The study is concerned with Physical sciences subject only.

5. The effect of only a few Psycho-Sociological variables on the scholastic achievement in Physical sciences has been studied.
6. The Scholastic achievement scores in Physical sciences are taken only from the achievement test constructed and standardized by the investigator.
7. The study is based on survey research where in the techniques of analyzing the data are based on the questionnaires only
8. The scholastic achievement of IX class students in physical sciences depends upon a number of psychological, sociological, demographic, environmental etc., variables. It is not possible to include each and every factor in this investigation.
9. It is only a presage-product study in the area of scholastic achievement.

CHAPTER 4 Methods of Investigation

This chapter deals with various procedures followed in the construction and standardization of data gathering instruments to measure the different variables, included in the present investigation. A brief description of methods adopted in the selection of the sample, collection of data, scoring, analysis and statistical techniques employed, are presented here under.

The flow chart showing the procedure followed in the present investigation is given in Fig. 4.1.

Tools used in the Present Study

The tools used in the present study are shown here under:

1. Objective Achievement Test (OAT)
2. Dr. B.V. Patels' Study Habits Inventory.
3. Dr. (Miss) Muktha Rani Rastogi's Self-concept Scale.
4. Cattell's High School Students Personality Questionnaire (HSPQ).
5. Personal Data sheet Prepared by the Investigator.

Construction of Objective Achievement Test (OAT)

An achievement test is essentially a tool or a device of measurement that helps in ascertaining quantity and quality of learning at the end, in a subject of study or group of subjects, after a period of instruction. *Dictionary of Education* (1998) refers it, to the performance in a school or a college in a standardized

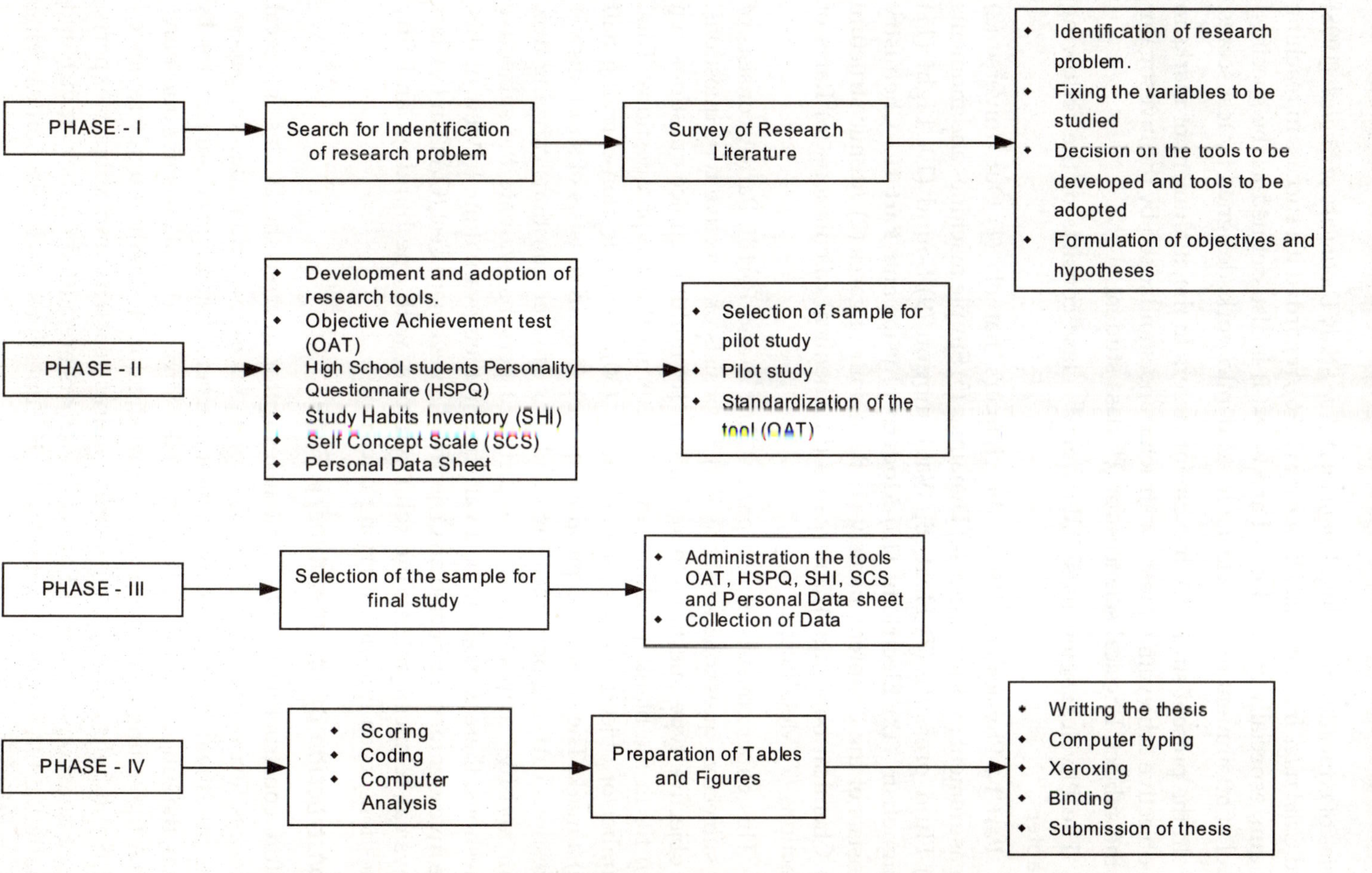

Fig. 4.1 : Flow Chart showing the Procedures Followed in the Present Study

series of educational testing. *Longman Active Study Dictionary of English* (1998) and *Cambridge International Dictionary* (1996), regarded it a success in reaching an aim, especially after a lot of hard work. It is also defined as the specified level of attainment or proficiency in academic work, designed by test scores.

In the present study "Achievement" refers to the attainment of marks in an objective achievement test constructed and standarised by the investigator in the subject, Physical sciences for 9th class students

The Physical sciences syllabus of 9th class consists of the following chapters:

Part I : Physics consists of the chapters, namely (1) Our universe (2) Measurement (3) Kinematics (4) Dynamics (5) Simple machines and moments (6) Fluid pressure (7) Heat (8) Wave motion (9) Sound (10) Light (11) Magnetism (12) Electricity (13) Modern physics and **Part II :** Chemistry consists of the Chapters, namely (1) Behaviour of gases (2) Atomic structure (3) Chemical bonding (4) Energetics (5) Chemical calculations (6) Rates of reactions (7) Metallurgy.

This paper consists of two parts - Part A and Part B. Part-A consists of all subjective questions where as Part B consists of objective type questions. In objective type questions there are ten (10) multiple choice questions, ten (10) fill in the blank questions and ten (10) matching type questions. Total number of objective questions are thirty (30), each question carrying half (½) a mark. The subjective questions in Part A again consists of short answer questions carrying one mark each and long answer questions carrying two, four and five marks each. If two different persons evaluate the subjective questions, there is likely to be a variation in their evaluation. In view of this, the investigator constructed an Objective Achievement Test (OAT) in IX Class Physical sciences, taking the total syllabus, with one hundred and fifty questions, each question carrying one mark.

Construction of the Preliminary Form

Before constructing the OAT, the investigator referred the IX class physical sciences text book, the syllabus and previous examination question papers. The investigator consulted the senior teachers, teaching the subject, for IX class, the subject experts and experts in the construction of objective questions. After the setting of questions by the investigator, it was thoroughly reviewed with the help of senior physical sciences teachers and subject experts. Some questions are deleted and some others are added on their advice and finally the OAT is constructed, with 150 questions, each question carrying one mark.

All the questions are multiple choice questions, with four alternatives for each question. Only one alternative is the correct answer out of the four alternatives. The pupils are asked to choose the correct alternative for each question.

Pilot Study

The Telugu version of the preliminary form of OAT, is administered on 370 students of different schools. The schools are selected at random. The sample design for pilot study is shown in the Table-1. The schools selected are from four educational divisions in Chittoor District.

Table 4.1 : Sample Design for Pilot Study

Sl. No.	Name of the school	Educational Division	Girls	Boys	Total
1.	Z.P. High School, Madanapalle	Madanapalle	20	30	50
2.	Muncipal High School Punganur	Madanapalle	18	22	40
3.	S.K.M Z.P. High School, P.R. Mangalam	Puttur	19	31	50
4.	G.H.S. Nagalapuram	Puttur	22	23	45
5.	Z.P.H School Santhipuram	Chittoor	18	27	45
6.	Muncipal High School Chittoor	Chittoor	30	20	50
7.	P.M. High School Renigunta	Tirupati	27	23	50
8	S.G.S. School Tirupati	Tirupati	16	24	40
	Total		**170**	**200**	**370**

Administration of the Pilot Study

The investigator obtained the prior permission from the heads of the institutions, selected for pilot study, to conduct the test, after explaining them the purpose of the study and convincing them. The investigator explained the purpose of the test to the students and asked them to prepare well on the total syllabus. The test is conducted, after giving sufficient time for preparation. The test is conducted with the help of the teachers and all the answer sheets are collected. The investigator visited the different schools on different dates and conducted the test according to the schedule, given earlier.

Scoring Procedure

One mark is awarded for each correct answer and the total marks obtained by each student is marked on the right top corner of the sheet.

Item Analysis

This procedure of item analysis is adopted from the prescribed standardized procedure, for construction and use of tests for class room examinations. For the present study, the difficulty index and validity index of each item are computed, by following the procedure in the text book "Statistics in psychology and Education" by Garrett (1973) given in the pages 365 to 368.

On the basis of total marks obtained in the OAT, the answer sheets are arranged in descending order. The upper 27 per cent of papers and lower 27 per cent of the papers are separated and are named as High group and Low group. These two groups of papers are taken for analysis and the rest are excluded from analysis. Papers of High group are then computed to find out how often, the correct answer to each question has been chosen by the pupils in the group. The numbers thus obtained are recorded. Papers of low group are also corrected in the same procedure. Percentages of correct responses are also recorded.

If the validity index approaches to 1.00, the question tends to discriminate perfectly between high and low achievers. As the validity index approaches to zero, the question does not discriminate between high and low achievers.

After ascertaining the difficulty Index and validity index for each item in the preliminary test as per the guidelines given by Garrett (1973) fifty questions whose validities are less than 0.30 are deleted and a final test is constructed. The difficulty index and validity index (Discriminating power) of OAT are given in the Table 4.2.

The questions deleted from the preliminary OAT are also shown in the Table 4.2.

Table 4.2 : Difficulty index and Validity Index of the Items of Pilot form of Objective Achievement Test

Item No.	Percentage of correct response is		Difficulty Index (Difficulty Value)	Validity Index (Discriminating power)	Remarks
	High Group	Low Group			
1	2	3	4	5	6
1	92	42	0.67	0.58	Retained
2	84	32	0.58	0.53	Retained
3	97	56	0.77	0.61	Retained
4	90	80	0.85	0.18	Deleted
5	56	18	0.37	0.41	Retained
6	75	63	0.69	0.15	Deleted
7	63	21	0.42	0.43	Retained
8	68	20	0.44	0.45	Retained
9	71	66	0.69	0.05	Deleted
10	82	41	0.62	0.44	Retained
11	68	22	0.45	0.47	Retained
12	72	35	0.54	0.41	Retained
13	85	76	0.81	0.16	Deleted
14	90	79	0.85	0.19	Deleted
15	55	18	0.37	0.40	Retained
16	67	30	0.49	0.38	Retained
17	69	29	0.49	0.40	Retained
18	76	65	0.71	0.09	Deleted
19	90	35	0.63	0.59	Retained
20	62	25	0.44	0.38	Retained
21	67	30	0.49	0.38	Retained
22	71	61	0.66	0.10	Deleted
23	72	28	0.50	0.43	Retained
24	32	25	0.29	0.06	Deleted
25	49	13	0.31	0.43	Retained
26	53	20	0.37	0.37	Retained
27	66	54	0.55	0.13	Deleted

1	2	3	4	5	6
28	62	22	0.44	0.42	Retained
29	53	61	0.57	- ve	Deleted
30	62	56	0.59	0.06	Deleted
31	74	58	0.66	0.18	Deleted
32	90	46	0.69	0.51	Retained
33	94	82	0.88	0.26	Deleted
34	86	94	0.90	- ve	Deleted
35	46	34	0.40	0.13	Deleted
36	50	18	0.34	0.36	Retained
37	62	22	0.42	0.42	Retained
38	70	62	0.66	0.09	Deleted
39	38	26	0.32	0.14	Deleted
40	53	14	0.34	0.44	Retained
41	46	38	0.42	0.08	Deleted
42	66	25	0.46	0.42	Retained
43	62	30	0.46	0.33	Retained
44	68	58	0.63	0.11	Deleted
45	78	33	0.56	0.46	Retained
46	65	74	0.70	- ve	Deleted
47	73	34	0.54	0.40	Retained
48	61	50	0.56	0.12	Deleted
49	62	29	0.46	0.34	Retained
50	74	65	0.70	0.10	Deleted
51	69	30	0.55	0.39	Retained
52	57	36	0.47	0.22	Deleted
53	68	26	0.47	0.43	Retained
54	60	50	0.55	0.11	Deleted
55	60	18	0.39	0.45	Retained
56	58	14	0.36	0.48	Retained
57	42	30	0.36	0.13	Deleted
58	65	46	0.56	0.20	Deleted

1	2	3	4	5	6
59	78	30	0.54	0.49	Retained
60	81	42	0.62	0.42	Retained
61	86	50	0.68	0.42	Retained
62	70	30	0.50	0.40	Retained
63	91	46	0.69	0.53	Retained
64	69	26	0.48	0.43	Retained
65	80	70	0.75	0.13	Deleted
66	66	30	0.48	0.37	Retained
67	59	18	0.39	0.44	Retained
68	61	30	0.46	0.32	Retained
69	68	30	0.49	0.38	Retained
70	72	42	0.57	0.31	Retained
71	78	42	0.60	0.38	Retained
72	82	38	0.60	0.47	Retained
73	72	30	0.56	0.42	Retained
74	54	26	0.40	0.30	Retained
75	66	50	0.58	0.17	Deleted
76	75	26	0.51	0.49	Retained
77	62	46	0.54	0.16	Deleted
78	74	34	0.54	0.41	Retained
79	94	52	0.73	0.54	Retained
80	74	38	0.56	0.37	Retained
81	82	45	0.64	0.40	Retained
82	70	38	0.54	0.33	Retained
83	53	22	0.38	0.33	Retained
84	60	34	0.47	0.27	Deleted
85	54	22	0.38	0.34	Retained
86	77	26	0.52	0.51	Retained
87	83	38	0.61	0.48	Retained
88	88	34	0.61	0.57	Retained
89	58	22	0.40	0.38	Retained

1	2	3	4	5	6
90	66	26	0.46	0.41	Retained
91	70	22	0.46	0.49	Retained
92	78	54	0.66	0.27	Deleted
93	65	26	0.46	0.40	Retained
94	71	22	0.47	0.50	Retained
95	85	42	0.64	0.47	Retained
96	93	30	0.62	0.67	Retained
97	80	38	0.59	0.45	Retained
98	51	26	0.39	0.27	Deleted
99	66	22	0.44	0.45	Retained
100	46	42	0.44	0.04	Deleted
101	58	22	0.40	0.38	Retained
102	62	20	0.41	0.45	Retained
103	72	54	0.63	0.20	Deleted
104	82	58	0.70	0.28	Deleted
105	89	42	0.66	0.52	Retained
106	70	30	0.50	0.40	Retained
107	66	38	0.52	0.29	Deleted
108	70	32	0.51	0.38	Retained
109	78	34	0.56	0.45	Retained
110	90	50	0.70	0.48	Retained
111	86	68	0.77	025	Deleted
112	62	82	0.72	- ve	Deleted
113	78	34	0.56	0.45	Retained
114	58	36	0.47	0.22	Deleted
115	83	42	0.63	0.44	Retained
116	91	46	0.69	0.53	Retained
117	75	30	0.53	0.45	Retained
118	69	34	0.52	0.36	Retained
119	90	42	0.66	0.54	Retained
120	69	46	0.58	0.24	Deleted

1	2	3	4	5	6
121	74	42	0.58	0.33	Retained
122	50	22	0.36	0.31	Retained
123	62	30	0.46	0.33	Retained
124	78	32	0.55	0.47	Retained
125	86	40	0.63	0.49	Retained
126	74	40	0.57	0.35	Retained
127	74	54	0.64	0.22	Deleted
128	82	58	0.70	0.28	Deleted
129	90	44	0.67	0.52	Retained
130	92	78	0.85	0.26	Deleted
131	67	34	0.51	0.34	Retained
132	72	50	0.61	0.23	Deleted
133	85	46	0.66	0.44	Retained
134	74	50	0.62	0.26	Deleted
135	58	18	0.38	0.43	Retained
136	72	50	0.61	0.23	Deleted
137	78	38	0.58	0.42	Retained
138	62	34	0.48	0.29	Deleted
139	82	38	0.60	0.47	Retained
140	90	58	0.74	0.41	Retained
141	58	22	0.40	0.38	Retained
142	66	34	0.50	0.33	Retained
143	73	58	0.66	0.17	Deleted
144	82	42	0.62	0.43	Retained
145	79	54	0.67	0.28	Deleted
146	92	34	0.63	0.63	Retained
147	72	26	0.49	0.46	Retained
148	62	22	0.42	0.42	Retained
149	84	30	0.57	0.55	Retained
150	66	42	0.54	0.25	Deleted

Validity

The validity of a test is concerned with, what is measured. It refers to the degree to which extent, the test scores predict some practical criterion measures. There are various methods of estimating the validity of a measuring instrument.

Table 4.2 shows the difficulty index and validity index of each item of the OAT. The following validities are established for the OAT.

1. ***Content validity:*** This form of validity is estimated by evaluating the relevance of the test items, individually and as a whole. Validity of content should not depend upon the subjective judgement of only one specialist. In the present case, the previous question papers were thourouly reviewed, views of specialists in the subject were taken, the investigator thoroughly referred the total syllabus, the items in the test were thoroughly scrutinized with respect to the subject matter and hence it is assumed that the OAT has content validity.

2. ***Item validity:*** The validity index calculated for each of the items is a measure of the extent, to which a given item differentiates the low group and high group. Thus the items in the inventory with validity index, equal to or greater than 0.30 ensure the item validity of the OAT. Hence the OAT has item validity.

3. ***Intrinsic Validity***: Guilford (1954) defined intrinsic validity as, "The degree to which a test measures what it purports to measure". This can also be stated in terms of how well, the obtained scores measure the test's true score component. This validity is given by the square root of its reliability. Hence the intrinsic validity of the OAT is 0.96 $\left(\sqrt{0.92}\right)$.

4. ***Face validity:*** If a common thread of achievement runs through all the items of the test, then the test is said to have face validity. All items in the OAT have a common thread for measuring the achievement of IX Class pupils in Physical sciences. Hence the OAT has face validity.

5. ***Construct Validity:*** Construct validity of a test measures particular characteristics of the individual taking the test. A test is valid from the construct point of view, if it can indicate the individual's actual achievement of instructional objectives. All the questions in the Objective Achievement Test (OAT) are based on the objectives of instruction. Hence there is construct validity for the OAT.

6. ***Concurrent validity and predictive validity:*** In a situation of some observable criterion, the scale's validity can be investigated by seeing how good an indicator it is. This approach leads to two categories of validity (i.e.) 'Predictive Validity' and 'Concurrent Validity'.

Predictive validity is concerned with how the scale can forecast a future criterion and concurrent validity with how well it can describe a present one. The results in the succeeding chapter show that the OAT has both concurrent and predictive validities.

Final Study

The final OAT paper is prepared after deleting, the invalid fifty items whose validity index is less than 0.30, from the preliminary inventory. Garrett (1973), suggested that the items with validity index less than 0.20 are invalid. In the present investigation, the investigator wants to retain one hundred items for the final study. Hence the items with validity index equal to or more than 0.30 are retained for final study. The final version of the OAT paper is translated into English. The translation is observed by three experts in English and they confirmed that there is no ambiguity in the translation.

Reliability

Next to validity, reliability is the most indispensable characteristic of any measuring instrument. It refers to the consistency of scores obtained by the same individuals at different occasions or with different sets of equivalent items.

A tool is said to be reliable, if it reveals similar results in various situations. The test-retest and parallel form methods of estimating reliability may be common and legitimate for both power and speed tests. In the power test each student has enough time to write what he knows. The Split-Half technique is not proper for speed test, in which he does not have time to respond to some questions, for which he knows the correct answer. Speed test usually yields spuriously high reliability co-efficient, when split half and internal consistency methods are employed. (Stanley *et al.* 1978).

Split-Half reliability is some times called as co-efficient of equivalence. The test is split into two equivalent halves, usually by pooling the odd numbered items for one half where as, the even numbered items forming the second half of the test. This usually makes the two scores obtained from a single test reasonably equivalent.

The reliability of the OAT is tested by employing

1. Test-Retest method on a sample of 370 with a gap of 15 days for retest,
2. Split-Half Technique, and
3. K.R. Formula-20. The Reliability coefficients of the OAT are presented in Table 4.3.

Table 4.3 : The Reliability Co- efficient of the Objective Achievement Test

Sl.No.	Type of the Reliability	Mangnitude of Reliability
1.	Test – Retest method	0.89
2.	Split – Half Technique	0.86
3.	K.R. formula-20	0.92

The magnitude of the coefficient of correlation in all the above three methods is more than 0.85. Hence the reliability of the OAT is very high.

Study Habits Inventory

A few definitions of a study habits are presented hereunder

The complex of reading behaviour of a person resulting from varying degrees of interaction of a number of variable factors, may be defined as a study habits.

The ability to schedule his aims, the habit of note taking, reviewing, judicious application of the whole and part method etc. form learner's study habits.

The word 'study habits' is used to refer students' way of studying systematic or unsystematic - efficient or inefficient (Good, 1973).

Study habits include student's habit of concentration, note taking, time budgeting and study methods (Smith, 1961).

Study habits mainly depend on motivation for reading, interest in the subject, attitude, encouragement by others, personality traits etc. Effective learning takes place only with good study habits.

Factors Affecting the Study Habits

Some of the noteworthy factors affecting the study habits are presented here under

1. *Home:* Parents are the first teachers and home is the first place of learning for every child. Parents and other family members may influence the children's learning methods and study habits. The level of education and occupation of the parents may also have some influence on children's study habits.

2. *Intelligence :* Intelligent students can more quickly develop good study habits than dull students.

3. *Personality :* Students with better adjustments to the environment, can develop better study habits.

4. *Community :* Community resources like library facilities, meetings with learned people inculcate good study habits among children.

5. *School :* The school atmosphere and teachers play an important role in developing good or bad study habits.

6. *Curriculum :* The curriculum should be suitable for the standard of the child. If the curriculum is above the standard of the children, pupils may be frustrated and may develop bad study habits.

7. *Demographic factors* : Locality, sex, education of parents, income of the family, number of members in the family, social status of the family etc. influence the study habits of the pupils.

Factors Helping for Developing Good Study Habits

"Study is nothing but a passion of Mind" -*Thomous Hobbs*

1. *Efficient use of time*: The first and most important thing for success in the class room is efficient use of time, outside the class-room. There are twenty four hours a day. Two or three hours each day are to be set aside for studying. It is not the amount of time spent on study that matters much, but it is how effectively time is spent.

2. *The power of Co-operation*: Education often looks like competition. Pupils compete for marks or, for graces when they are in school. They compete for jobs, when they leave school. In such a climate, it is easy to overlook the power of co-operation that is developed through study groups. Hence pupils are to remember, their friends, classmates and support group, when they study.

3. *Mixing with Social Activities*: The most successful students balance school activities with good study habits. A diversion from studies will alleviate stress and help prevent from becoming fatigued. Hence pupils have to take small breaks after some hours of study for sharpening their concentration.

4. *Setting a Comfortable Pace:* A good grade, in a course is almost never the result of luck. The key is to set a comfortable pace of study. Each pupil will have his own pace of learning. Hence planning a convenient study schedule and adhering to it, will guarantee better grades.

5. *Changing Habits*: Some students may have very poor study habits. Those poor study habits such as not completing assignments, missing classes, not regular at studying, etc. Hence changing these poor habits will result in better life.

6. *Immediate Review of Class Notes*: Reviewing as soon as possible what they have heard and learnt in the class, improve their retention of the sub-matter for long. Otherwise eighty percent of what was learnt, will be forgotten. Hence the pupils must review the class notes before they go to next chapter.

7. *Time Management*: Time management is one of the most important factor in the student life. Research indicates that unless a lesson is reviewed

within twenty four hours, eighty per cent of the material can be forgotten. Hence reviewing information as soon as possible, decrease the hours of study, needed before examinations. Using small amounts of time for reviewing and avoiding marathon study sessions are advisable. Learning to budget the time, will give more time for frequent reviewing, so that less time is spent for cramming. A large part of time spent in study, would, however, need to be spent in repetition and in drill.

The teachers are to keep the above points in mind and popularize them among the pupils, for their benefit.

8. Parents involvement to improve study habits: Parents should try to encourage their children's natural curiosity about the world. Parents can do this by talking to their children, by listening to their children and by answering their questions. Parents should also try to expose their children to as many exciting, stimulating things, as possible. Parents should take an interest in their children's education by joining Parents-Teachers Association meetings or by becoming involved in their school activities. This will help to reinforce what they are learning.

Every Student can Learn, Just not on the Same Day or the Same Way

Construction of the Study Habits Inventory

Study habits of an individual play an important role in his/her scholastic achievement. The review of related literature showed that there were a number of studies which established the relation between study habits and academic achievement at school level. Very few studies were found which showed the relationship between study habits and achievement in the subject physical sciences of 9th class students. Hence the investigator felt it necessary to find a relationship between study habits of 9th class students and achievement in physical sciences.

Though there were many Study Habits Inventories (SHI), constructed by Wrenn in 1933, ST Mary Esther in 1945, Jammur in 1958, on the students concentration, note taking, time budgeting; the investigator felt that the Study Habits Inventory (SHI) constructed and standardized by Dr. B.V. Patel (1975), is worth using for the present investigation. The inventory consists of 45 statements which are classified into seven areas. The seven areas are :

1. Home environment and planning of the work
2. Reading and note taking.
3. Planning of the subject.
4. Habits of concentration.

5. Preparation for examination
6. General habits and attitudes
7. School environment.

Adoption of Study Habits Inventory

On examination of various instruments, developed to measure the study habits of secondary school children the study habits inventory developed and standardized by Dr. B.V. Patel in 1975, is adopted to measure the study habits of the subjects included in the sample (N=1800), for the present study. The SHI consists of 45 items, out of which 27 items are positive and 18 are negative. The positive items are 1, 2, 3, 4, 8, 9, 10, 11, 12, 13, 16, 17, 18, 19, 22, 26, 32, 33, 36, 37, 38, 39, 40, 41, 42, 43 and 44. The negative items are : 5, 6, 7, 14, 15, 20, 21, 23, 24, 25, 27, 28, 29, 30, 31, 34, 35 and 45.

Scoring Procedure

There are five alternatives for each item. The alternatives are always, often, some times, seldom and never. For 'Positive' items marks are awarded 5 to 1 in the descending order and for negative items 1 to 5 marks in the ascending order. The above method of scoring is followed, while evaluating the SHI answer sheets. The English version of SHI is translated into Telugu, the regional language of the subjects. Five judges who are well versed with psychological testing, cheeked the translation. Terms which are ambiguous, are discussed and resolved.

The numerical values for different alternatives of positive and negative items are presented in Table 4.4.

Table 4.4 : Numerical Values for Different Alternatives of Positive and Negative Items of SHI

Item	Alternatives				
	Always	Often	Some-times	Seldom	Never
Positive	5	4	3	2	1
Negative	1	2	3	4	5

Administration of SHI

The Telugu version thus prepared is administered on all the subjects of the sample. (N=1800) in the fore noon session. Necessary instructions are given to the pupils for answering the items and with the help of teachers the sheets are collected and scoring is done according to the weightage given by the author.

Reliability and Validity

For calculating reliability and validity of SHI, the procedure suggested by H.E. Garrett (1973) is followed. The reliability of SHI is tested by employing split-half technique on a sample of 370. The reliability coefficient for half test is 0.91 and for the full test is 0.95. Test-retest reliability on a sample of 370 with a gap of 15 days is 0.97. This shows that the reliability of SHI is very high.

The validity of a test is an estimate of the correlations between the raw test scores and true criterion scores. There are various methods of estimating the validity of a measuring instrument. For the present study the following validities are established:

1. ***Intrinsic validity***: Guilford (1954) stated that the square root of reliability gives the validity and hence it is 0.98.
2. ***Face validity:*** If a common thread runs through all the items of an inventory, the resultant test has face validity. All the items in the SHI of Dr. B.V. Patel have a common thread for measuring the study habits. Hence there is face validity in SHI.

Self-concept Scale

Self concept has been variously defined as "The self as known to the self" (Murphy, 1947)

"Those aspects of the individual which seem most vital and important to the person". (Jersield 1960)

An infant does not bring Self-Concept with him/her at the time of it's birth. Children acquire it by means of accidental or incidental learning. In the process of learning from interaction with others, the child not only develops self-concept but also develops an ideal towards which, it has to strive. Thus self-concept is a key variable in the behaviour of an individual.

In psychological discussion, the word self has been used in many ways. Two chief meanings emerge- the 'self' as the subject or agent and the 'self' as the individual, who is known to himself/herself.

The term self –concept has come into common use, to refer to the second meaning, which refers to the phenomenological approach. Self-concept refers to "The pictures or images a person has himself" (Taneja, 1991).

Allport (1961) has described self-concept as "Some thing of which we are immediately aware. We think of it as the warm, central, private region of our life. As such it plays a crucial part in our consciousness (a concept broader in itself), in our personality (a concept broader than consciousness), and in our organism (a concept broader than personality). Thus it is some kind of core in our being.

Research studies have shown, how self-concept built in early years of life and reinforced in later experience, influence behaviour and characteristic reactions to the people and situations.

Because self-concept is dominant in personality pattern, the measurement of self-concept becomes very essential. If we want to understand the personality of an individual, to understand and predict his life adjustment and his success and failure, we can not proceed further without knowing this "self-concept". Thus it is some kind of core in our being.

Adoption of the Self-concept Scale

On examination of the various instruments developed to measure self-concept, the investigator felt that the self-concept scale (SCS) developed by **Dr. (Miss) Mukta Rani Rastogi** (1974) is more suitable for the purpose of present study. This scale consists of 51 items, divided into 10(ten) areas. Out of these 51 items, 23 are positive and 28 are negative. It is a five-point attitude scale with alternatives, Strongly Agree (SA), Agree (A), Doubtful (D), Disagree (DA), and Strongly Dis-Agree (SDA). The ten areas are:

1. Health and sex appropriateness
2. Abilities
3. Self-confidence
4. Self- acceptance
5. Worthiness
6. Present, past and future
7. Beliefs and convictions
8. Feeling of shame and guilt
9. Sociability
10. Emotional maturity

This scale is translated into Telugu Version with experts in psychological tests and is used for the present investigation. The item numbers of each area of self-concept scale are presented in the Table 4.5.

The self-concept inventory consists of 51 items of which 23 are positive and 28 are negative.

Table 4.5 : The item Numbers in Each Area of the Self-concept Scale

Sl.No.	Description	Item Numbers							
1.	Health and Sex Appropriateness	6P	20P	29N	22N	34P	46P		
2.	Abilities	4P	8P	12N	23N	36P	38N	39N	42P
3.	Self-Confidence	7P	9P	14N	15N	44P			
4.	Self Acceptance	2P	10N	17N	35N				
5.	Worthiness	1P	3N	19N	25P	27P	41N	48P	
6.	Present, Past and Future	18P	22P	26N	31N	40P			
7.	Beliefs and Convictions	24N	47P	49P					
8.	Feeling of Shame and guilt	5N	13N	28N	30N	50N			
9.	Sociability	33N	37P	43P	45N				
10.	Emotional Maturity	11N	15N	21N	51N				

Note: The letters P or N shown below indicate positiveness or negativeness.

Scoring Procedure

The adopted SCS is a Five Point Scale with alternatives, Strongly Agree, Agree, Undecided, Disagree and Strongly Disagree. For the purpose of scoring, numerical values were assigned for each of the above shown alternatives, which are shown in the Table 4.6.

Table 4.6 : Numerical Values for Different Alternatives of the Positive and Negative Items of the SCS

Item	Alternatives				
	Strongly Agree (SA)	Agree (A)	Undecided (U)	Disagree (DA)	Strongly Disagree (SDA)
Positive	5	4	3	2	1
Negative	1	2	3	4	5

Validity of the Scale

The validity of the scale or tool refers to its "accuracy", how closely it measures, what it actually intends to measure. For this self-concept scale, the author **Mukta Rani Rastogi** (1974) reported the following validities:

(*i*) Content validity
(*ii*) Criterion validity and
(*iii*) Construct validity.

Reliability

Reliability can be defined as the degree of consistency between two measures of the same thing. Several methods are used to estimate the reliability. The more common ones reported in the text manuals are:

1. Measures of stability (test-retest)
2. Measures of equivalence
3. Measures of internal consistency
4. Split-Half method
5. Kurder-Richardson's estimates.

Split-Half Reliability

In this study internal consistency is measured through Split-Half method. The procedure described by Garrett (1973) is employed. The correlation coefficient for half test(rh), with a sample of 370, is 0.8565. The correlation coefficient for full test $\left(r = \frac{2r_h}{1+r_h}\right)$ is also calculated which is equal to 0.9227.

It shows the reliability of the instrument is very high

Administration of Self-Concept Scale

The Telugu Version of SCS is administered on all the subjects (N=1800) of the sample, in the forenoon session of the school. Necessary instructions for answering the items, are given to the students. Teacher's help is taken in conducting the test and collecting all the data sheets. Scoring is done according to the weightage, given by the Author.

Personality Questionnaire

Personality of an individual plays an important role in his / her scholastic achievement. The review of related literature showed that there are a number of studies showing the relationship between personality and scholastic achievement at school level. Hence the investigator felt a need to investigate the relationship between personality of the child and its scholastic achievement particularly, the achievement in physical sciences of IX class students. This motivated the investigator to search for a suitable personality questionnaire.

The investigator studied all the personality theories and searched for a suitable means of measuring the total behaviour of an individual and is convinced that cattle's theory, of all the various theories, is the only theory based on the principle of totality of behaviour of an individual.

Selection of the Tool (HSPQ)

Different psychologists have given different definitions for the term "personality".

Personality is a dynamic organization within the individual of those psycho-physical systems that determine his unique adjustment to his environment (Allport, 1949)

According to Cattell (1950), 'personality is that which permits a prediction of what a person will do in a given situation'. One can not pass a judgment over one's personality, by just looking through one's physique or sociability. One has to go carefully into all the aspects, biological and social and then only one can assess the personality of an individual. Sometimes some researchers and even psychologists fall easily into the mistake of settling, on a single test, dealing with any one dimension of personality, for example extroversion, self realization etc. and from that they try to asses all kinds of behaviour, which is not advisable.

For the individual all aspects of behaviour, thought and feeling that make the person unique. For psychologists, it is a major area of theory and research (Derek Rowntree, 1981).

Keeping this in view, the personality of the students in the present study is assessed using Cattell's Junior-Senior High School Students Personality Questionnaire (HSPQ). It is applicable to the age group of students 12 to 18 years. It is a culture free test. It helps to obtain scores on 14 dimensions of the personality. They represent basic concepts, which are understood by psychologists, so that insightful understandings of the individual and his development as well as statistical predictions are possible. The above point weighted in favour of selecting the HSPQ for assessing the personality traits of the students. Cattell's 14 personality factors are given here under.

A brief description of Cattell's fourteen HSPQ personality factors is given below.

Description of the HSPQ Factors

Factor A: Reserved vs. outgoing

The person, who scored low on Factor-A tends to be stiff, cool and alone. He likes things rather than people, working alone and avoiding class of view points. He is likely to be precise and rigid in his way of doing things and personal standards.

The person who scores high on Factor-A, tends to be more matured, easy going, emotionally expressive ready to co-operate, attentive to the people, soft hearted, kindly adaptable. He readily forms active groups. He is generous in personal relations, less afraid of criticism and better able to remember the names of the people.

Factor B: Less Intelligent vs. More Intelligent

Less intelligent, concrete thinking vs. more intelligent, abstract thinking.

The person scoring low on Factor-B tends to be a slow learner, dull and sluggish. He tends to have little capacity for higher forms of knowledge.

The person who scores high on Factor -B tends to be more intelligent, quick in grasping, and a fast learner. Low score, in contrast indicate deterioration of mental functions in pathological conditions.

Factor C: Emotionally Less Stable vs. Emotionally Stable

The person who scores low on Factor -C tends to be low in frustration, tolerance for un-satisfactory conditions and neurotically fatigued.

The person who scores more on Factor-C tends to be emotionally mature, more stable, calm, and be able to maintain high group morale.

Factor D: Phlegmatic vs. Excitable

Phlegmatic, Deliberate, Inactive vs. excitable, Impatient, Demanding, Overactive.

The person scoring low on Factor-D is thought of same as 'C' with which it has some behaviour in common. However it is distinguishable by more immediate, "temperate mental" quality of excitability and by an irresponsible, positive, assertive emphasis in the emotionality.

The person who scores high on 'D' tends to be a restless sleeper, easily distracted from work by noise. He is hurt and angry, if he is not given important positions.

Factor E: Obedient, Mild, Conforming, submissive vs. Assertive, Independent, Aggressive, Stubborn, Dominant.

The person who scores low on Factor-E tends to be dependent, a follower, and takes action which goes along with the group. This, positively, is part of many neurotic syndromes.

The person who scores high on Factor-E tends to be assertive, self assumed, independent, bold in his approach to the situations. He may at times, be hard, a law to himself, hostile, authoritarian and dis-regards authority.

Factor 'F': Sober Vs. Happy - Go-Lucky, Gay, Enthusiastic, Impulsively Lively.

The person who scores low on Factor-F tends to be restrained and introspective. He is some times pessimistic, anxious and considered to be swung. He tends to be a sober, dependable person.

The person who scores high on this factor tends to be cheerful, active, talkative, frank, expressive, quick and un-perturbable. He is frequently chosen as an elected leader. He may be impulsive and mercurial.

Factor 'G': Moral standards Vs. super ego-strength.

Expedient, rules vs. Conscientious, preserving and rule bound.

The person who scores low on factor 'G' tends to be unsteady in purpose. He is often casual and lacking in effort for group undertakings and cultural demands.

The person who scores high on this factor tends to be strong in character, preserving, responsible, determined, consistent, playful and well organized. He prefers hard working people to witty companions.

Factor 'H': Shy VS. Venturesome

Shy, Restrained, Different, Timid Vs. Venture Some, Socially Bold, Uninhibited, Spontanious.

The person who scored low on 'H' tends to be shy, with-drawing, cautious, retiring, and cooling. He usually has inferiority feelings. He tends to be slow in speech, dislikes occupations with personal contacts and prefers one or two close friends to large groups and is not given to keeping in contact with all that is going on around him.

The person who scores high on this factor tends to be more sociable, bold, ready to try new things, spontaneous and abundant in emotional response. His "thickskinnedness" enables him to face wear and tear in dealing with people. He tends to be pushy and actively interested in the opposite sex.

Factor 'I': Though Minded VS. Tense Minded

Though Minded, Self Realistic Vs. Tender Minded,Dependent, over Protected and Sensitive.

The person who scores low on Factor-I tends to be practical, realistic, masculine, independent, responsible but skeptical of subjective and "uncultured". He is some times unmoved, hard, cynical, and smug.

The person who scores high on this factor tends to be tender-minded, day dreaming, artistically fastidious. He is sometimes demanding of attention and help, impatient, dependent and impractical. He dislikes crude people and rough occupations. He tends to be slow in group performance.

Factor 'J': Vigorous Vs. Doubting

Vigorous, justify to action Vs. Doubting, Obstructive, Individualistic, Reflective and unwilling etc.

The person who scores low on Factor-J has 'no' for a difficult pattern to interpret. It has been called variously the Hamlet factor neurasthenia, etc.

The person who scores high on this trait prefers to do things on his own in physically and intellectually fastidious, thinks over his mistakes and how to avoid them, tends not to forget if he is unfairly treated, has private views differing from the groups, but prefers to keep himself in the back ground and avoid argument, knows he has fewer friends.

Factor 'O': Placid Vs. Apprehensive

Placid, confident, serene, untroubled Vs. Apprehensive, worrying, depressive, troubled, Guilt proneness.

The person who scores low on Factor-O tends to be placid, calm, with unshakable nerve. He has a mature, unanxious, confidence in himself and has capacity to deal with things. He is resilient and secure.

The person who scores high on Factor-O tends to be depressed, moody, worried, suspicious, brooding and avoiding people. He has a child like tendency to anxiety in difficulties. He does not feel accepted in groups or free to participate.

Factor 'Q_2': Group dependent Vs. self-sufficient

The person who scores low on Factor-Q_2 prefers to work and make decisions with other people and depends on social approval and administration. He tends to go alone with the group and may be lacking individual resolution. He needs group support.

The person who scores high on this trait, is temperamentally independent, accustomed to go in his own way, making decisions and taking action on his own. He discounts public opinion, but is not necessarily dominant in his relation with others. He does not dislike people but simply does not mind their agreement or support.

Factor Q_3: Undisciplined Vs. controlled

Undisciplined, self conflict, careless of protocol follows own urges, low integration Vs. controlled, socially precise, self disciplined, compulsive, high self concept, control.

The person who scores low on Factor-Q_3 will not be bothered with will-control and regard for social demands. He is not over considerable, careful or painstaking. He may feel, maladjusted.

The person who scores high on Factor- Q_3 tends to have strong control of his emotions and general behaviour, inclined to be socially aware and careful and regards for social reputations. Effective leaders and some paranoids are high on Q_3.

Factor Q_4: Relaxed Vs. Tensed

Relaxed, tranquil, torpid, unfrustrated Vs. Tense, driven over, wrought, frustrated.

The person who scores low on factor Q_4 tends to be sedate, relaxed, composed, and satisfied. In some situations, his over satisfaction may lead to laziness and low performances in the sense that low motivation produces little trail and error.

The person who scores high on this trait, tends to be tense, excitable, restless, fruitful, and impatient. He is often fatigued, but unable to remain inactive. In groups, he likes a poor view of the degree or unity, orderliness and leadership.

One of the Unique features of HSPQ and other personality scales developed by cattell, is that each of the items in any factor is selected on the basis of their own correlation with pure factors. In other words the HSPQ of cattell has factorial validity. The research carried out over years with these factors, has produced constant and substantial correlation of these primary factor scales, to a wide arrary of criteria in educational, clinical, occupational and other areas establishing its criterion of validity.

Having decided to make use of HSPQ (cattell), the questionnaire is translated into telugu, the mother tongue and the regional language of the subjects on whom, it has to be applied. Five judges who are well versed with psychological testing, checked the translation. Necessary instructions are given to the students and they were asked to answer the items as per the instructions given to them.

Adoption of the Instrument (HSPQ)

Junior- senior high school personality questionnaire (HSPQ) Form-A, prepared and standardized by cattell (1950) is adopted for the study. Telugu version of HSPQ Form-A is used for the present study.

Validity and Reliability of HSPQ

For calculating Validity and Reliability, the procedure suggested by Garrett (1973) is followed. Reliability of two subjects of each factor as obtained by the split half technique and validity, which is the square root of reliability are presented in Table 4.7. The split half reliability is calculated on a sample of 370 students.

Table 4.7 : Reliability and Validity of HSPQ Form-A, Using Split-Half Method

Factor	A	B	C	D	E	F	G
Reliability	0.623	0.747	0.752	0.683	0.799	0.771	0.749
Validity	0.789	0.864	0.867	0.826	0.894	0.878	0.865
Factor	**H**	**I**	**J**	**O**	**Q2**	**Q3**	**Q4**
Reliability	0.713	0.686	0.735	0.609	0.775	0.663	0.672
Validity	0.844	0.828	0.857	0.780	0.880	0.814	0.820

Re-test was also conducted on a sample of 370 pupils with a gap of 15 days. The test-retest Validity and Reliability for each factor is presented in the Table 4.8.

Table 4.8 : Reliability and Validity of HSPQ- Form A Using Test- Retest Method

Factor	A	B	C	D	E	F	G
Reliability	0.593	0.735	0.794	0.668	0.863	0.752	0.772
Validity	0.770	0.857	0.891	0.817	0.929	0.867	0.879
Factor	**H**	**I**	**J**	**O**	**Q2**	**Q3**	**Q4**
Reliability	0.809	0.656	0.709	0.719	0.753	0.662	0.736
Validity	0.899	0.810	0.842	0.848	0.868	0.814	0.858

The results of Validity and Reliability of HSPQ Form-A show that all the factors of HSPQ are highly valid and reliable.

Scoring Procedure for HSPQ

There are 142 items in the HSPQ. Three alternatives are given for each item. The student has to choose only one alternative which he feels appropriate for him. The scoring is done for each student and for each factor using the scoring key given by the author.

Administration of HSPQ

The Telugu version of HSPQ is administered on all the pupils (N=1800) with the help of the teachers in the morning session. Thorough inspection is done whether the students are following the instructions or not. All the answer sheets are collected and evaluated, as per the scoring key.

Personal Data Sheet

The personal data sheet prepared by the investigator with the help of experts in the field of education consists of the following particulars, with regard to the pupil's personal, socio-demographic variables:

1. Name of the pupil
2. Name of the school/Educational divisions
3. Age
4. Annual income of the family
5. Father's education
6. Father's occupation
7. Mother's education
8. Mother's occupation
9. Number of children in the family
10. Birth order
11. Number of members in the family
12. Sex
13. Religion
14. Caste
15. Nativity/Locality
16. Economic Position
17. Separate Room for study
18. Study hours at home
19. Works at home

Final Study

The final study is conducted after the construction and standardization of all the tools and adoption of the tools as described in the preceding pages.

Selection of Sample for Final Study

After the construction, standardization and adoption of all the test tools, the investigator has planned for the selection of the sample for the final study. Geographically the district is divided into four educational divisions namely, Madanapalle, Puttur, Chittoor and Tirupati. The investigator selected 36 schools, in the four educational divisions, following the stratified random sampling procedure. The total sample consists of 1800 students of 9th class. The sample design for the final study is shown in the Table-4.9.

Table 4.9 : Sample Design for Final Study

Sl. No.	Name of the School	Educational division	Total No. of students	Remarks
1	2	3	4	5
1.	Hope Municipal High School, Madanpalle	Madanapalle	50	Co-education
2.	Basavaraju Govt. High School, Punganur	Madanapalle	50	Boys
3.	Hope. High School, Madanapalle	Madanapalle	50	Co-education
4.	G.H.S.Kalikiri	Madanapalle	50	Boys
5.	Municipal . High School, Punganur	Madanapalle	50	Co-education
6.	Z.P. High School, C.T.M	Madanapalle	50	Co-education
7.	Z.P. High School, Madanapalle	Madanapalle	50	Co-education
8.	P.V.C.Govt. High School, Vayalpadu	Madanapalle	50	Co-education
9.	Z.P. High School, Basinikonda	Madanapalle	50	Co-education
10.	S.K.M.Z.P. High School, P.R. Mangalam	Puttur	50	Co-education
11.	Govt. High School, Nagalapuram	Puttur	50	Co-education
12.	Z.P. High School, K.B.R.Puram	Puttur	50	Co-education
13.	Z.P. High School, Nindra	Puttur	50	Co-education
14.	Sarvani Vidya Nikethan, Nagari	Puttur	50	Co-education

1	2	3	4	5
15.	Z.P.H. School, Dasukuppam	Puttur	50	Co-education
16.	Z.P.High School, Gate Puttur	Puttur	50	Co-education
17.	P.C.N.H.School, Nagari	Puttur	50	Boys
18.	Z. P.H.School D.M.Puram	Puttur	50	Co-education
19.	Z.P.H.School, Nelapalle	Chittoor	50	Co-education
20.	Z.P.H. School, Bandapalle	Chittoor	50	Co-education
21.	Ksthuriba G.H. School, Chittoor	Chittoor	50	Co-education
22.	Municipal High School, Greampet, Chittoor	Chittoor	50	Co-education
23.	Govt.High School Boys,Kuppam	Chittoor	50	Boys
24.	G.H.School, Santhipuram	Chittoor	50	Co-education
25.	Z.P.H.School, Santhambakkam	Chittoor	50	Co-education
26.	Z.P.H.School, Ugranapalle	Chittoor	50	Co-education
27.	Z.P.H.School, Gudipalle	Chittoor	50	Co-education
28.	M.C.H.School, Tirupati	Tirupati	50	Co-education
29.	S.G.S.High School, Tirupati	Tirupati	41	Co-education
30.	Z.P.H.School, Perumalpalle	Tirupati	40	Co-education
31.	M.C.H.School, Tirupati	Tirupati	50	Co-education

1	2	3	4	5
32.	Z.P.H.School, Cherllopalle	Tirupati	50	Co-education
33.	Z.P.Boys High School,Renigunta	Tirupati	50	Boys
34.	P.M.High School, Renigunta	Tirupati	50	Co-education
35.	Govt.High School Boys, Chandragiri	Tirupati	50	Boys
36.	S.P.Z.P.H.School, Girls,Chandragiri	Tirupati	70	Girls

Educational Division-wise Schools

Nine schools from Madanapalle Division, Nine schools from Puttur Division, Nine Schools from Chittoor Division and Nine Schools from Tirupati Division are selected for final study. The sample design for Educational division Vs. caste Vs. Sex is shown in Table 4.10.

Table 4.10 : The Sample Design for Educational Divisions Vs. Castes Vs. Sex

Educational Devisions	Caste→	SC/ST		BC		OC		Total
	Sex→	Girls	Boys	Girls	Boys	Girls	Boys	
Madanapalle		48	65	57	132	65	83	450
Puttur		78	65	107	154	23	23	450
Chittoor		40	68	126	107	64	45	450
Tirupati		45	59	100	129	70	47	450
Total		**211**	**257**	**390**	**522**	**222**	**198**	**1800**

The Geographical map showing Chittoor District in Andhra Pradesh is presented in the Figure 4.2.

Administration of Tools

Having selected the schools, following stratified random sampling method, the investigator consulted the selected Heads of Institutions personally and explained them, the purpose of the test and took their permission for holding the test. The test dates for different schools were intimated sufficiently in advance. The students were thoroughly motivated for the tests and they were given proper instructions for answering the different sets of test tools.

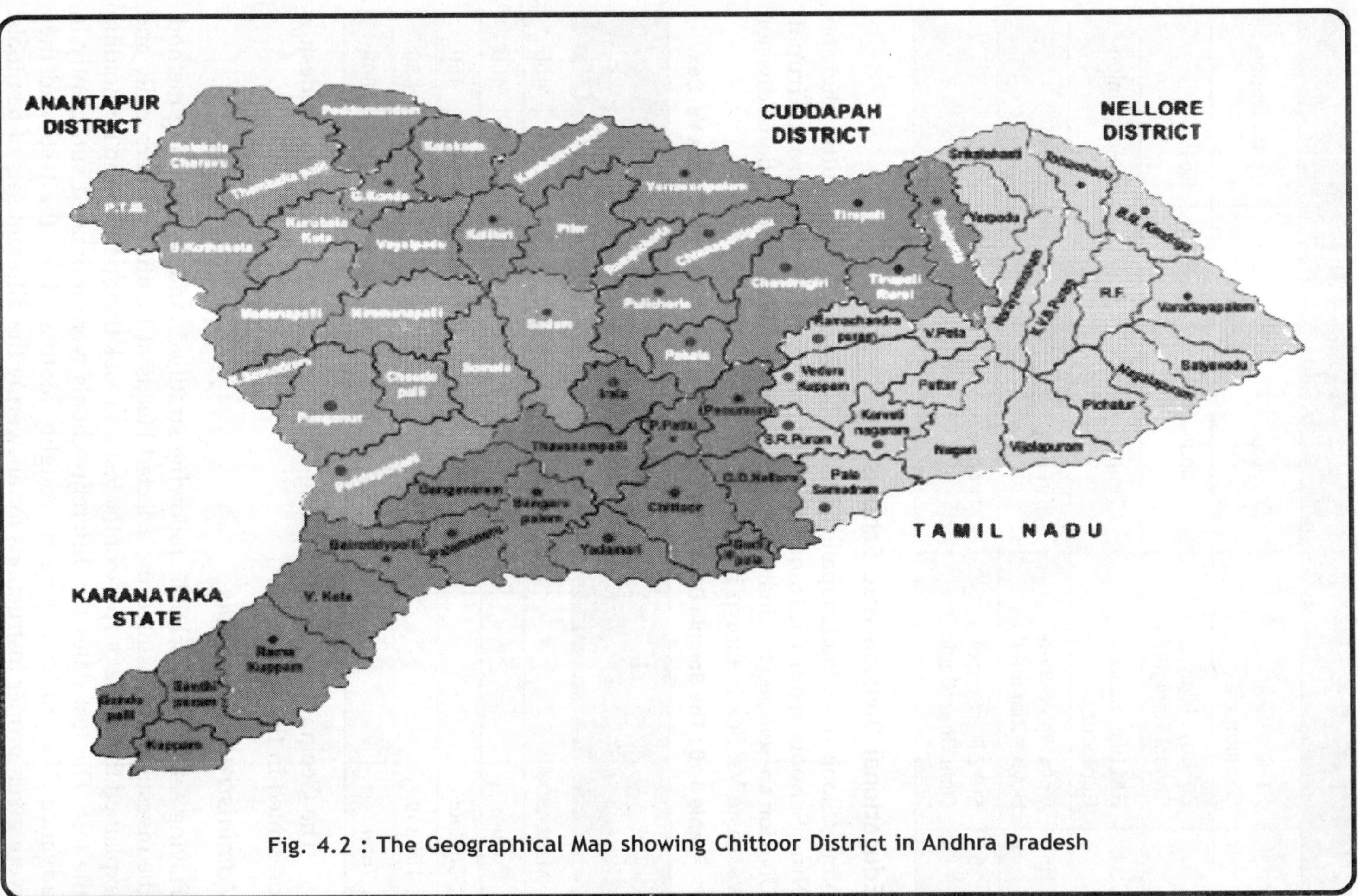

Fig. 4.2 : The Geographical Map showing Chittoor District in Andhra Pradesh

The investigator visited all the schools personally, as decided and intimated earlier. In the morning session, the sets of HSPQ, self-concept scale and study habits inventories are given to the students and with the help of teachers of concerned schools, the tests are administrated. In the afternoon session, the OAT paper and personal data sheets are given to the students. Thorough inspection is made with the help of concerned school teachers, when the students are answering the different test tools. The students who attended the school on the day of collection of data are considered for the purpose of investigation. All the data gathering instruments are collected from the students and they are evaluated following the weightages given by the test constructing authorities concerned. All the collected data are given for statistical analysis.

Scoring

Scoring is done as already explained in the preceding pages, under each tool.

Coding of the Data

The data on each variable is properly coded to suit for computer analysis.

Statistical Analysis

On the basis of the objectives of the investigation, statistical analysis is carried out by employing appropriate statistical techniques.

Frequency distribution tables, on the scholastic achievement are prepared for the total sample, for different educational divisions, for girls and, boys students, for castes. Measures of central tendency, measures of dispersion, skewness, kurtosis, co-efficient of variation and standard error of mean are computed and used wherever necessary. The inferential statistical techniques like 't' test and 'F' tests are employed to test the different Hypotheses. Multiple "R" is computed by carrying out, step-wise multiple regression analysis to find out, whether it would be possible to predict scholastic achievements in physical sciences of IX class students. The services of S.V. University computer centre are utilized. The obtained numerical values are adumberated by graphical representations. For dividing the groups, quartile values and Sten values are used wherever necessary. Sufficient number of tables are prepared.

For Statistical Formulae, the following Text Books were consulted:

1. "Applied Regression Analysis" by Drapper and Smith (1981).
2. "Fundamental Statistics in Psychology and Education" by Guilford (1950).
3. "Non-Parametric Statistics for the Behavioural Science" by Sidney Siegel (1956).

4. "Psychometric Methods" by Guilford (1954).
5. "Statistical Methods for research workers" by Fisher (1950).
6. "Statistics in Psychology" by Yate (1965).
7. "Statistical Principles in Experimental Design" by Winer (1971).
8. "Statistics in Psychology and Education" by Henry Garrette, (1973).
9. "Statistical Methods" by Gupta (1974).
10. "Statistics in Psychology and Education" by Mangal (2002).
11. Techniques of Attitude scale construction by Edwards (1969).

The significant levels employed with respective symbols are given here under:

1. ** Indicates significant at 0.01 level
2. * Indicates Significant at 0.05 level
3. @ Indicates in-significant at 0.05 level

Chapter 5 Analysis and Interpretation of the Data

This chapter deals with analysis and interpretation of the data. The analysis is presented in the following form:

1. Frequency Distribution Tables
2. Factorial Designs
3. 't' values and 'F' Ratios with respect to the influence of the independent variables on the dependent variable and
4. Regression Analysis.

Frequency Distribution Tables

The frequency distribution Tables for the Scholastic Achievement scores of IX class students in Physical sciences are presented in the following pages.

Frequency Distribution of Scholastic Achievement Scores for the Whole Group

Frequency distribution of scholastic achievement scores for the whole group is presented in Table-5.1. The Distribution characteristics namely Mean (M), Median (Md), Mode (Mo), Range (E), Quartile Deviation (QD), Standard Deviation (SD), Skewness (S_k), Kurtosis (K_u), Coefficient of variation (CV) and standard error of Mean (SE_M) are also presented in Table-5.1.

Table 5.1 : Frequency Distribution of Scholastic Achievement Scores of IX Class Students in Physical Sciences for the Total Sample

Sl.No.	CI	Limits	Midpoint	f	Cf	Cpf
1.	6 – 13	5.5 – 13.5	9.5	1	1	0.05
2.	14 – 21	13.5 – 21.5	17.5	94	95	5.28
3.	22 - 29	21.5 – 29.5	25.5	531	626	34.78
4.	30 – 37	29.5 – 37.5	33.5	537	1163	64.61
5.	38 – 45	37.5 – 45.5	41.5	284	1447	80.38
6.	46 – 53	45.5 – 53.5	49.5	188	1635	90.83
7.	54 – 61	53.5 – 61.5	57.5	123	1758	97.67
8.	62 – 69	61.5 – 69.5	65.5	31	1789	99.38
9.	70 – 77	69.5 – 77.5	73.5	9	1798	99.89
10.	78 - 85	77.5 – 85.5	81.5	1	1799	99.94
11.	86 - 93	85.5 – 93.5	89.5	1	1800	100

N=1800, M=35.55, Md=33.00, Mo=27.90, R=81.00, QD=7.50, SD=11.31, S_k=0.81, K_u=3.53, CV=31.81, SE_M = 0.27

The Scholastic Achievement test in Physical sciences is conducted for 100 marks. The test consists of 100 multiple choice questions. The data are collected on 1800 students studying under four educational divisions It is clear from the Table 5.1 that the mean value is 35.55. The median and mode values are 33.00 and 27.90. The values of skewness is 0.81 and kurtosis is 3.53. For normal distribution the value of skewness is 0.00 and kurtosis is 3.00. Hence the frequency distribution is positively skewed and leptokurtic. (The values of skewness and Kurtosis are computed based on moments; Aggarwal, 1990). It implies that the scores are massed at the low/ left end of the scale, and are spread out gradually towards high right end of the scale. The distribution is more peaked than the normal distribution. On the whole the performance of the IX class students in Physical sciences is poor, because mean achievement is less than 50.

The Histogram for the distribution of Scholastic Achievement scores in Physical sciences for the whole group is presented in Figure 5.1.

The frequency polygon for the distribution of Scholastic Achievement scores in physical sciences is shown in Figure 5.2.

The Ogive for the distribution of Scholastic Achievement scores in physical sciences is presented in Figure 5.3.

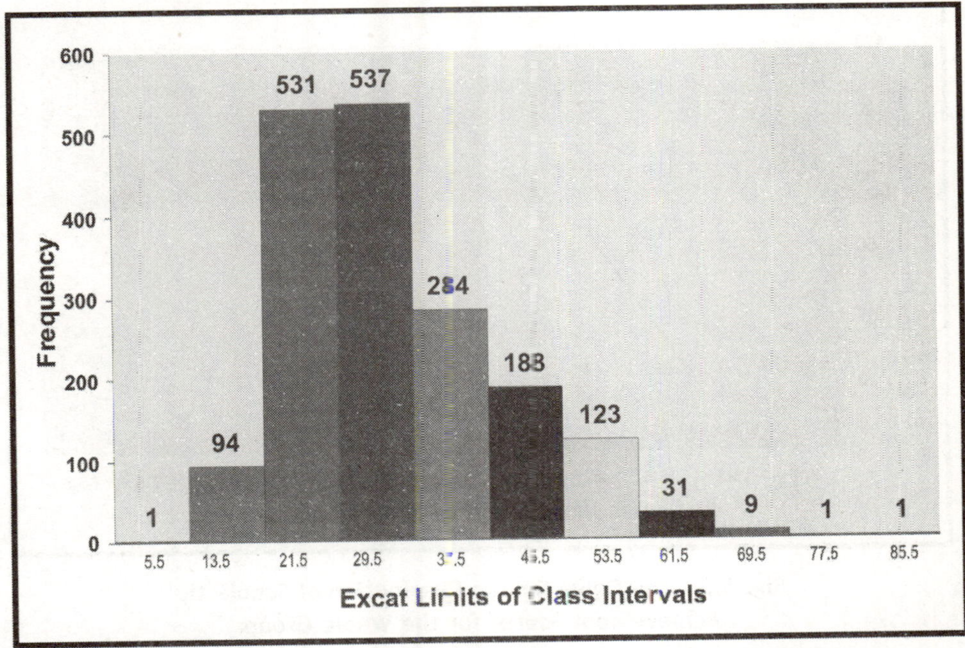

Fig. 5.1 : The Histogram for the Distribution of Schoolastic Achievement Scores in Physical Sciences for the Whole Group

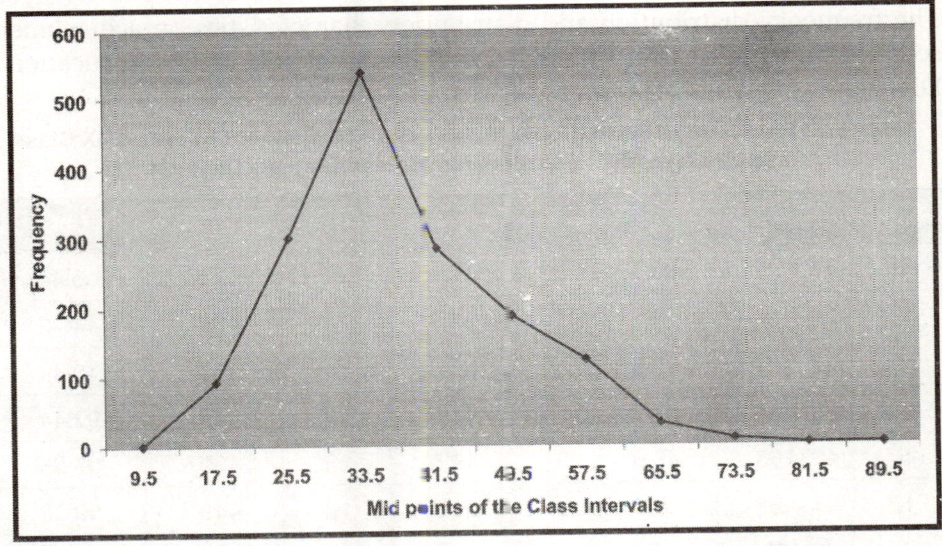

Fig. 5.2 : Frequency Polygon for the Distribution of Scholastic Achievement Sores for the Whole Group

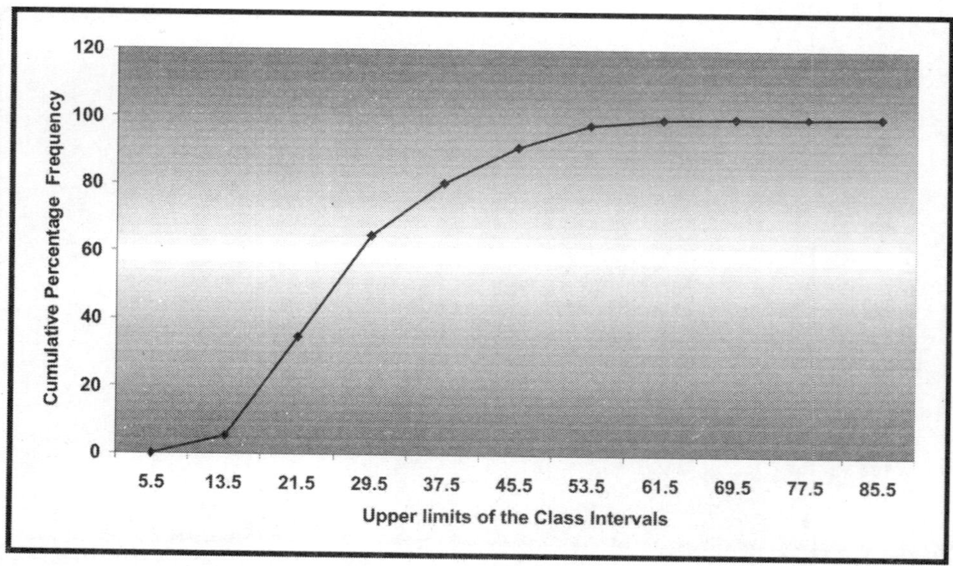

Fig. 5.3 : The Ogive for the Distribution of Scholastic Achievement Scores for the Whole Group

Frequency Distribution of Scholastic Achievement Scores for the Variable Educational Divisions

There are four 'Educational Divisions' in Chittoor District namely 1. Madanapalle Division, 2. Puttur Division, 3. Chittoor Division and, 4. Tirupati Division. The frequency distribution and distribution characteristics on achievement scores for the students studying in the above schools of four Educational Divisions are presented from Tables 5.2 to 5.3.

Table 5.2 : Frequency Distribution of Scholastic Achievement Scores of IX Class Students in Physical sciences for Madanapalle Division

Sl.No.	CI	Limits	Midpoint	f	Cf	Cpf
1.	14 – 21	13.5 – 21.5	17.5	29	29	6.44
2.	22 – 29	21.5 – 29.5	25.5	170	199	44.22
3.	30 – 37	29.5 – 37.5	33.5	154	353	78.44
4.	38 – 45	37.5 – 45.5	41.5	63	416	92.44
5.	46 – 53	45.5 – 53.5	49.5	23	439	97.56
6.	54 – 61	53.5 – 61.5	57.5	10	449	99.78
7.	62 - 69	61.5 - 69.5	65.5	1	450	100

N=450, M=31.80, Md=30.00, Mo=26.41, R=51.00,QD=5.00, SD=8.39, Sk=0.93, Ku=4.08, CV=26.00, SEM = 0.40

Table 5.3 : Frequency Distribution of Scholastic Achievement Scores of IX Class Students in Physical Sciences for Puttur Division.

Sl.No.	CI	Limits	Midpoint	f	Cf	Cpf
1.	14 - 21	13.5 - 21.5	17.5	12	12	2.67
2.	22 - 29	21.5 - 29.5	25.5	82	94	20.89
3.	30 - 37	29.5 - 37.5	33.5	82	176	39.11
4.	38 - 45	37.5 - 45.5	41.5	52	228	50.67
5.	46 - 53	45.5 - 53.5	49.5	92	320	71.11
6.	54 - 61	53.5 - 61.5	57.5	93	413	91.78
7.	62 - 69	61.5 - 69.5	65.5	28	441	98.00
8.	70 - 77	69.5 - 77.5	73.5	8	449	99.78
9.	78 - 85	77.5 - 85.5	81.5	1	450	100

N=450, M=43.52, Md=45.00, Mo=47.96, R=67.00 QD=12.00, SD=13.78, Sk=0.091, Ku=2.06, CV=31.67, SEM = 0.65

Table 5.4 : Frequency Distribution of Scholastic Achievement Scores of IX Class Students in Physical Sciences for Chittoor Division.

Sl.No.	CI	Limits	Midpoint	f	Cf	Cpf
1.	14 - 21	13.5 - 21.5	17.5	30	30	6.67
2.	22 - 29	21.5 - 29.5	25.5	131	161	35.78
3.	30 - 37	29.5 - 37.5	33.5	157	318	70.67
4.	38 - 45	37.5 - 45.5	41.5	79	397	88.22
5.	46 - 53	45.5 - 53.5	49.5	42	439	97.56
6.	54 - 61	53.5 - 61.5	57.5	9	448	99.56
7.	62 - 69	61.5 - 69.5	65.5	2	450	100

N=450, M=33.39, Md=32.00, Mo=29.21, R=47.00,QD=6.00, SD=8.96, Sk=0.35, Ku=2.99, CV=26.83, SEM =0.42

It is observed from the above tables that the students studying in Puttur Division schools have better achievement than the students in other divisions of schools. The achievement of the students studying in Madanapalle division schools is the lowest as compared to the achievement of the students studying in other divisions of schools.

Table 5.5 : Frequency Distribution of Scholastic Achievement Scores of IX Class Students in Physical Sciences for Tirupati Division

Sl.No.	CI	Limits	Midpoint	f	Cf	Cpf
1.	6 - 13	5.5 - 13.5	9.5	1	1	0.22
2.	14 - 21	13.5 - 21.5	17.5	23	24	5.33
3.	22 - 29	21.5 - 29.5	25.5	148	172	38.22
4.	30 - 37	29.5 - 37.5	33.5	144	316	70.22
5.	38 - 45	37.5 - 45.5	41.5	90	406	90.22
6.	46 - 53	45.5 - 53.5	49.5	31	437	97.11
7.	54 - 61	53.5 - 61.5	57.5	11	448	99.55
8.	62 - 69	61.5 - 69.5	65.5	0	448	99.55
9.	70 - 77	69.5 - 77.5	73.5	1	449	99.78
10.	78 - 85	77.5 - 85.5	81.5	0	449	99.78
11.	86 - 93	85.5-93.5	89.5	1	450	100

N=450, M=33.49, Md=32.00, Mo=29.03, R=81.00,QD=6.00, SD=9.18, Sk=1.08, Ku=5.76, CV=27.42, SEM =0.43

The Standard Deviation of the achievement scores in Puttur Division schools is more than all others. The Standard Deviation of the achievement scores in Madanapalle division Schools is the least. The value of skewness is positive for all the distributions. It implies that the scores are massed at low/

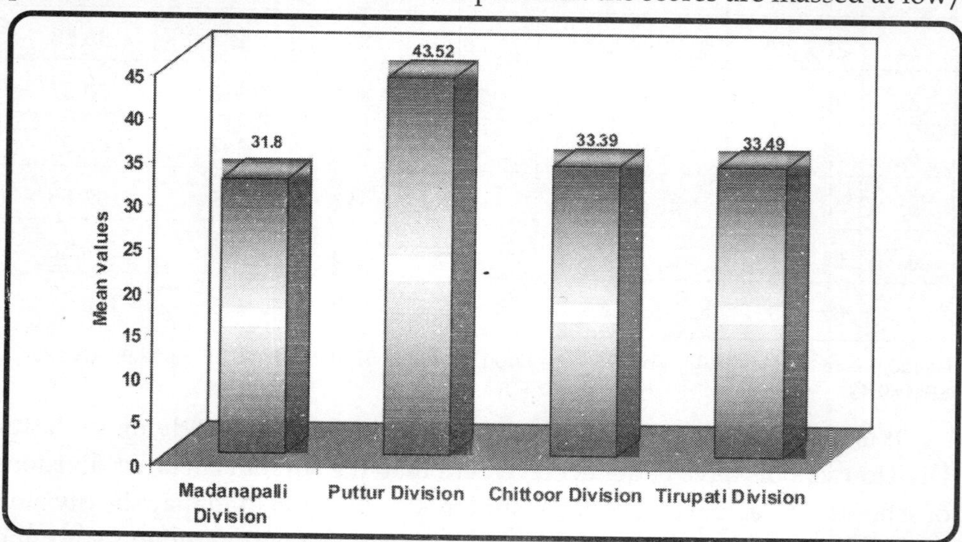

Fig. 5.4 : The Bar Diagram for the Mean Achievement Socres for Different Educational Divisions

left end of the scale and are spread out gradually towards the high/ right end of the scale. The distributions of achievement scores are leptokurtic for the students studying in Madanapalle division and Tirupati division Schools where as the distribution of achievement scores are platykurtic for the students studying in Puttur division schools. The distribution of achievement scores for Chittoor Division schools are very nearer to normal distribution

The bar diagram for the mean achievement scores for the different 'Educational divisions' is shown in Figure 5.4.

Frequency Distribution Tables for the Scholastic Achievement Scores for the Variable 'Sex'

There are two divisions in the variable 'sex' namely, 1. Girls and 2. Boys. The frequency distribution and distribution characteristics of achievement scores for both the groups are presented in Tables 5.6 and 5.7.

Table 5.6 : Frequency Distribution of Scholastic Achievement Scores of IX Class Students in Physical Sciences for Girls

Sl.No.	Ci	Limits	Midpoint	f	Cf	Cpf
1.	14 - 21	13.5 - 21.5	17.5	41	41	4.98
2.	22 - 29	21.5 - 29.5	25.5	216	257	31.23
3.	30 - 37	29.5 - 37.5	33.5	238	495	60.15
4.	38 - 45	37.5 - 45.5	41.5	150	645	78.37
5.	46 - 53	45.5 - 53.5	49.5	86	731	88.82
6.	54 - 61	53.5 - 61.5	57.5	74	805	97.81
7.	62 - 69	61.5 - 69.5	65.5	17	822	99.88
8.	70 - 77	69.5 - 77.5	73.5	1	823	100

N=823, M=36.43, Md=34.00, Mo=29.13, R=55.00,QD=8.00, SD=11.29, Sk=0.40, Ku=2.65, CV=30.99, SEM = 0.39

It is observed from the Tables 5.16 and 5.17 that there are 823 girls and 977 boys. The mean of girls is 36.43 and that of boys is 34.80. Hence the girls performance is slightly better than boys. The standard deviations of achievement scores of both girls and boys are almost equal (11.29 and 11.26 respectively). The values of skewness are positive for both the distributions. It implies that the scores are massed at low/left end of the scale and are spread out gradually towards the high/ right end of the scale for both the groups.

The values of Kurtosis for girls and boys are 2.65 and 4.42. respectively. Hence the distribution of achievement scores for boys is lefto-kurtic and girls is platy kurtic.

Table 5.7 : Frequency Distribution of Scholastic Achievement Scores of IX Class Students in Physical Sciences for Boys

Sl.No.	CI	Limits	Midpoint	f	Cf	Cpf
1.	6 - 13	5.5 - 13.5	9.5	1	1	0.10
2.	14 - 21	13.5 - 21.5	17.5	53	54	5.53
3.	22 - 29	21.5 - 29.5	25.5	315	369	37.77
4.	30 - 37	29.5 - 37.5	33.5	299	668	68.37
5.	38 - 45	37.5 - 45.5	41.5	134	802	82.09
6.	46 - 53	45.5 - 53.5	49.5	102	904	92.53
7.	54 - 61	53.5 - 61.5	57.5	49	953	97.54
8.	62 - 69	61.5 - 69.5	65.5	14	967	98.98
9.	70 - 77	69.5 - 77.5	73.5	8	975	99.79
10.	78 - 85	77.5 - 85.5	81.5	1	976	99.89
11.	86 - 93	85.5 - 93.5	89.5	1	977	100

N=977, M=34.80, Md=32.00, Mo=26.39, R=81.00,QD=7.00, SD=11.26, Sk=1.29, Ku=4.42, CV=32.37, SEM = 0.36

The bar diagram for the mean achievement scores for girls and boys is given in Figure 5.5.

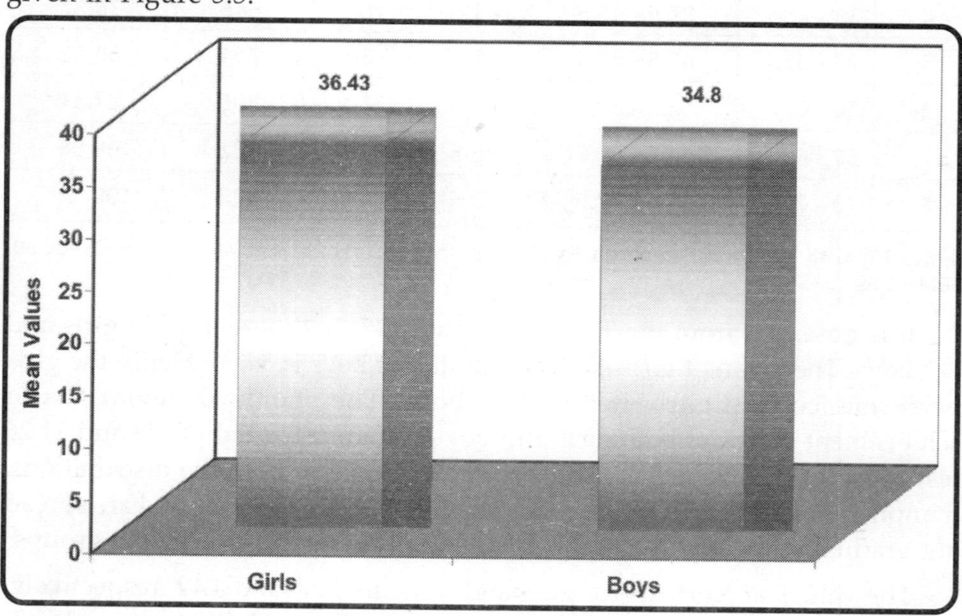

Fig. 5.5 : The Bar Diagram for the Mean Achievement Scores for Girls and Boys

Frequency Distribution Tables for the Scholastic Achievement Scores for the variable "Caste"

There are three divisions in the variable 'Caste' namely 1. Schedule Caste/ Tribes (SC/ST) 2. Backward caste (B.C) and 3. Other Castes (OC). The Frequency distributions and distribution characteristics of achievement scores for the students of students of the above three types, are presented from Tables 5.8 to 5.10.

Table 5.8 : Frequency Distribution of Scholastic Achievement Scores of IX Class Students in Physical Sciences for SC/ST Students

Sl.No.	CI	Limits	Midpoint	f	Cf	Cpf
1	14 – 21	13.5 – 21.5	17.5	30	30	6.41
2	22 – 29	21.5 – 29.5	25.5	153	183	39.10
3	30 – 37	29.5 – 37.5	33.5	138	321	68.59
4	38 – 45	37.5 – 45.5	41.5	63	384	82.05
5	46 - 53	45.5 – 53.5	49.5	51	435	92.95
6	54 – 61	53.5 – 61.5	57.5	23	458	97.86
7	62 – 69	61.5 – 69.5	65.5	7	465	99.36
8	70 - 77	69.5 – 77.5	73.5	3	468	100

N=468, M=34.46, Md=32.00, Mo=27.08, R=52.00,QD=7.50, SD=11.03, S_k=0.91, K_u=3.67, CV=32.01, SE_M=0.51

Table 5.9 : Frequency Distribution of Scholastic Achievement Scores of IX Class Students in Physical Sciences for B.C Students

Sl.No.	CI	Limits	Midpoint	f	Cf	Cpf
1	6 – 13	5.5 – 13.5	9.5	1	1	0.11
2	14 – 21	13.5 – 21.5	17.5	46	47	5.15
3	22 – 29	21.5 – 29.5	25.5	273	320	35.09
4	30 – 37	29.5 – 37.5	33.5	259	579	63.49
5	38 – 45	37.5 – 45.5	41.5	129	708	77.63
6	46 – 53	45.5 – 53.5	49.5	98	806	88.34
7	54 – 61	53.5 – 61.5	57.5	80	886	97.15
8	62 – 69	61.5 – 69.5	65.5	18	904	99.12
9	70 – 77	69.5 – 77.5	73.5	6	910	99.78
10	78 – 85	77.5 – 85.5	81.5	1	911	99.89
11	86 - 93	85.5 – 93.5	89.5	1	912	100

N= 912, M=36.09, Md=32.00, Mo=23.82, R=8 .00,QD=8.50, SD=12.05, S_k=0.82, K_u=3.39, CV=33.39, SE_M = 0.40

Table 5.10 : Frequency Distribution of Scholastic Achievement Scores of IX Class Students in Physical Sciences for O.C Students

Sl.No.	CI	Limits	Midpoint	f	Cf	Cpf
1.	14 – 21	13.5 – 21.5	17.5	18	18	4.28
2.	22 – 29	21.5 – 29.5	25.5	105	123	29.28
3.	30 – 37	29.5 – 37.5	33.5	140	263	62.62
4.	38 – 45	37.5 – 45.5	41.5	92	355	84.52
5.	46 – 53	45.5 – 53.5	49.5	39	394	93.81
6.	54 – 61	53.5 – 61.5	57.5	20	414	98.57
7.	62 – 69	61.5 – 69.5	65.5	6	420	100

N= 420, M=35.58, Md=34.00, Mo=30.82, R=48.00,QD=6.00, SD=9.75, S_k=0.45, K_u=3.15, CV=27.40, SE_M =0.47

From Tables 5.8, 5.9 and 5.10, it is observed that there are 468 SC/ST students, (as the number of S.T students are very less, SC and ST are clubbed), 912 BC students and 420 OC students (Total sample N=1800).

It is observed from the above tables that there is slight difference in the mean performance of SC/ST (34.46) , B.C (36.09) and OC (35.58) students. The standard deviations of the achievement scores of OC students is less than all others. The value of skewness is positive for all the distributions. It implies that the scores are massed at low/ left end of the scale and are spread out gradually towards the high/ right end.

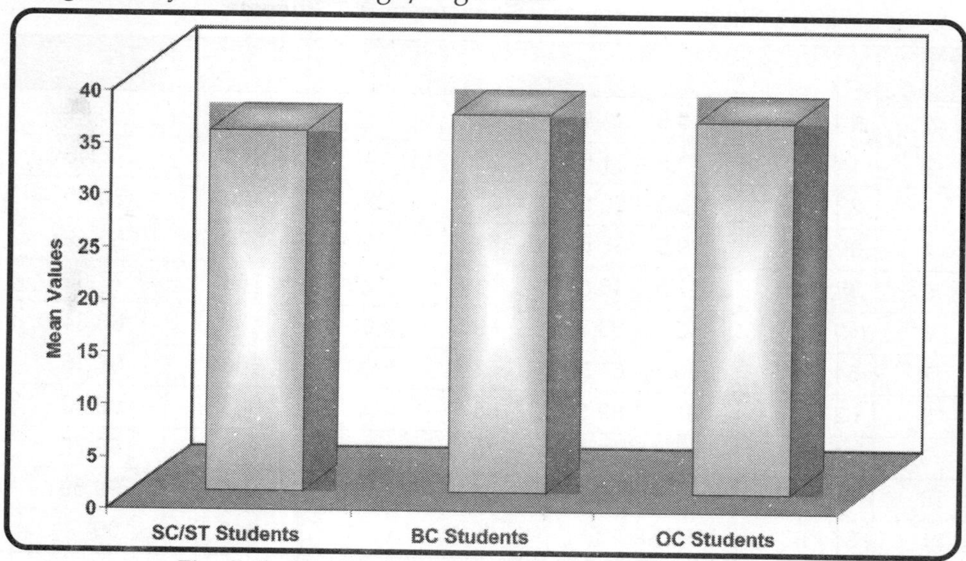

Fig. 5.6 : The Bar Diagram for the Mean Achievement Scores of SC/ST, BC and OC Students

The values of kurtosis for SC/ST, BC and OC students are 3.67, 3.39 and 3.15 respectively. Hence the distributions of achievement scores for SC/ST, BC and OC students are slightly leptokurtic.

The bar diagram for the mean achievement scores of SC/ST, BC and OC students is presented in Figure 5.6.

The values of N, M, SD, S_k, K_u, R and SE_M for the distribution of Scholastic Achievement scores for different groups of the sample

The values of N, M, S.D, S_k, K_u, R and SE_M for the distribution of Scholastic Achievement scores in Physical Sciences of IX class students for the different groups of the sample are presented in Table 5.11.

Table 5.11 : The Values of N, M, SD, S_k, K_u, R and SE_M for the Distribution of Scholastic Achievement Scores in Physical Sciences of IX Class Students for the Different Groups of the Sample

Sl.No.	Group	N	M	SD	Sk	Ku	R	SE_M
1.	Whole group	1800	35.55	11.31	0.81	3.53	81	0.27
2.	Madanapalle division schools	450	31.80	8.39	0.93	4.08	51	0.40
3.	Puttur division Schools	450	43.52	13.78	0.09	2.06	67	0.65
4.	Chittoor Division schools	450	33.39	8.96	0.35	2.99	47	0.42
5.	Tirupati division schools	450	33.49	9.18	1.08	5.76	81	0.43
6.	Girls	823	35.43	11.29	0.40	2.65	55	0.39
7.	Boys	977	34.80	11.26	1.29	4.42	81	0.36
8.	SC/ST	468	34.46	11.03	0.91	3.67	62	0.51
9.	B.C	912	35.09	12.05	0.82	3.39	81	0.40
10.	O.C	420	35.58	9.75	0.45	3.15	48	0.47

It is clear from Table 5.1 that the mean Scholastic Achievement for the students of Puttur division schools is the highest (43.52) among all the groups and the lowest (31.80) for the students of Madanapalle division schools. The standard deviation of achievement scores for the students of Puttur division schools is the highest (13.78) among all the groups and the lowest (8.39) for the students of Madanapalle division schools. The values of skewness for all the groups is positive. It implies that the scores are massed at low/left end of the scale and slowly spread over towards the high/right end of the scale. The values of kurtosis for the students of Puttur division schools (2.06) Chittoor division Schools (2.99) and girls (2.65) are less than the normal value (3.00) and hence the distributions are platy kurtic. The value of kurtosis for the remaining groups is more than 3.00 and hence the distributions are leptokurtic. The value of kurtosis for the students of Tirupati division schools (5.76) is the highest among all the groups and the distribution is highly leptokurtic. For the remaining groups, the values of kurtosis are slightly greater than the normal value (3.00) and hence the distributions are slightly leftokurtic.

Factorial Designs

The influence of the variables Educational division, sex and caste and their interactions on the Scholastic Achievement of IX class students in Physical sciences is studied with the help of Factorial Design.

Factorial Design for Educational Division, Sex and Caste

The influence of educational division, sex and caste on Scholastic Achievement of IX class students in physical sciences is investigated by employing 4 × 2 × 3 Factorial Design.

The following hypotheses are formulated:

Hypothesis-1

There would be no significant influence of main effects namely educational divisions, sex and caste on the Scholastic Achievement of students in physical sciences.

Hypothesis-2

There would be no significant impact of interaction effect of educational division, sex and caste on the Scholastic Achievement.

The above hypotheses are tested through 4 × 2 × 3 factorial design. The results of Analysis of variance (ANOVA) of 4 × 2 × 3 factorial design for Scholastic Achievement scores are presented in Table 5.12.

It is observed from Table 5.12 that the computed value of 'F' for the main effect 'Educational division' is 77.23. The Table / critical value of 'F' for 3 and 1776 degrees of freedom (df) at 0.05 level is 2.60 and at 0.01 level is 3.78. The computed value is far greater than the critical value at 0.01 level of significance. Hence the Hypothesis-1 is rejected for the main effect educational division. Hence it is concluded that the educational division has significant influence on the achievement of IX class students in physical sciences. The performance of students in Puttur educational division is significantly better than the students in other three educational divisions.

Table 5.12 : Results of ANOVA of 4 × 2 × 3 Factorial Design for Scholastic Achievement Scores of IX Class Students in Physical Sciences

Factor A : Educational divisions (4 Levels)

Factor B : Sex (2 Levels)

Factor C : Caste (3 Levels).

Sl. No.	Source of variance	Sum of squares	df	Mean Squares	F-Value	Level of Significance
1.	A	23864.6800	3	7954.8940	77.2342	* *
2.	B	944.8041	1	944.8041	9.1731	* *
3.	C	1564.5400	2	782.2702	7.5951	* *
4.	AB	360.9946	3	120.3315	1.1683	@
5.	AC	3066.4390	6	511.0732	4.9620	* *
6.	BC	94.5380	2	47.2690	0.4589	@
7.	ABC	620.4271	6	103.4045	1.004	@
8.	Error	182922.80	1776	102.9971		

The computed value of 'F' for the mean effect 'Sex' is 9.17. The critical value of 'F' for 1 and 1776 df at 0.05 level is 3.84 and 0.01 level is 6.64. The computed value is for greater than critical value at 0.01 level of significance. Hence Hypothesis – 1 is rejected for the main effect 'Sex'. Therefore it is concluded that 'Sex' has significant influence on the Scholastic Achievement of IX class students in Physical sciences. The performance of girls is significantly better than boys.

The computed value of 'F' for the main effect 'Caste' is 7.60 The Table / Critical value of F for 2 and 1776 df at 0.05 level is 2.99 and at 0.01 level is 4.60. The computed value of 'F' is far greater than the critical value. Hence hypothesis -1 is rejected for the main effect 'Caste' at 0.01 level of significance. Therefore it is concluded that Caste has significant influence on the Scholastic Achievement of IX class students in Physical sciences. It is found that Back ward caste students performance is significantly better than SC/ST and other caste students.

Similar results are reported by Dubey and Mishra (1977), Jagannadham (1983), Gopalacharyulu (1984) , Singh (1993), Mehra (1992) and Dash (2002).

Contradictory results were revealed by Kumaraswamy (1992), Jayachandrama naidu (1998), and Govindareddy (2002).

The computed value of 'F' for the two factor interaction effect namely educational division × caste is 4.96. The Table/Critical value of 'F' is for 6 and 1776 df at 0.05 level is 2.09 and at 0.01 level is 2.80. The computed value of 'F' is far greater than the critical value. Therefore, Hypothesis-2 is rejected for the two factor interaction effect namely educational division × caste at 0.01 level of significance. Hence it is concluded that the two factors interaction namely educational division x caste has significant influence on the Scholastic Achievement of IX class student in Physical sciences.

The computed value of 'F' for the two factor interaction effect (i) Educational division × sex and (ii) sex × caste are less than critical values of 'F' for 3 and 1776 df and 2 and 1776 df at 0.05 level. Therefore Hypothesis-2 is accepted at 0.05 level for the two factor interactions effects namely (i) Educational division × sex and (ii) sex × caste. Hence it is concluded that the two factors interactions namely (1) Educational division × sex and (2) Sex × caste do not have significant influence on the Scholastic Achievement of IX class students in physical sciences.

The computed value of 'F' For three factor interaction effect namely Educational division × sex × caste is 1.00 which is less than Table/Critical value of 'F' for 6 and 1776 df at 0.05 level of significance (2.09). Hence, Hypothesis -2 is accepted for three factor interaction effect at 0.05 level of significance. Therefore ,it is concluded that the three factor interaction namely Educational division × sex × caste does not have significant influence on Scholastic Achievement of IX class students in physical sciences.

Factorial Design for Age, Religion and Nativity

The impact of Age, Religion and Nativity on the Scholastic Achievement of 9th class students in physical sciences is studied by using 3 × 3 × 3 factorial design. The following Hypotheses is formulated.

Hypothesis-3

There would be no significant influence of main effects namely age, religion and nativity, on the Scholastic Achievement of IX class students in physical sciences.

Hypothesis-4

There would be no significant influence of interaction effect of age, religion and nativity on the achievement.

The above hypotheses are tested through 3×3 ×3 factorial design. The results of Analysis of variance (ANOVA) of 3×3×3 factorial design for Scholastic Achievement scores are presented in the Table 5.13.

Table 5.13 : Results of ANOVA of 3 × 3 × 3 Factorial Design for Scholastic Achievement scores of IX class students in Physical sciences.

Factor A : Age (3 Levels)

Factor B : Religion (3 Levels)

Factor C : Nativity (3 Levels).

Sl. No.	Source of variance	Sum of squares	df	Mean Squares	F – Value	Level of Significance
1	A	421.9588	2	210.9794	1.6444	@
2	B	361.6378	2	180.8189	1.4093	@
3	C	134.7880	2	67.3940	0.5253	@
4	AB	245.7818	4	61.4454	0.4789	@
5	AC	71.0026	4	17.7507	0.1384	@
6	BC	335.6252	4	83.9063	0.6540	@
7	ABC	616.8248	8	77.1031	0.6010	@
8	Error	227477.8000	1773	128.3011		

It is observed from Table 5.13 that the computed values of 'F' for all the main effects namely 1. Age 2. Religion and 3. Nativity are less than the Table/ critical value of 'F' for 2 and 1773 df at 0.05 level of significance (2.99). Hence Hypothesis-3 is accepted for all the main effects. Therefore it is concluded that the main effects namely 1. Age 2. Religion and 3. Nativity do not have significant influence on the Scholastic Achievement of IX class students in physical sciences.

It is also seen from Table 5.13 that all the two factor interaction effects namely 1. Age × Religion 2. Age × Nativity and 3. Religion × Nativity do not have significant influence on the Scholastic Achievement of IX class students in physical sciences at 0.05 level of significance.

It is also noticed from Table 5.13 that the computed value of 'F' for three factors interaction effect namely Age × Religion × Nativity is 0.60. The Table/ critical value of 'F' for 8 and 1773 df at 0.05 level is 1.94. The computed value of 'F' is less than critical value. Therefore Hypothesis-4 is accepted for the three factor interaction effect at 0.05 level of significance. Hence it is concluded that the three factor interaction namely, Age × Religion × Nativity does not have significance effect on Scholastic Achievement of IX class students in physical sciences.

The Influence of Socio-Demographic, Psychological Variables

The influence of socio-demographic variables and psychological variables namely socio-demographic (personal) variables, study habits, self concepts and personality factors on Scholastic Achievement of the IX class students in physical sciences is investigated.

The Impact of Socio-Demographic Variables on the Scholastic Achievement

The influence of socio-demographic variables on the Scholastic Achievement of students is studied. The following socio-demographic variables are considered for the analysis:

1. Educational divisions
2. Age
3. Income of the family
4. Father's education
5. Father's Occupation
6. Mother's education
7. Mother's Occupation
8. Number of children
9. Birth order
10. Number of members in the family
11. Sex
12. Religion
13. Caste
14. Nativity
15. Economic Position
16. Separate Room for study
17. Study hours at home
18. works at home

The following Hypothesis is framed.

Hypothesis-5

There would be no significant influence of socio-demographic variables on the Scholastic Achievement of IX class students in physical sciences.

The above Hypothesis is tested for each variable from 1 to 18 as shown above by employing one way Analysis of variance (ANOVA).

1. Educational Divisions

The needed data is collected from the schools of Chittoor District. Chittoor District is divided in to four Educational Divisions. Namely 1. Madanapalle 2.Puttur 3. Chittoor and 4.Tirupathi

The impact of educational division on the Scholastic Achievement of IX class students in physical sciences is investigated. By employing one way ANOVA and the results are presented in Table 5.14.

Table 5.14 : Influence of Educational Divisions on the Scholastic Achievement

Sl. No.	Educational Division	N	M	SD	F	Level of Significance
1.	Madanapalle	450	31.7956	8.3986	121.8594	**
2.	Puttur	450	43.5178	13.7967		
3.	Chittoor	450	33.3933	8.9708		
4.	Tirupati	450	33.4867	9.1919		

It is observed from Table 5.14 that the computed value of ' F' (121.86) is far greater than Table/critical value of 'F' (3.78) for 3 and 1796 df at 0.01 level of significance. Therefore Hypothesis-5 is rejected for the variable 'Educational Division' at 0.01 level of significance. It is concluded that 'Educational Division' has significance influence on the Scholastic Achievement of IX class students in physical sciences.

If any one is interested to know which mean differs significantly from the other Duncan's New Multiple range test for equal number or 't' test may be applied and the results may be drawn accordingly because the needed data is already available in Table 5.14.

2. Age

The age of IX class students in this investigation varies from 13 to 17 years. On the basis of age, the students are divided into three groups namely Group-I is formed with 13 years age, Group-II is formed with 14 years age and Group-III is formed with 15 years and above age. The influence of age on Scholastic Achievement is investigated by employing one way ANOVA. The number of students in each age group, the values of mean, standard deviation and 'F' values are presented in the Table 5.15.

It is seen from Table 5.15 that the computed value of 'F' (2.95) is less than Table / critical value of 'F' (2.99) for 2 and 1797 df at 0.05 level of significance. Therefore Hypothesis-5 is accepted at 0.05 level of significance for the variable 'Age'. Hence it is concluded that 'Age' does not have significant influence on the Scholastic Achievement of IX class students in physical sciences.

Table 5.15 : Influence of Age on the Scholastic Achievement

Sl. No.	Age	N	M	SD	F	Level of Significance
1	13 Years	245	34.47	11.9975		
2	14 Years	1280	35.97	11.2833	2.9514	@
3	15 Years & Above	275	34.52	10.6997		

Similar results were reported by Hara Govinda Guptha (1968), Asudulla, Prakasham *et al.* (1982), Quraishi and Bhat (1986), Biswas (2001), Govindha Reddy (2002) and Krishna reddy (2008).

Contradictory results were reported by Srivastava (1967), Vyas (1982), Dowson *et al.* (1999), Suneetha and Mayuri (2002), and Manchala (2007).

3. Annual Income of the Family

The impact of 'Annual income of the family' on the Scholastic Achievement of students in physical sciences is studied. On the basis of annual income of the family the students are divided in to three groups. Group-I is formed with annual income below Rs. 25,000. Group-II is formed with annual income from Rs. 25,000 to Rs. 50,000. Group-III is formed with annual income above Rs. 50,000. One way ANOVA is employed and the results are shown in Table 5.16.

Table 5.16 : Influence of Annual Income on the Scholastic Achievement

Sl. No.	Annual Income	N	M	SD	F	Level of Significance
1.	Below Rs. 25,000	1648	35.8113	11.3220		
2.	Rs.25,000 to 50,000	68	36.8235	12.9407	13.6519	**
3.	Above Rs. 50,000	84	29.3571	7.2305		

It is evident from the Table 5.6 that the computed value of 'F' (13.65) is far greater than the critical value of 'F' (4.60) for 2 and 1797 df at 0.01 level of significance. Therefore Hypothesis-5 is rejected for the variable 'annual income of the family' at 0.01 level of significance. Hence it is concluded that 'annual income of the family' has significance influence on Scholastic Achievement of the students in physical sciences. Kramer's test r 't' test may be employed for further analysis.

Similar results were revealed by Fraser (1959), Gopal Rao (1965), Hara Govinda Gupta (1968), Jagannadhan (1986), Vijayakumar Sethi (1990),

Bujendranatha Panda (1991), Govinda Reddy (2002), Selvan and Sundaravalli (2002), Manchala (2007) and Krishna Reddy (2008).

Contradictory results were revealed by Wiseman (1964), Jayachandrama Naidu (1998) and Krishna Moorthy (1999).

4. *Father's Education*

The influence of 'Father's Education' on the Scholastic Achievement of IX class students in physical sciences is investigated. On the basis of Father's Education the students are divided in to three groups Group-I is formed with Father's Education up to X class. Group II is formed with Father's Education Intermediate and Degree and Group-III is formed with Father's Education Post Graduation and other professionals. One way ANOVA is used and the results are reported in Table 5.17.

Table 5.17 : Influence of Father's Education on the Scholastic Achievement.

Sl. No.	Fathers Education	N	M	SD	F	Level of Significance
1.	Up to X Class	1640	35.4573	11.2675	0.6633	@
2.	Inter & Degree	145	36.5862	11.6378		
3.	P.G & Other Professions	15	35.4667	13.0157		

It is clear from Table 5.17 that the computed value of 'F' (0.66) is less than the critical value of 'F' (2.99) for 2 and 1797 df at 0.05 level of significance. Therefore Hypothesis-5 is accepted for the variable Father's Education. Hence it is concluded that the Father's Education does not have significant influence on Scholastic Achievement of IX class students in physical sciences.

Similar results were reported from Hara Govinda Gupta (1968), Ranga swamy and Visveswara (1977) and N.C.E.R.T Report (2008).

Contradictory results were reported by Sarma (1984), Jagannadhan (1986), Vijayakumar Sethi (1990); Bhupendra Nath Panda (1991), Krishna Moorthy (1999), Chakrabarthi and Samanstha (2002), Govinda Reddy and Panda (2002a), Manchala (2007) and Krishna reddy (2008).

5. *Father's Occupation*

The impact of 'Father's Occupation' on the Scholastic Achievement of IX class students in physical sciences is investigated. On the basis of Father's Occupation the students are divided into three groups. Group-I is formed with Father's Occupation mainly Labour, Group-II is formed with Father's Occupation Agriculture and caste occupation. Group-III is formed with the Father's Occupation namely Employees and other professions. One way ANOVA is employed and the results are presented in Table 5.18.

Table 5.18 : Influence of Father's Occupation on the Scholastic Achievement

Sl. No.	Father's Occupation	N	M	SD	F	Level of Significance
1	Labour	798	36.084	11.702	1.78	@
2	Agriculture & Caste occupation	900	35.192	10.977		
3	Employees and other Professions	102	34.500	10.994		

It is clear from Table 5.18 that the computed value of 'F' (1.78) is less than critical value of 'F' (2.99) for 2 and 1797 df at 0.05 level of significance. Therefore Hypothesis-5 is accepted for the variable Father's Occupation at 0.05 level of significance. Hence, it is concluded that fathers occupation has no influence on Scholastic Achievement of IX class students in physical sciences.

Har Govinda Gupta (1968), Ranga Swamy and Visveswara (1977) and Panda (2002), found similar results.

Pavithran and Feroze (1965), Bujendranatha Panda (1991), Govinda Reddy (2002), Manchala (2007) and Krishna reddy (2008) reported contradictory results.

6. Mother's Education

The effect of Mother's education on Scholastic Achievement of IX class students in physical sciences is studied. On the basis of Mother's education the students are divided into two groups. Group-I is formed with Mothers education up to X class. Group II is formed with Mother's education Intermediate and above. 't' technique is employed and the results are shown in Table 5.19.

Table 5.19 : Influence of Mother's Education on the Scholastic Achievement.

Sl. No.	Mother's Occupation	N	M	SD	't'	Level of Significance
1.	Up to 10 Class	1740	35.5057	11.2687	0.8594	@
2.	Inter and above	60	36.7833	12.4942		

It is observed from Table 5.19 that the computed value of 't' (0.86) is less than the Table value of 't' (1.96) for 1798 df at 0.05 level of significance. Therefore Hypothesis-5 is accepted for the variable Mother's education at 0.05 level of significance. Hence it is concluded that Mother's education does not have significant influence on Scholastic Achievement of IX class students in physical sciences.

Hara Govinda Gupta (1968) and Rangaswamy and Visweswara (1977) reported similar results.

Sarma (1984), Jagannadham (1986), Vijaya Kumar Sethi (1990), Bhajendranath Panda (1991), Krishna Moorthy (1999), Govindha Reddy (2002), Manchala (2007), N.C.E.R.T (2008) and Krishna Reddy (2008) reported contradictory results

7. Mother's Occupation

The influence of 'Mother's Occupation' on the Scholastic Achievement of IX class students in physical sciences is investigated. On the basis of Mother's occupation the students are divided into three groups. Group-I is formed with Mother's occupation as a Labour. Group -II is formed with Mother's occupation as a house wife and, Group -III is formed with Mother's occupation as Employee. One way ANOVA is employed and the results are presented in Table 5.20.

Table 5.20 : Influence of Mother's Occupation on the Scholastic Achievement

Sl. No.	Mother's Occupation	N	M	SD	F	Level of Significance
1.	Labour	579	35.4767	11.2575	0.2138	@
2.	House wife	1185	35.6177	11.3090		
3.	Employee	36	34.4167	12.4174		

It is evident from Table 5.20 that the computed value of 'F' (0.21) is less than the critical value of 'F' (2.99) for 2 and 1797 df at 0.05 level of significance. Therefore hypothesis-5 is accepted at 0.05 level of significance. Hence it is concluded that 'Mother's Occupation' does not have significance influence on the Scholastic Achievement of IX class students in physical sciences. .

Har Govinda Gupta (1968), Ford Dawson (1970), Rangaswamy and Visveswara (1977), Ayishabi and Moly Kuruvilla (1998), Panda (2002), and Manchala (2007) reported similar results

Pavithran and Feroze (1965), Bujendranatha Panda (1991), Goswamy Minakshi (2002), Govinda Reddy (2002), N.C.E.R.T. Report (2008) and Krishna reddy (2008) reported contradictory results.

8. Number of Children in the Family

The impact of number of children in the family on Scholastic Achievement of IX class students in physical sciences is studied. On the basis of 'Number of Children in the family' the students are divided in to three groups. Group-I is formed with number of children in the family 3 and above, Group-II is formed with number of children in the family as 2. Group-III is formed with number of children in the family as 1. One way ANOVA is employed and the results are given in below:

Table 5.21 : Influence of Number of Children on the Scholastic Achievement

Sl. No.	Number's Children	N	M	SD	F	Level of Significance
1.	3 & above	931	35.5940	11.4530		
2.	2 Children	734	35.4155	10.9924	0.1455	@
3.	1 Child	135	35.9556	12.0731		

It is clear from Table 5.21 that the computed value of 'F' (0.15) is less than the critical value of 'F' (2.99) for 2 and 1797 df at 0.05 level of significance. Therefore Hypothesis-5 is accepted at 0.05 level of significance. Hence number of children in the family does not have significance influence on Scholastic Achievement of IX class students in physical sciences.

Jaya Chandra Naidu (1988) and Manchala (2007) reported are similar results.

Bhujendra Nath panda (1991) observed that pupils coming from small family were better in academic achievement than the pupils living in big families.

9. Birth Order

The impact of Birth order on the Scholastic Achievement of IX class students in physical sciences is investigated. 'Birth order' means order of a child like first child, second child, third child and so on. On the basis of birth order the students are divided in to three groups. Group-I is formed with birth order 3 and above. Group-II is formed with birth order as 2. Group-III is formed birth order as 1. One way ANOVA is used and the results are given Table 5.22.

Table 5.22 : Influence of Birth Order on the Scholastic Achievement

Sl. No.	Birth order	N	M	SD	F	Level of Significance
1	3& Above	487	34.9076	11.2845		
2	2	669	35.1719	11.1654	3.0892	*
3	1	644	36.4239	11.4416		

It is seen from Table 5.22 that the computed value of 'F' (3.09) is greater than the critical value of 'F' (2.99) for 2 and 1797 df at 0.05 level of significance. Therefore Hypothesis-5 is rejected at 0.05 level of significance for the variable 'birth order'. Hence it is concluded that birth order has significant influence on the Scholastic Achievement on the IX class students in physical sciences.

Govindha Reddy (2002) reported similar results.

Jagnnadhan (1983), Bujendra Nadh Panda (1991), Manchala (2007) and Krishna Reddy (2008) reported contradictory results.

10. Total Members in the Family

The influence of total members in the family on the Scholastic Achievement of IX class students in physical sciences is investigated. On the basis of total members in the family, the students are divided in to three groups. Group-I is formed with 5 and above member in the family. Group-II is formed with 4 members in the family. Group-III is formed with 3 and below members in the family. One way ANOVA technique is employed and the results are reported in the Table 5.23.

Table 5.23 : Influence of Total Members in the Family on the Scholastic Achievement

Sl. No.	Members in the family	N	M	SD	F	Level of Significance
1.	5 And above	1182	35.3706	11.3622	0.9292	@
2.	4	575	35.7635	11.0013		
3.	3 and below	43	37.5581	13.7621		

It is observed from Table 5.23 that the computed value of 'F' (0.93) is less than the critical value of 'F' (2.99) for 2 and 1797 df at 0.05 level of significance.

Therefore Hypothesis-5 is accepted at 0.05 level of significance for the variable total members in the family. Hence it is concluded that total members in the family does not have significant influence on the Scholastic Achievement of IX class students in Physical sciences.

This view was supported by Bhujendranath Panda (1991) by observing that students coming from small families have better academic achievement than students from big families.

Similar results were reported by Jayachandrama Naidu (1998) and Manchala (2007).

11. Sex

The impact of sex on the Scholastic Achievement of IX class students in physical sciences is studied by employing 't' technique and the results are given in Table 5.24.

Table 5.24 : Influence of Sex on the Scholastic Achievement

Sl. No.	Sex	N	M	SD	't'	Level of Significance
1.	Girls	823	36.4313	11.2992	3.0471	**
2.	Boys	977	34.8045	11.2716		

It is evident from Table 5.24 that the computed value of 't' (3.05) is greater than critical value of 't' (2.58), for 1798 df at 0.01 level of significance.

Therefore Hypothesis-5 is rejected at 0.01 level of significance for the variable sex. Hence it is concluded that sex has significant influence on the Scholastic Achievement of IX class students in physical sciences. It is observed that girls performed significantly better than the boys.

Similar reports were given by Padmanabhan Nayar and Visweswaran (1966), Hara Govinda Gupta (1968), Vasantha Rama Kumar (1969), Roach (1979), Gupta (1983), Watkins, Hattie and Astilla (1984), Suneetha and Mayuri (2002) and Mohammad Khayyer and Philip Lacey (2005).

Contradictory results were reported by Farquhar (1963), Gupta (1968), Rangaswamy and Visweswaran (1977), Dholakia (1980), Asudullakhan *et al.* (1982), Jagannadhan (1983), Rangaswamy(1990), Govindha Reddy (2002), Panda (2002), Gakhar and Aseema (2004), Panday, Md Faiz Ahmad (2008) and Paavala Sapiyonja (2008).

Religion/Community

The impact of 'Religion' on the Scholastic Achievement of IX class students in physical sciences is investigated. On the basis of 'Religion' the students are divided into three groups. Group-I is formed with Muslims. Group-II is formed with Hindus and Group-III is formed with Christians. One way ANOVA technique is employed and the results are reported in Table 5.25.

Table 5.25 : Influence of Religion on the Scholastic Achievement

Sl. No.	Religion	N	M	SD	F	Level of Significance
1.	Muslim	158	35.2785	10.1554		
2.	Hindu	1520	35.6086	11.3984	0.1425	@
3.	Christian	122	35.1475	11.6942		

It is observed from Table 5.25 that the computed value of 'F' (0.14) is less than the critical value of 'F' (2.99) for 2 and 1797 df at 0.05 level of significance. Therefore Hypothesis-5 is accepted at 0.05 level for the variable 'Religion'.

Hence it is concluded that 'religion' does not have significant influence on the scholastic achievement of IX class students in physical sciences.

Similar results were reported by Nair (1974), Asudulla Khan *et al.* (1982), Krishna Moorthy (1999) and Manchala (2007).

Contradictory results were reported by Radha Mohan (1998), Kobal-public *et al.* (1999) and Regnerus and Mark (2000).

13. Caste

The influence of caste on scholastic achievement of IX class students in physical sciences is investigated. The students are divided in to three groups. Group-I is formed with scheduled Caste (SC) and Scheduled Tribes (ST) students. Group-II is formed with Backward Caste (BC) students and Group-III is formed with other Caste (OC). One way ANOVA technique is employed and the results are presented in Table 5.26.

Table 5.26 : Influence of Caste on the Scholastic Achievement

Sl. No.	Caste	N	M	SD	F	Level of Significance
1.	SC/ST	468	34.4573	11.0411	3.2376	*
2.	BC	912	36.0910	12.0578		
3.	OC	420	35.5857	9.7609		

It is evident from Table 5.26 that the computed values of 'F' is 3.24 which is greater than critical values of 'F' (2.99) for 2 and 1797 df at 0.05 level of significance. Therefore Hypothesis-5 is accepted at 0.05 level of significance for the variable caste. Hence it is concluded that caste has significant influence on the scholastic achievement of IX class students in physical sciences.

Dubey and Mishra (1977), Jagannadham (1983), Gopalacharyulu (1984), Singh (1993), Mehra (1992) and Dash (2002), Manchala (2007), and Krishnareddy (2008) reported similar results.

Kumarswamy (1992), Jayachandrama Naidu (1998) and Govindareddy (2002) reported contradictory results. Dubey and Mishra (1999) revealed that there was no consistency in the predictors of academic success across the three groups SC/ST, BC and OC students.

Nativity

The impact of nativity on the Scholastic Achievement of IX class students in physical sciences is studied. Students are divided in to three groups on the basis of their nativity. Group-I is formed with the students whose nativity is village. Group-II is formed with the students whose nativity is small town. Group-III is formed with the students whose nativity is Municipality/

Corporation. One way ANOVA technique is employed and the results are shown in Table 5.27.

Table 5.27 : Influence of Nativity on the Scholastic Achievement

Sl. No.	Nativity	N	M	SD	F	Level of Significance
1	Village	1145	35.7659	11.3262	1.2785	@
2	Small town	326	34.6442	11.1052		
3	Municipality / Corporation	329	35.6869	11.4451		

It is found from Table 5.27 that the computed value of 'F' is 1.28 which is less than critical value of 'F' (2.99) for 2 and 1797 df at 0.05 level of significance. Therefore Hypothesis-5 is accepted at 0.05 level at significance. Hence it is concluded that nativity does not have significant influence on Scholastic Achievement of IX class students in physical sciences.

Krishnamurthy (1999), Anice James and Marice (2004) and Panchalingappa (2004) reported similar results.

Jagannadham(1983), Narayana Kotewara and Ramachandra Reddy (1998), Kumar (1998), Prakash (2000), Gupta (2002), Panda (2002), Singh (2003), Sunil Kumar Singh, Saheem Malik, Gakhar and Aseema (2004), Dwivedi (2005), Manchala (2007) and Krishna Reddy (2008) reported contradictory results.

15. Economic Position

The impact of the economic position of the family on Scholastic Achievement is investigated. The 'economic position of the family is divided into three divisions namely 1. Poor 2. Middle and 3. Rich. One way ANOVA techniques is used for and the results are reported in Table 5.28.

Table 5.28 : Influence of Economic Position of the Scholastic Achievement

Sl. No.	Economic Position	N	M	SD	F	Level of Significance
1.	Poor	742	35.7345	12.1527	0.1777	@
2.	Middle	1031	35.4248	10.6245		
3.	Rich	27	35.1481	12.9784		

It is observed from Table 5.28 that the computed values of 'F' is 0.18 which is less than the critical value of 'F' (2.99) for 2 and 1797df. at 0.05 level of significance. Therefore Hypothesis-5 is accepted at 0.05 level for the variable economic position. Hence it is concluded that economic position of the family does not have significance influence on the scholastic achievement of IX class students in physical sciences.

Pavithran and Feroze (1965), Rao (1965), Srivastava (1967), Berrnstein (1968), Sudama (1973), Sharma and Bhargava (1980), Ramana Sood (1990), Saxena (2002) and Manas Ranjan Panigrahi (2005) revealed similar results.

Gupta (1968), Anand (1973), Menon (1973), Shakiba-Nejad *et al.* (1983), Quaraishi and Bhat (1986), Young (1999), Harikrishnan (1992), Natesan (1992), Karla and Pyari (2004), Malvinder Ahuja (2006), and Krishna Reddy (2008) revealed contradictory results.

16. Separate Room for Study

The influence of the variable 'separate room for study' on scholastic achievement is studied. The students are divided into two groups namely 1. having separate room for study and 2. not having separate room for study. 't' technique is employed for the analysis and the results are reported in Table 5.29.

Tale 5.29 : Influence of Separate Room for Study on the Scholastic Achievement

Sl. No.	Separate Room for study	N	M	SD	t	Level of Significance
1.	Yes	1509	35.7064	11.2611	1.3506	@
2.	No	291	34.7285	11.5462		

It is clear from Table 5.29 that computed value of 't' is 1.35 for 1798 df at 0.05 level of significance. Therefore Hypothesis-5 is accepted at 0.05 level for the variable separate room for study. Hence it is concluded that the variable separate room for study does not have significance influence on this Scholastic Achievement of IX class students in physical sciences.

Similar results were reported by Mishra (1980) and contradictory results were reported by Krishna Reddy (2008).

17. Study Hours at Home

The impact of study hours at home on Scholastic Achievement of the students is studied. The students are divided into three groups namely 1. one hour and less than one hour, 2.2 hours and less than three hours and 3.3 hours and above. One way ANOVA is employed for the analysis and results are presented in Table 5.30.

It is observed from Table 5.30 that the computed value of 'F' is 1.34 which is less than critical value of 'F' (2.99) for 2 and 1797 df. at 0.05 level of significance. Therefore Hypotheis-5 is accepted at 0.05 level of significance.

Therefore Hypothesis-5 is accepted at 0.05 level of significance for the variable study hours at home. Hence study hours at home does not have significance influence on the Scholastic Achievement of IX class students in physical sciences.

Table 5.30 : Influence of Study hours at home on the Scholastic Achievement

Sl. No.	Study Hours at Home	N	M	SD	F	Level of Significance
1.	One hour and less than 1 hour	464	36.2672	11.9472		
2.	2 to 3 hours	832	35.2043	10.7496	1.3402	@
3.	3 and above Hours	504	35.4544	11.5991		

Contradictory results were reported by Krishna Reddy (2008).

18. Works at Home

The impact of the variable works at home on Scholastic Achievement of the students is investigated. Students are divided into two groups namely 1. Having works at home and 2. Not having works at home. For the analysis 't' technique is used and the results are shown in Table 5.31.

Table 5.31 : Influence of Works at Home on the Scholastic Achievement

Sl. No.	Works at Home	N	M	SD	't'	Level of Significance
1.	Yes	1603	35.61	11.31	0.7003	@
2.	No	197	35.01	11.36		

It is clear from Table 5.31 that the computed value of 't is 0.70 which is less than critical value of 't'(1.96) for 1798 df at 0.05 level significance. Therefore Hypothesis-5 is accepted for the variable 'works at home' at 0.05 level of significance. Hence, it is concluded that works at home does not have significance influence on the scholastic achievement of IX class students in physical sciences.

Contradictory results were reported by Desai (1979) and Krishna Reddy (2008).

The Impact of Study Habits on Scholastic Achievement

Study habits play an important role in academic achievement of the students. The study habits of the IX class students are investigated by adopting Dr. B.V.Patel's study habits inventory. To study the influence of study habits on achievement one way analysis of variance (ANOVA) technique is employed. The criterion in the division of groups is based on quartile values. Group-I is formed with scores of study habits up to Q1, Group-II is formed with scores of study habits above Q1 and up to Q3. Group-III is formed with scores of study habits above Q3. The corresponding Scholastic Achievement scores of the students in physical sciences for the above three groups are analyzed accordingly using one way ANOVA technique. The mean values of Scholastic Achievement scores for the above three groups for each area of study habits inventory (SHI) and for total scores of SHI are tested for significance, through one way ANOVA technique. The following Hypothesis is formulated.

Hypothesis-6

There would be no significant influence of different areas of SHI and total score of SHI on the Scholastic Achievement of IX class students in physical sciences.

The above Hypothesis is tested by employing one way ANOVA. The results are presented in Table 5.32.

The impact of study habits on Scholastic Achievement of IX class students in physical sciences is evident from Table 5.32. It is seen from Table 5.32 that the computed values of 'F' for all the seven areas of SHI and for total scores of SHI are far greater than critical value of 'F' (4.60) for 2 and 1797 df at 0.01 level of significance. Hence Hypothesis 6 is rejected for all the seven areas of study habits namely: (1) Home environment and planning work (SH_1), (2) Reading and note taking (SH_2), (3) Planning of the subject (SH_3), (4) Habits of concentration (SH_4), (5) Preparation for examination (SH_5), (6) General habits and attitudes (SH_5), and (7) School environment (SH_7)and for Study Habits Total scores (SH_T) at 0.01 level of significance. It is observed from Table 4.32, that the mean values of Group-II for all the areas of SH_1 except SH_2 are greater than Group-I and the mean values of Group-III are greater than Group-II. Hence it is concluded that students who have better study habits achieved significantly better in physical sciences.

Similar results were reported by Asha Bhatnagar (1980), Patel (1981), Chopra (1982), Tiwari (1982), Deb and Gravel (1990), Aruna (1994), Narayana Koteswar (1997) , Gordan Darlene (1998) Syam Sunanda Rai and Sreethi (2000), Kumaran and Kamala (2001), Nagaraju (2001) , Shinde (2001), Govindha Reddy (2002), Vamdevappa (2002), Rajani (2004), Arockiadass (2005), Manchala (2007), and Ramana Sood and Dalvinder Kumar (2007) and Krishna Reddy (2008).

Contradictory results were reported by Wood Ruff (1940), Nortan (1959), Harbans Singh (1989), Ravath and Leela (1995), Verma (1996) and Guravaiah (2004).

Table 5.32 : Impact of Study Habits on the Scholastic Achievement

Sl. No.	Study Habits	No. of Observations			Mean			S.D. Values			Fvalues	Level of Significance
		I	II	III	I	II	III	I	II	III		
1.	SH_1	584	786	430	33.93	36.20	36.55	10.93	11.53	11.21	9.05	**
2.	SH_2	472	879	449	37.02	34.32	36.40	12.49	10.64	11.04	10.55	**
3.	SH_3	554	880	366	33.61	35.72	38.07	11.05	11.40	10.98	17.70	**
4.	SH_4	460	928	412	33.05	36.10	37.08	10.43	11.53	11.34	16.36	**
5.	SH_5	581	843	376	34.85	35.17	37.48	10.95	11.23	11.85	7.09	**
6.	SH_6	473	881	446	34.23	35.18	37.67	10.60	10.98	12.37	11.68	**
7.	SH_7	517	918	365	33.79	35.50	38.16	10.17	11.32	12.31	16.30	**
8.	SH_T	451	901	448	34.28	34.58	38.76	11.22	10.94	11.54	24.81	**

The Influence of Self-Concepts on Scholastic Achievement

The Self-concept Scale (SCS) developed by Dr. (Miss) Muktha Rani Rastogi (1974) is adopted to examine the self-concepts of high school students and to find the influence of self-concepts on the Scholastic Achievement of IX class students. The influence of self-concepts on the Scholastic Achievement of IX class students in physical sciences is investigated. The areas of SCS and the scoring procedure have already been described in Chapter 4. The raw scores on each area of self-concept scale and the total score have been divided into three groups on the basis of quartiles. Group-I is formed with the values up to Q_1, Group-II is formed with values above Q_1 and up to Q_3 and Group-III is formed with the values above Q_3. The corresponding Scholastic Achievement scores of the three groups are analyzed accordingly. The mean values of Scholastic Achievement scores for the three groups for each area of self-concepts and for total score of self- concepts are tested for significance, by employing one-way ANOVA technique. The following Hypothesis is formulated.

Hypothesis-7

There would be no significant influence of different areas of self-concepts scale and for total score of self concept scale on the Scholastic Achievement of IX class students in physical sciences.

The above Hypothesis is tested by employing one way ANOVA technique. The results are presented in Table 5.33.

It is observed from Table 5.33 that the computed values of 'F' for the areas of Self-Concepts scales namely, (1) Health and sex Appropriateness (SC_1), (2) Abilities (SC_2), (3) Worthiness (SC_5), (4) Present, Past and Future (SC_6), (5) Beliefs and convictions (SC_7), (6) Emotional maturity (SC_{10}) and (7) Self-Concepts Total score (SC_T) are far greater than the critical value of 'F' (4.60) for 2 and 1797 df at 0.01 level of significance. Therefore Hypothesis- 7 is rejected for the above areas of SCS at 0.01 level of significance. It is clear from mean values that who are better in Health and sex appropriateness, Abilities, worthiness, present, past and future, Belief's and convictions, emotional maturity and Total self-concepts are also significantly better in Scholastic Achievement.

The computed values of 'F' for the areas of SCS namely (1) Self-confidence (SC_3) and (2) Sociability (SC_9) are greater than the critical value of 'F' (2.99) for 2 and 1797 df at 0.05 level of significance. Therefore Hypothesis-7 is rejected for the above two areas at 0.05 level. It is observed from Table 5.33 who are better in Self-Confidence and less in sociability are significantly better in Scholastic Achievement.

Table 5.33 : Impact of Self-concepts on the Scholastic Achievement

Sl. No.	Self-Concept	No. of Observations			Mean			S.D. Values			F values	Level of Significance
		I	II	III	I	II	III	I	II	III		
1.	SC_1	553	930	317	33.64	35.98	37.61	10.83	11.61	10.76	14.00	**
2.	SC_2	597	785	418	33.27	35.60	38.71	10.35	11.05	12.32	29.33	**
3.	SC_3	648	772	380	34.64	35.79	36.61	11.48	11.08	11.40	3.93	*
4.	SC_4	455	925	420	35.52	35.29	36.16	11.61	11.27	11.07	0.89	@
5.	SC_5	570	850	440	34.73	35.32	36.95	10.9	11.22	11.85	4.93	**
6.	SC_6	525	924	351	34.66	35.39	37.28	11.48	11.00	11.69	5.88	**
7.	SC_7	539	971	290	34.12	36.01	36.68	11.01	11.60	10.65	6.60	**
8.	SC_8	587	780	433	35.68	35.61	35.25	10.82	11.31	11.97	0.21	@
9.	SC_9	793	660	347	36.19	35.38	34.41	11.65	10.70	11.58	3.12	*
10.	SC_{10}	464	891	445	36.74	35.51	34.39	12.28	11.05	10.66	4.93	**
11.	SC_T	481	898	421	33.14	35.73	37.91	11.03	10.94	11.88	20.60	**

It is evident from Table 5.33 that the computed values of 'F' for the areas namely: (1) self acceptance (SC_4) and (2) Feeling of shame and guilt (SC_8), are less than critical value of 'F' (2.99) for 2 and 1797 df at 0.05 level of significance. Therefore Hypothesis-7 is accepted for the above two areas at 0.05 level. Hence it is concluded that the areas namely: (1) self acceptance (SC_4) and (2) Feeling of shame and guilt (SC_8), do not have significant influence on the Scholastic Achievement of IX class students in physical sciences.

The Impact of 14 Personality Factors (HSPQ) on the Scholastic Achievement

The Cattell's Junior-senior High-school personality questionnaire (HSPQ) Form-A is adopted as a tool to asses the personality of IX class students in the present investigation. The raw scores on each factors are converted into sten values as recommended by Cattell (1970) for the purpose of analysis.

The influence of HSPQ on the Scholastic Achievement of IX class students in physical sciences is studied. One way analysis of variance (ANOVA) is employed. As recommended by Cattell, the criterion in the divisions of the groups based on the sten values is used. The sten values 1 to 4 are grouped as low scorers (Group-I), 5 and 6 as average scorers (Group-II) and 7 to 10 as high scorers (Group-III). The corresponding Scholastic Achievement test scores of the three groups are analized The mean values of Scholastic Achievement test scores of the three groups are analized. The mean values of Scholastic Achievement test scores for each personality factor are tested for significance by employing the technique of one-way analysis of variance (ANOVA). The following Hypothesis is formulated.

Hypothesis-8

There would be no significant influence of personality factors on the achievement of IX class students in physical sciences. Employing the technique of one-way Analysis of variance, the above Hypothesis is tested. The results are presented in the Table 5.34.

It is evident from Table 5.34 that the computed values of 'F' for the personality factors B, D,E, H, I, and Q_3 are far greater than the critical value of 'F' (4.60) for 2 and 1797 df at 0.01 level of significance. Therefore Hypothesis-8 is rejected for the above personality factors at 0.01 level.

The computed values of 'F' for the personality factors A and F are greater than critical value of 'F' (2.99) for 2 and 1797 df at 0.05 level of significance. Therefore Hypothesis-8 is rejected for the above personality factors at 0.05 level.

The computed value of 'F' for the personality factors C, G, J, O, Q_2 and Q_4 are less than critical value of 'F' (2.99) for 2 and 1797df at 0.05 level of

Table 5.34 : Impact of 14 Personality Factors on the Scholastic Achievement

Sl. No.	Personality factors	No. of Observations			Mean			S.D. Values			F values	Level of Significance
		I	II	III	I	II	III	I	II	III		
1.	FA	650	683	467	35.23	35.10	36.65	10.91	11.05	12.15	3.00	*
2.	FB	584	695	521	32.17	35.79	39.01	9.02	11.01	12.83	53.70	**
3.	FC	487	675	638	35.49	35.74	35.39	11.59	11.28	11.13	0.16	@
4.	FD	603	641	556	34.46	35.47	36.81	10.64	11.14	12.07	6.31	**
5.	FE	702	576	522	36.95	35.47	33.74	12.21	11.15	9.91	12.24	**
6.	FF	575	642	583	34.49	36.08	36.00	10.66	11.17	12.01	3.70	*
7.	FG	563	649	588	35.38	36.00	35.21	11.34	11.46	11.11	0.84	@
8.	FH	528	626	646	33.66	35.42	37.22	10.07	10.98	12.31	14.68	**
9.	FI	511	818	471	34.27	35.40	37.18	10.62	11.45	11.61	8.30	**
10.	FJ	668	640	492	35.77	35.90	34.79	11.59	11.57	10.54	1.53	@
11.	FO	667	620	513	36.01	35.69	34.77	11.79	11.30	10.65	1.82	@
12.	FQ_2	678	611	511	35.65	35.41	35.59	11.22	11.51	11.21	0.08	@
13.	FQ_3	534	800	466	33.39	35.24	38.55	9.57	10.86	13.14	27.19	**
14.	FQ_4	584	647	569	36.23	35.44	34.97	11.73	11.25	10.91	1.85	@

significance. Therefore Hypothesis-8 is accepted for the above personality factors. Hence it is concluded that the above personality factors namely 1. emotionally less stable - Vs emotionally stable - (C), 2. moral standards Vs Super ego-strength(G), 3. Vigorous Vs Doubting(J), 4. Placid Vs Apprehensive (O), 5.Group dependent Vs Self-sufficient (Q_2) and 6. Relaxed Vs tensed (Q_4) do not have significant influence on this Scholastic Achievement of IX class students in physical sciences.

It is clear from the above discussion that the students having the following personality characteristics namely 1. Out going, 2. More intelligent, 3. Exicitable, 4 Obedient, 5.Happy – Go-Lucky, 6. Venturesome, 7. Tense minded, and 8. Controlled have achieved significantly better than the students having personality characteristics Namely 1. Reserved, 2. Less intelligent, 3. Inactive, 4. Aggressive, 5. Sober, 6. Shy, 7. Though minded and 8. Undisciplined.

Similar results were reported by Cattell, *et al.* (1966), Vyas (1982) Vijayakumar Shethi (1990), Koteswara Rao and Rama Chandra Reddy (1998), Panchanandam (1999), Govindha Reddy (2002), Kagade(2002), Guru Basappa (2005), Manchala (2007) and Krishna Reddy (2008).

Contradictory results were formed by Anuradha Joshi (1990), Mavi and Iswara Patel (1997), Natesan and Suseela (2000), Ayodya (2007), and Subramanyam and Sreenivasa Rao (2008).

Step-wise Multiple Regression Analysis

This section deals with the analysis of relative contribution of magnitude of the effect of each of the independent variables on the dependent variable. The Scholastic Achievement of IX class students in physical sciences is predicted with the help of different sets of independent variables.

In this regard, it is appropriate to know the meaning and nature of regression analysis. Regression means to predict one variable with the help of other variable/variables. The dictionary meaning of the term "regression" is 'act of returning' or 'going back'. In 19th century Francis Galton used the term 'regression' for the first time, while studying the relationship between the height of fathers and their off springs. Galton found that the children of abnormally tall or short parents tend to 'regress' or 'step back' to the height of average population. But now, in statistics, the term "regression" is used only as a convenient term without having any reference to the biometry.

In regression analysis, there are two types of variables. The variable whose value is influenced or is to be predicted is called dependent variable and variable which influences values or is used for prediction, is called independent variable. The independent variable is also called the 'regressor' or 'predictor'.

Nowadays regression analysis is used widely in all the scientific disciplines, such as physical and social sciences.

Correlation is a tool of ascertaining the degree of relationship between two variables. The objective of regression analysis is to find the 'nature of relationship' between two variables. The cause and effect relation is clearly indicated through the regression analysis, rather than by correlation. The stepwise multiple regression analysis is employed in the present study to predict the dependent variable with the help of independent variables.

There are 52 variables in the step-wise multiple regression analysis, in the present investigation. The variable number, description of the variable and symbols used are presented in the Table 5.35.

Table 5.35 : Variables used for Regression Analysis

Variable Number (VN)	Description of the variable	Symbol used
1	2	3
1.	Educational Division	ED
2.	Age	A
3.	Income of the family	I
4.	Father's education	FED
5.	Father's occupation	FOP
6.	Mother's education	ME
7.	Mother's occupation	M.O
8.	Number of children in the family	NC
9.	Birth Order	BO
10.	Number of members in the Family	MF
11.	Sex	S
12.	Religion	RN
13.	Caste	C
14.	Nativity	N
15.	Economic Position	EP
16.	Separate Room for study	SR
17.	Study Hours at Home	SHH

1	2	3
18.	Works at Home	WH
19.	Home environment and planning	SH_1
20	Reading and Note taking	SH_2
21	Planning of the subjects	SH_3
22	Habits of concentration	SH_4
23	Preparation for examinations	SH_5
24	General Habits and Attitudes	SH_6
25	Social Environment	SH_7
26	Study Habits Total score	SH_T
27	Health and Sex Appropriateness	SC_1
28	Abilities	SC_2
29.	Self-confidence	SC_3
30.	Self-acceptance	SC_4
31.	Worthiness	SC_5
32.	Past, Present and Future	SC_6
33.	Beliefs and convictions	SC_7
34.	Feelings of shame and guilt	SC_8
35.	Sociability	SC_9
36.	Emotional Maturity	SC_{10}
37.	Self-concepts Total	SC_T
38.	14 PF Factor A	FA
39.	14 PF Factor B	FB
40.	14 PF Factor C	FC
41.	14 PF Factor D	FD
42.	14 PF Factor E	FE
43.	14 PF Factor F	FF
44.	14 PF Factor G	FG
45.	14 PF Factor H	FH
46.	14 PF Factor I	FI

1	2	3
47.	14 PF Factor J	FJ
48.	14 PF Factor O	FO
49.	14 PF Factor Q_2	FQ_2
50.	14 PF Factor Q_3	FQ_3
51.	14 PF Factor Q_4	FQ_4
52	Achievement Test Score	ATS

Scholastic Achievement in Physical sciences (ATS) *i.e.* variable number 52 in the Table 5.35 is the dependent variable in the present investigation. Scholastic Achievement of students in physical sciences is very important and is related to a number of psycho-sociological and Demographic variables.

Prediction of Scholastic Achievement in Physical Sciences

The prediction of achievement test scores (ATS) and the relative contribution of various variables namely 1. socio-demographic variables, 2. Study Habits 3. Self-Concepts 4. Personality factors (HSPQ) and 5. All independent variables on the dependent variable (ATS) is studied, with the help of step-wise multiple regression analysis.

Prediction of Scholastic Achievement with the help of Socio-Demographic Variables (1-18)

The achievement test score (ATS) variable number-52 in the Table 5.36 is predicted with help of socio-demographic variables (1-18) using step-wise multiple regression analysis. The results of the regression analysis are presented in the Table 5.36.

It is observed from the Table 5.36 that the first variable entered into the step-wise regression analysis is Income of the family(I).The multiple correlation (R) obtained is 0.104. It implies that the strength of the relationship between the two variables (ATS and I) is about 10.4 per cent. It could be seen that R is significant (F=19.24) beyond 0.01 level of significance for 1 and 1798 df. The critical value of 'F' is 3.84 at 0.05 level and 6.64 at 0.01 level for 1 and 1798 df. The coefficient of multiple R^2 is 0.011. This shows that 1.10 percent of the variance in ATS is accounted by I.

The standard error of Multiple R (SER) is 11.253. From this it may be inferred that nearly 68 per cent of actual ATS value would lie with in M ± 11.253 of ATS value predicted with the help of this variable (I).

Table 5.36 : Prediction of Scholastic Achievement in Physical Sciences with the Help of Socio-demographic Variables (1-18)

Step No.	IV (VN)	R	R^2	SER	F value for R	b (VN)	't' value for b	Constant	B	r	% variance
1	2	3	4	5	6	7	8	9	10	11	12
1.	I (3)	0.103	0.0106	11.253	19.24** (1,1798)	- 2.56 (3)	4.39**	38.439	- 0.103	- 0.103	1.06
2.	ED (1)	0.126	0.0158	11.226	14.46** (2,1797)	- 2.93 (3) - 0.75 (1)	4.94** 3.10**	40.735	- 0.118 - 0.074	- 0.050	1.21 0.37
3.	S(11)	0.140	0.0197	11.207	12.04** (3,1796)	-2.73(3) -0.79(1)	4.56** 3.27**	42.816	-0.110 -0.078	-0.072	1.13 0.39
4.	FOP(5)	0.150	0.0224	11.195	10.28** (4,1795)	-2.71(3) -0.86(1) -1.45(11) -1.00(5)	4.54** 354** 2.70** 2.21*	44.614	-0.109 -0.085 0.061 0.062	-0.04	1.12 0.43 0.46 0.23
5.	BO (9)	0.157	0.0248	11.185	9.12** (5,1794)	-2.68(3) -0.86(1) -1.42(11) -0.98(5) 0.70(9)	4.49** 3.52** 2.66* 2.18* 2.10*	43.031	-0.108 -0.085 -0.063 -0.051 0.049	0.055	1.11 0.42 0.45 0.23 0.27
6.	SR (6)	0.163	0.0266	11.177	8.17** (6,1703)	-2.72(3) -0.92(1) -1.44(11) -0.95(5) 0.69(9) -1.33(16)	3.56** 3.76** 2.69** 2.11* 2.07* 1.83@	44.781	-0.110 -0.091 -0.063 -0.050 0.048 -0.043	-0.032	1.13 0.46 0.45 0.22 0.26 0.14

1	2	3	4	5	6	7	8	9	10	11	12
7.	C (13)	0.167	0.0281	11.72	7.41**	-2.77(3)	4.64**	43.647	-0.112	0.037	1.15
					(7,1792)	-0.93(1)	3.79*		-0.092		0.46
						-1.36(11)	2.54*		-0.060		0.43
						-0.98(5)	2.18*		-0.051		0.23
						0.68(9)	2.02*		0.047		0.26
						-1.39(16)	1.91@		-0.045		0.14
						-1.36(13)	1.68@		-0.040		0.15
8.	FE (4)	0.172	0.0295	11.167	6.79**	-2.82(3)	4.71*	42.588	-0.113	0.023	1.17
					(8,1791)	-0.97(1)	3.92**		0.096		0.48
						-1.35(11)	2.51*		-0.059		0.43
						-1.05(5)	2.32*		-0.055		0.24
						0.65(9)	1.95@		0.046		0.25
						-1.46(16)	2.01*		-0.048		0.15
						0.64(13)	1.70@		0.040		0.15
						1.28(4)	1.55@		0.037		0.08

The partial regression coefficient (b) presented in the column '7' is 2.53. This value indicates that ATS value would change by 2.56 units for every one unit of change in I. The 't' value for 'b' is 4.39 which is highly significant at 0.05 level. The value of the constant that could be written to predict ATS at this stage is 38.439.

The general form of multiple regression equation may be written as.

$$Y = A + b_1 (X_1) + b_2 (X_2) + b_3 (X_3) + \ldots + b_n (X_n)$$

Where Y is predicted score on the dependent variable, $b_1, b_2, b_3 \ldots b_n$ are partial regression coefficients $X_1, X_2, X_3 \ldots X_{n-}$ are scores on different independent variables and A is constant.

Thus the multiple regression equation at the end of this step, could be written as: ATS = 38.439 – 2.56 (I)

Educational Division (ED) is entered into the step-wise regression analysis as the second most significant variable. The multiple correlation (R) between ATS on one side and I and ED on other side is 0.126. Thus the strength of the relationship between ATS and the two independent variables (I&ED) put together is 12.6 per cent. R is significant at 0.01 level (F = 14.46 for df 2 and 1797).

The value of R^2 is 0.016. This shows that the two variables put together could explain 1.60 per cent of variance in the dependent variable (ATS). Out of this 1.21 per cent of variance is explained by I. The remaining 0.37 per cent of variance is accounted for by ED (Table 5.36 Col 12).

The regression equation to predict ATS with these two variables (I and ED) as predictor variables is:

ATS = 40.735 – 2.93 (I) -0.75 (ED)

Where 40.735 is the constant to be considered at this step and -2.93 and -0.75 are the partial regression coefficients, and I and ED are scores on Income of the family and Educational Division. The 'b' values for the variables are significant at 0.01 level of significance.

There are 8 steps in this step wise multiple regression analysis. The regression equation at the end of 8th step could be written as:

ATS = 42.588 - 2.82 (I) - 2.82 (I) – 0.97(ED) – 1.35 (S) - 1.05(FOP) + 0.65 (BO)-1.46(SR)+0.64(C) +1.28(FE)

It is observed from the Table - 46 that it could be possible to explain 2.90 per cent of variance in the dependent variable ATS, with the help of the above eight variables. Hence it is concluded that Achievement Test Scores (ATS) in Physical sciences could best be predicted with the help of 1. Income of the family(I), 2. Educational division (ED), 3. sex(S), 4. Fathers occupation (FO), 5. Birth order (BO), 6. Separate room for study (SR), 7. Caste (C) and

8. Fathers Education (FE) among the eighteen (1-18) socio-demographic variables.

Prediction of Scholastic Achievement in Physical Sciences with the Help of Study Habits

Achievement Test Score (ATS), the variable 52, in the Table 5.37 (VN-52), is predicted with the help of study habits (VN 19 to 26), using step-wise multiple regression analysis. The results of the regression analysis are presented in the Table 5.37.

It could be seen from the Table 5.37 that the first variable entered into the step-wise regression analysis is 'Study Habits Total' (SHT). The multiple correlation 'R' obtained is 0.148. It indicates that the strength of the relationship between the two variables (ATS and SHT) is about 14.8 per cent. It could be seen that R is significant (F=40.26) beyond 0.01 level of significance for 1 and 1798 df. The coefficient of multiple R^2 is 0.022. This shows that 2.19 per cent of variance in ATS is contributed by SH_T.

The standard error of estimation (SER), as seen from the Table 5.37 is 11.189. From this, it may be inferred that nearly 68 per cent of the actual ATS value would lie within M±11.189 of ATS value, predicted with the help of this variable (SH_T).

The partial regression coefficient presented in Column 7 of Table 5.37 is 0.11. This value indicates that the value of ATS would change by 0.11 units for every unit of change in SH_T. The 't' value for 'b' is 6.34 (col.8) which is significant at 0.01 level. The value of constant that could be written to predict ATS at this stage is 18.206..

The multiple regression equation at the end of this step could be written as

$$ATS = 18.206 + 0.11 (SH_T)$$

There are five steps in this regression analysis as shown in Table 5.37. The regression equation at the end of 5th step would be the best to predict the dependent variable ATS (VN-52) and could be written as:

$$ATS = 16.630 +0.17 (SH_T) - 0.54 (SH_2) + 0.27 (SH_3) + 0.19 (SH_7)+0.16(SH_4)$$

With the help of above five variables namely 1. Study Habits Total (SH_T) 2. Reading and note taking (SH_2). 3. Planning of the subjects (SH_3) 4. Social environment (SH_7), and 5. Habits of Concentration (SH_4), it is possible to explain 7.29 per cent of variance in the dependent variable *i.e.* Scholastic Achievement in physical sciences.

Table 5.37 : Prediction of Scholastic Achievement in Physical Sciences with the Help of Study Habits (19-20)

Step No.	IV (VN)	R	R^2	SER	F value for R	b (VN)	't' value for b	Constant	B	r	% variance
1.	SHT	0.148	0.0219	11.189	40.26**	0.11	6.34**	18.206	0.148	0.148	2.19
	(26)				(1,1798)	(26)					
2.	SH_2	0.259	0.0669	10.931	64.46**	0.26	11.09**	15.275	0.344	-0.055	5.09
	(20)				(2,1797)	-0.61(20)	9.31**		-0.289		1.60
3.	SH_3	0.263	0.0694	10.919	44.68*	0.23(26)	8.67**	15.316	0.307	0.144	4.54
	(21)				(3,1796)	-0.59(20)	8.95*		-0.280		1.55
						0.22(21)	2.20*		0.059		0.85
4.	SH_7	0.268	0.0716	10.910	34.62**	0.20(26)	6.26**	15.906	0.261	0.139	3.87
	(25)				(4,1795)	-0.57(20)	8.49**		-0.269		1.49
						0.25(21)	2.53*		0.069		1.00
						0.16(25)	2.04*		0.058		0.81
5.	SH_4(22)	0.270	0.0729	10.905	28.24**	0.17(26)	4.63**	16.630	0.223	0.133	3.29
					(5,1794)	-0.54(20)	7.76**		-0.255		1.41
						0.27(21)	2.65**		0.073		1.04
						0.19(25)	2.36*		0.069		0.96
						0.16(22)	1.62@		0.044		0.59

Prediction of Scholastic Achievement in Physical Sciences with the Help of Self-concepts

Scholastic Achievement of IX class students in physical sciences is predicted (Dependent variable, VN. 52) with the help of ten areas of Self-concepts and Self-Concepts Total scores (Independent variables, variable numbers 27 to 37 in Table 5.35 using step wise multiple regression analysis. The results of the regression analysis are presented in Table 5.38.

It is observed from the Table 5.38 the most important independent variable that entered first into the step-wise regression analysis is 'Abilities' (SC_2). The multiple correlation 'R' is obtained is 0.198. It indicates that the strength of the relationship between the two variables ATS and SC_2 is about 19.8 percent. It could be seen that 'R' is significant (F = 73.66) beyond 0.01 level of significance for 1 and 1798 df. The coefficient of R^2 is 0.0394. This shows that 3.94 per cent of variance in ATS is accounted by SC_2.

The standard error of estimation (SER) is 11.088. From this it can be inferred that nearly 68 per cent of the actual ATS value would lie within M ± 11.088 of ATS value predicted with the help of this variable (SC_2).

The partial regression coefficient (b) presented in column 7 of Table 5.38 is 0.50. this value indicates that the ATS value would change by 0.50 units for every unit of change in SC_2. The 't' value for 'b' (col 8) is 8.58 which is significant beyond 0.01 level of significance for 1798 df. The value of constant that could be written to predict ATS at this stage is 22.287. The multiple regression equation at the end of this step could be written as:

$$ATS = 22.287 + 0.50 (SC_2).$$

The second important predictor variable that entered into the step-wise regression analysis is SC_1 (VN 27) i.e 'Health and Sex appropriateness . The value of R and R^2 at this stage from the Table 5.38 are 0.220 and 0.0485 respectively. Thus the amount of variance in ATS contributed by these two variables put together is 4.85 per cent out of which SC_2 has contributed 3.44 per cent of variance and the remaining 1.41 per cent of variance is contributed by SC_1 .

The multiple regression equation with these two predictor variables SC_2 and SC_1 could be written as

$$ATS = 17.509 + 0.44(SC_2) + 0.32 (SC_1).$$

There are six steps in this regression analysis. The value of R^2 in the 6th step from the Table 5.38 is 0.0615. This shows that these six variables put together could explain 6.15 percent of variance in the dependent variable (ATS). The regression equation at the end of 6th step could be written as:

Table 5.38 : Prediction of Scholastic Achievement in Physical Sciences with the Help of Self Concepts (27-37)

Step No.	IV (VN)	R	R^2	SER	F value for R	b (VN)	't' value for b	Constant	B	r	% variance
1.	SC_2 (28)	0.198	0.0394	11.088	73.66** (1,1798)	0.50(28)	8.58**	22.287	0.198	0.198	3.94
2.	SC_1 (27)	0.220	0.0485	11.038	45.87** (2,1797)	0.44(28)	7.30**	17.509	0.174	0.143	3.44
						0.32(27)	4.17**		0.099		1.41
3.	SC_{10} (36)	0.233	0.0545	11.006	34.54** (3,1796)	0.45(28)	7.50**	20.695	0.178	-0.083	3.53
						0.27(27)	3.76**		0.090		1.28
						-0.30(36)	3.37**		-0.078		0.64
4.	SC_6 (32)	0.240	0.0578	10.001	27.54** (4,1795)	0.43(28)	7.10**	10.104	0.170	0.097	3.37
						0.27(27)	3.52**		0.084		1.20
						-0.30(36)	3.38**		-0.078		0.64
						0.22(32)	2.49*		0.058		0.57
5.	SC_5 (31)	0.245	0.0600	10.980	22.94** (5,1794)	0.26(28)	6.71**	15.248	0.162	0.088	3.22
						0.41(27)	3.41**		0.082		1.16
						-0.31(36)	3.47**		-0.080		0.66
						0.21(32)	2.35*		0.055		0.53
						0.16(31)	2.08*		0.049		0.43
6.	SC_7 (33)	0.248	0.0615	10.975	19.60** (6,1793)	0.40(28)	6.50**	14.010	0.158	0.93	3.13
						0.24(27)	3.10**		0.075		1.07
						-0.30(36)	3.36**		-0.078		0.64
						0.20(32)	2.30*		0.054		0.52
						0.16(31)	2.02*		0.047		0.42
						0.20(33)	1.67@		0.040		0.37

$$ATS = 14.010 + 0.4. (SC2) + 0.24 (SC1) - 0.30 (SC10) +0.20 (SC6) +0.16 (SC5) + 0.20 (SC7)$$

With the help of the above six variables namely 1. Ability (SC_2) 2. Health and sex appropriateness $(SC_1)_3$. Emotional maturity (SC_{10}) 4. Present, past, future, (SC_6), 5. Worthiness (SC_5), and 6. Beliefs and convictions (SC_7) , it is possible to explain 6.15 percent of variance in the dependent variable.

Prediction of Scholastic Achievement in Physical Sciences with the help of 14 Personality Factors (HSPQ)

The Achievement Test score in Physical sciences, the variable number 52 in the Table 5.35 is predicted with the help of HSPQ (VN 38 to 51) using step-wise multiple regression analysis. The results of the regression analysis are presented in the Table 5.39.

It could be seen from the Table 5.39 that the first independent variable that entered into the step-wise regression analysis is 'Factor B' (FB). The multiple correlation 'R' obtained is 0.224. It indicates that the strength of the relationship between the two variables (ATS and FB) is about 22.4 per cent. From the Table 5.39 it is clear that 'R' is significant (F=95.22) beyond 0.01 level of significance for 1 and 1798 df. The coefficient of R^2 is 0.0503. This shows that 5.03 per cent of variance in ATS is accounted for by FB.

The standard error of multiple 'R' (SER) is 11.025. From this it can be inferred that nearly 68 per cent of the actual value of ATS would lie within M±11.025 of ATS value predicted with the help of this variable.

The partial regression coefficient (b), presented in the column 7 in Table 5.39 is 1.31. This value indicates that the value of ATS would change by 1.31 units for every one unit of change in FB. The value of 't' for 'b' is 9.76 (Col 8) which is significant beyond 0.01 level of significance. The value of the constant that could be written to predict ATS at this stage is 29.686.

The multiple regression equation at the end of this step could be written as:

$$ATS = 29.686 + 1.31 (FB)$$

The second most predictor variable that entered into the step-wise regression analysis is $Q_3(FQ_3)$. The values of R and R^2 at this stage from the Table 5.39 are 0.271 and 0.0735 respectively. Thus the amount of variance in ATS contributed by these two variables in combination is 7.35 per cent. Out of this the contribution of FB is 4.53 per cent and the remaining 2.82 per cent of variance is contributed by FQ_3.

The multiple regression equation with these two predictor variables FB and FQ_3 could be written as

$$ATS = 29.925 + 1.18 (FB) + 0.51 (FQ_3)$$

Table 5.39 : Prediction of Scholastic Achievement in Physical Sciences with the help of 14 Personality Factors (HSPQ).

Step No.	IV (VN)	R	R^2	SER	F value for R	b (VN)	't' value for b	Constant	B	r	% variance
1	2	3	4	5	6	7	8	9	10	11	12
1.	FB(39)	0.224	0.0503	11.025	95.22**	1.31(39)	9.76**	29.686	0.224	0.224	5.03
					(1,1798)						
2.	FQ_3(50)	0.271	0.0735	10.892	71.27**	1.18(39)	8.79*	29.925	0.202	0.183	4.5
					(2,1797)	0.51(50)	*6.71**		0.154		32.82
3.	FH(45)	0.290	0.0843	10.832	55.15**	1.15(39)	8.61**	21.597	0.197	0.138	4.41
					(3,1796)	0.47(50)	6.10**		0.140		2.57
						0.38(45)	4.62**		0.105		1.45
4.	FD(41)	0.306	0.0937	10.779	46.37**	1.17(39)	8.81**	18.345	0.201	0.108	4.50
					(4,1795)	0.43(50)	5.64**		0.130		2.38
						0.38(45)	4.60**		0.105		1.44
						0.36(41)	4.29**		0.097		1.05
5.	FE(42)	0.310	0.0964	10.766	38.28**	1.15(39)	8.67**	20.667	0.197	-0.096	4.43
					(5,1794)	0.42(50)	5.49**		0.127		2.32
						0.36(45)	4.30**		0.098		1.35
						0.35(41)	4.25**		0.096		1.03
						- 0.19 (42)	2.34*		-0.053		0.51

1	2	3	4	5	6	7	8	9	10	11	12
6.	FF(43)	0.313	0.0978	10.760	32.42**	1.143(39)	8.62**	19.213	0.196	0.054	4.40
					(6,1793)	0.418(50)	5.44**		0.125		2.30
						0.35(45)	4.23**		0.097		1.33
						0.36(41)-	4.28**		0.096		1.04
						0.19(42)	2.31*		- 0.053		0.50
						0.35(43)	1.71@		0.038		0.21
7.	FI (46)	0.315	0.0990	10.756	28.17**	1.118(39)	8.37**	18.377	0.192	0.103	4.30
					(7,1792)	0.400(50)	5.14**		0.120		2.20
						0.145(45)	4.27**		0.098		1.34
						0.338(41)	4.03**		0.092		0.99
						- 0.189(42)	2.31*		- 0.053		0.50
						0.145(43)	1.65@		0.037		0.20
						0.127(46)	1.57@		0.036		0.37

There are 7 steps in this regression analysis. The value of R^2 at the end of 7th step is 0.0990. This shows that these seven variables put together could explain 9.90 per cent of variance in the dependent variable *i.e.* ATS. The regression equation at the end of 7th step could be written as

$$ATS = 18.377 + 1.118\ (FE) + 0.400(FQ3) + 0.145\ (FH) + 0.338\ (FD) - 0.189\ (FE) + 0.145\ (FF) + 0.127\ (FI)$$

The above multiple regression equation at the end of 7th step would be the best equation to predict ATS It is concluded that the Scholastic Achievement in Physical sciences could best be predicted with help of

1. Factor-B, (Less Intelligence Vs more Intelligence)
2. Factor-Q_3 (Undisciplined Vs Controlled)
3. Factor-H, (SHy Vs Venture some)
4. Factor-D, (Inactive Vs Excitable -)
5. Factor-E (Obedient Vs Aggressive)
6. Factor-F (Sober Vs Happy-Go-Lucky) and
7. Factor-I (Though Minded Vs Tense minded)among 14 personality factors.

It is possible to explain 9.90 per cent variance in the dependent variable with the help of the above 7 variables

Prediction of Scholastic Achievement in Physical Sciences with the help of all 51 Independent Variables

The relative contribution of all 51 independent variables, (VN 1 to 51 in the Table 5.35) to the Scholastic Achievement in Physical sciences (VN 52 in the Table 5.35) is predicted with the help of step-wise multiple regression analysis. The results of the regression analysis are presented in the Table 5.40.

It could be seen from the Table – 50 that the first Independent variable entered into the stepwise multiple regression analysis is 'Factor – B (FB)'. The multiple correlations 'R' obtained is 0.224. It indicates that the strength of the relationship between the two variables, (ATS and FB) is about 22.4 percent. From the Table 5.40, it is clear that 'R' is significant (F = 95.22) beyond at 0.01 level of significance for 1 and 1798 df. The coefficient of multiple R^2 is 0.0503. This shows that 5.03 percent of variance in ATS is accounted for by (FB).

The standard error of multiple 'R' (SER) is 11.025. From this it may be inferred that nearly 68 percent of the actual ATS value would be within M ± 11.025 of ATS value predicted with the help of this variable (FB).

The partial regression coefficient (b) presented in column 7 is 1.31. This value indicates that the ATS value would change by 1.31 units for every unit

Table 5.40 : Prediction of Scholastic Achievement in Physical Sciences with the Help of all the 51 Independent Variables

Step No.	IV (VN)	R	R^2	SER	F value for R	b (VN)	't' value for b	Constant	B	r	% variance
1	2	3	4	5	6	7	8	9	10	11	12
1.	FB (39)	0.224	0.0503	11.025	95.22** (1,1798)	1.31(39)	9.76**	29.686	0.224	0.224	5.03
2.	SC_2 (28)	0.279	0.0778	10.867	75.78** (2,1797)	1.16(39) 0.43(28)	8.65** 7.32**	19.146	0.198 0.168	0.198	4.45 3.33
3.	FQ_3 (50)	0.312	0.0975	10.753	64.72** (3,1796)	1.04(39) 0.40(28) 0.48(50)	7.83** 6.92** 6.27**	15.390	0.179 0.157 0.143	0.183	4.02 3.12 2.61
4.	FD (41)	0.330	0.1089	10.688	54.886** (4,1795)	1.06(39) 0.42(28) 0.43(50) 0.40(41)	8.01** 7.24** 5.74** 4.80**	11.354	0.182 0.033 0.024 0.012	0.108	4.09 3.25 2.39 1.16
5.	FH (45)	0.344	0.1185	10.634	48,226** (5,1794)	1.04(39) 0.41(28) 0.39(50) 0.39(41) 0.36(45)	7.86** 7.11** 5.18** 4.78** 4.40**	8.497	0.178 0.160 0.118 0.107 0.099	0.138	4.00 3.18 2.17 1.15 1.36
6.	SH_T (26)	0.357	0.1274	10.583	43.62** (6,1793)	1.01(39) 0.33(28) 0.41(50) 0.40(41) 0.37(45) 0.08(26)	7.67** 5.61** 5.37** 4.85** 4.50** 4.27**	- 1.283	0.173 0.132 0.122 0.108 0.100 0.099	0.148	3.89 2.61 2.24 1.16 1.38 1.46

1	2	3	4	5	6	7	8	9	10	11	12
7.	SH_2 (20)	0.398	0.1588	10.393	48.36** (7,1792)	0.96(39) 0.31(28) 0.40(50) 0.37(41) 0.33(45) 0.20(26) - 0.52(20)	7.38** 5.25** 5.32** 4.59** 4.12** 8.72** 8.19**	-2.467	0.164 0.121 0.119 0.100 0.090 0.267 -0.243	-0.055	3.68 2.40 2.17 1.08 1.24 3.96 1.35
8.	I (3)	0.409	0.1672	10.344	44.96** (8,1791)	0.95(39) 0.30(28) 0.39(50) 0.30(41) 0.32(45) 0.20(26) - 0.53(20) - 2.23(3)	7.34** 5.16** 5.25** 4.71** 4.09** 8.74** 8.34** 4.24**	0.801	0.162 0.119 0.116 0.103 0.089 0.267 -0.248 -0.092	-0.103	3.64 2.35 2.14 1.10 1.23 3.95 1.38 0.94
9.	SD (1)	0.420	0.1764	10.290	42.58** (9,1790)	0.99 (39) 0.33(28) 0.36(50) 0.36(41) 0.31(45) 0.21(26) - 0.50(20) - 2.75(3) - 1.03(1)	7.69** 5.66** 4.94** 4.51** 3.87** 9.06** 8.02** 5.04** 4.45**	1.714	0.170 0.130 0.109 0.098 0.084 0.276 -0.234 -0.111 -0.102	-0.050	3.80 2.58 2.01 1.05 1.16 4.08 1.31 1.14 0.51

of change in FB. The 't' value for 'b' is 9.76 which is highly significant at 0.01 level. The value of the constant that could be written to predict ATS at the end of this step is 29.686.

Thus the multiple regression equation at the end of this step could be written as:

$$ATS = 29.686 + 1.31(FB)$$

The results of the regression analysis up to 9th step are presented in the Table 5.40. It is seen from the Table 5.40 that there is no much increase in R^2 from 9th step onwards. Therefore, the regression equation at the end of 9th step would be the best to predict the dependent variable ATS and it could be written as

$$ATS = 1.714 + 0.99\ (FB) + 0.33\ (SC2) + 0.36\ (FQ3) + 0.36\ (FD) + 0.31(FH) + 0.21\ (SHT) - 0.50\ (SH2) - 2.75\ (I) - 1.03\ (SD).$$

With the help of above nine variables namely 1. Factor-B (Less Intelligence Vs more Intelligence), 2. SC_2 (Abilities), 3 Factor-Q_3 (Undisciplined Vs Controlled) 4. Factor-D, (Inactive Vs Excitable) 5. Factor-H, (Shy Vs Venture some) 6. SH_T (Study Habits Total scores) 7. SH_2 (Reading and Note taking) 8. Factor-I (Though Minded Vs Tense minded) 9. E.D (Educational Division), it is possible to explain 17.64 per cent of variance in the dependent variable namely Scholastic Achievement in physical sciences.

There are 24 steps in this regression analysis. The summary at the end of 24th step is presented in Table 5.41.

From the value of R^2 at the 24th step, it is inferred that 20.9 per cent of variance in ATS is, contributed by all these 24 Predictor variables put together.

The regression equation at the end of 24th step could be written as

$$ATS = -0.017 + 0.85\ (FB) + 0.28\ (SC_2) + 0.33\ (FQ_3) + 0.36\ (FD) + 0.26\ (FH) + 0.13\ (SH_T) - 0.45\ (SH_2) - 2.37\ (I) - 1.37\ (ED) + 0.22\ (SC_1) - 0.24\ (SC_{10}) + 0.21\ (SC_6) - 1.26\ (S) - 0.99\ (FOP) - 0.16\ (FE) + 0.17\ (FF) + 0.69\ (C) - 1.36\ (SR) + 1.39\ (FED) + 0.19\ (SC_7) + 0.19\ (SH_3) + 0.14\ (SH_5) + 0.11\ (SC_5) + 0.11\ (SH_7).$$

Table 5.41 : Summary of the Final Step (24th) of Regression Analysis with Scholastic Achievement Test Scores (ATS) as Dependent Variable and Remaining 51 Variables as Independent Variables.

Step No.	IV (VN)	R	R^2	SER	F value for R	b (VN)	't' value for b	Constant	B	r	% variance
1	2	3	4	5	6	7	8	9	10	11	12
1.	FB (39)	0.224	0.050	11.025	95.22** (1,1798)	0.85 (39)	6.59**	-0.017	0.146	0.224	3.27
2.	SC_2 (28)	0.279	0.078	10.867	75.78** (2,1797)	0.28 (28)	4.59**		0.109	0.198	2.15
3.	FQ_3 (50)	0.313	0.098	10.753	64.72** (3,1796)	0.33 (50)	4.50**		0.099	0.183	1.81
4.	FD (41)	0.330	0.109	10.688	54.886** (4,1795)	0.36 (41)	4.57**		0.098	0.108	1.06
5.	FH (45)	0.344	0.118	10.634	48.226 **(5,1794)	0.26 (45)	3.39**		0.074	0.138	1.01
6.	SH_T (26)	0.356	0.127	10.583	43.62 **(6,1793)	0.13 (26)	3.88**		0.173	0.148	2.55
7.	SH_2 (20)	0.399	0.159	10.393	48.36 **(7,1792)	-0.45 (20)	6.62**		-0.212	-0.055	1.18
8.	I (3)	0.409	0.167	10.344	44.961 **(8,1791)	-2.37 (3)	4.89**		-0.107	-0.103	1.10

1	2	3	4	5	6	7	8	9	10	11	12
9.	ED (1)	0.419	0.176	10.290	42.58** (9,1790)	-1.37 (1)	5.74**		-0.135	0.050	0.68
10.	SC_1 (27)	0.427	0.182	10.257	39.85 **(10,1789)	0.22 (27)	2.96**		0.067	0.143	0.96
11.	SC_{10} (36)	0.431	0.186	10.238	37.06** (11,1788)	-0.24 (36)	2.87**		-0.063	-0.083	0.52
12.	SC_6 (32)	0.435	0.189	10.219	34.73** (12,1787)	0.21	(32)	2.59**	0.056	0.097	0.55
13.	S (11)	0.438	0.192	10.205	32.61** (13,1786)	-1.26 (11)	2.56*		-0.056	-0.072	0.40
14.	FO (5)	0.440	0.194	10.192	30.74** (14,1785)	-0.99 (5)	2.42*		-0.052	-0.044	0.23
15..	FE (42)	0.444	0.197	10.179	29.14** (15,1784)	-0.16 (42)	2.12*		-0.046	-0.096	0.44
16..	FF (43)	0.446	0.199	10.168	27.67** (16,1783)	0.17 (43)	2.02*		0.043	0.054	0.23
17.	C (13)	0.448	0.201	10.161	26.29** (17,1782)	0.69 (13)	1.98*		0.043	0.037	0.16

1	2	3	4	5	6	7	8	9	10	11	12
18.	SR (16)	0.449	0.202	10.154	25.06** (18,1781)	-1.36 (16)	2.06*		-0.044	-0.032	0.14
19.	FED (4)	0.452	0.204	10.147	23.96** (19,1780)	1.39 (4)	1.85@		0.040	0.023	0.09
20.	SC_7 (33)	0.453	0.205	10.142	22.91** (20,1779)	0.19 (33)	1.68@		0.038	0.093	0.35
21.	SH_3 (21)	0.454	0.206	10.138	21.95** (21,1778)	0.19 (21)	1.97*		0.051	0.144	0.73
22.	SH_5 (23)	0.455	0.207	10.134	21.09** (22.1777)	0.14 (23)	1.93@		0.046	0.097	0.45
23.	SC_5 (31)	0.456	0.208	10.130	20.30 (22.1777**)	0.11 (31)	1.54@		0.034	0.088	0.30
24.	SH_7 (25)		0.209	10.127	19.55** (24,1775)	0.11 (25)	1.431@		0.040	0.139	0.55

Chapter

6

Summary, Findings, Conclusions, Recommendations and Suggestions

This chapter deals with the summary, major findings, conclusions, recommendations and suggestions for further research.

Summary

Science education is to a nation what protein is to a young organism. Former president of India A.P.J. Abdul Kalam called upon the Universities to turnout a global cadre of skilled professionals in Science and Technology to make India to realize its dreams of a developed nation by 2020. Education strengthens the powers of body and mind. It fits a man to perform justly, skillfully and magnanimously all the offices – private and public of peace and war. Physical sciences play a very important role in the life of all human beings. In the modern scientific world physical sciences occupies important place in the school curriculum.

Every body needs the knowledge of physical sciences in one way or other. Importance of Physical sciences is very clear, from its wide applications ranging from daily uses of even a common man, to its applications for the development of science, Engineering and Technology and even social sciences including languages. Physical sciences play a key role for the development of Science and Technology. National education commission observed "proper foundation in the knowledge of the subject should be laid down at the school level itself".

The scholastic achievement in physical sciences is related to various factors. The present investigation is to find out the relationship between achievement in physical sciences of IX class students and various Socio-Demographic and Psychological variables.

Introduction

Education is one of the potent instrument in the development process. It is properly geared for that purpose. A man without education is like a flower without fragrance. Education strengthens the powers of body and mind. It is a life long process. It is the most powerful and effective instrument for inducing radical changes in the behavior of students. It plays a significant role in the development of human resources. In a democratic country, Education can be used for giving training in a good citizenship.

Education is found to be an effective tool to bring the required changes in the society. The National Education Commission (1964-66) has emphasized that education is the one and only instrument that can be used to bring about a change towards the social and economic betterment of India. Further the commission quoted "India is now being shaped in her class rooms". It is not only a saying but also a reality. In the world, based on Science and Technology, it is the education that determines the level of prosperity, welfare and security of the people.

Science education has developed at an ever increasing pace, since the beginning of the 20th century so that the gap between the advanced and backward countries has reduced more and more. Modern science was introduced in India with the coming up of the British rule and it should in some opposition to the earlier traditions because the new system was to be learnt in foreign languages i.e. English.

Napoleon said, "The progress and improvement of Physical sciences are linked to the prosperity of the state". In view of the important role that physical sciences plays in the modern world, it had been imperative for any nation or world to promote physical sciences education in their respective countries.

In the daily life of the person, from the womb to the tomb, science education plays a vital role in all aspects such as food, clothing, shelter, social movability etc., Hence there is a need for each and every person to have a scientific knowledge which can be attained only through science education.

In view of the important role that physical sciences plays in the modern world, it has been imperative for any nation or the world to promote physical sciences education, in their respective countries. It is not possible for us to expect improved physical sciences education, in the higher education, unless, we succeed in providing a sound physical sciences education at the school level.

Secondary education has been considered as the weakest link between lower and higher education levels, in view of the low standards and more failures and dropouts after the secondary level of education. In this aspect, an achievement of the students in all the subjects is the most significant factor, in educational system. Among the different areas of research in education, scholastic achievement, is one of the most extensively investigated phenomena. The standards of education at schools and colleges would be refluxed by the performance of pupils in their academic subjects.

Scholastic achievement is the main concern of our educationists and the government. Achievement of the students depends upon several sociological, psychological and environmental aspects. This fact was established by several investigations in our country and aboard. The present study is aimed at establishing a meaningful relationship between achievement in physical sciences and various psychological and socio-demographic variables.

Statement of the Problem

The present study is concerned with the scholastic achievement of IX class students in physical sciences. It examines the main effects of educational divisions, sex, caste and their interaction effect on the scholastic achievement. It also examines the main effects of age, religion, nativity and their interaction effect on the scholastic achievement. It establishes the relationship between the scholastic achievement and other variables namely, study habits, self-concepts and personality factors. It also predicts the scholastic achievement with the help of different sets of psycho-sociological variables.

Title of the Problem

The title of the problem is "Scholastic Achievement of IX class pupils in Physical sciences in relation to Certain Psycho-Sociological Variables".

Scope of the Study

The main intention of the study is to find the relation of scholastic achievement of IX class-students with socio-demographic variables, study habits, self-concepts and personality factors. The marks obtained in an objective test, in physical sciences are taken as scholastic achievement in physical sciences which is regarded as dependent variable in the present study. The objective achievement test is developed and standardized by the investigator. The socio-demographic variables, study habits, self concepts and personality factors are measured by using the relevant instruments. The study is confined to only 36 schools of Chittoor District, belonging to the different educational divisions i.e. the four divisions of Chittoor District.

As already described in the earlier chapters, only a few variables have been included in this study. A number of factors will have their impact on the achievement, in physical sciences. Each and every variable having its influence on the achievement could not be included in this study.

The study also attempts to predict the scholastic achievement with the help of different sets of psycho- sociological variables.

Need for the Study

In one's life, the intellectual capacities and capabilities are assessed by his/her achievements in various subjects. In the present educational system, the various programmes are not confined, only to the text books. Using of libraries and laboratories for additional information, making arrangements for work-shops, seminars, various competitions, have come into school life. The unprecedented expansion of educational system, the enormous financial investments, made in educating the children, by individuals and governments, and the need to point out the priorities of educational expenditure, necessitate the identification of various factors, contributing most, for student learning and achievement levels. The achievement in various subjects, of learners, is the result of combined efforts of teachers, parents, managements of schools and students. Again there is an effect of various Psycho-sociological factors, on the achievement of students.

There is an urgent educational and social need to study and identify the influence of various factors, on the achievement of high school pupils, to draw up the conclusions for high/low achievements.

Scholastic achievement continues to be one of the most important variables held in high esteem in all cultures, countries and times. Hence the research related to the area of academic achievement is ever growing concern of the researchers, educationists and educational administrators.

In the present day, education is viewed seriously that there is every need to raise the standards of the pupils at all levels. A concerted effort is to be made to identify some of the significant socio-psychological factors that influence the academic achievement of the student and to explain the contribution of these factors.

An interesting feature observed is that majority of the studies in the area of scholastic achievement were confined to the simple correlation analysis between predictors and criterion variables. Individual and cumulative effects of several independent variables on the scholastic achievement could be assessed more accurately by employing regression analysis. Therefore the main aim of the present study is to identify, the influence of independent factors and to predict the multiple effect of independent factors on the achievement of IX class students, in physical sciences, with the help of various socio-psychological factors and further to suggest suitable regression equations, in the prediction of scholastic achievement. The study also aims at making some recommendations for further study in the field and some suggestions for teachers.

The above crucial conditions lead the investigator to make an attempt in this area of scholastic achievement of IX class pupils in physical sciences in relation to certain psycho-sociological factors.

Objectives of the Study

The present study has the following objectives:

1. To understand the present status of IX class students with regard to their achievement in Physical sciences.
2. To study the influence of the variables Educational Divisions, Sex, Caste and their interaction on scholastic achievement in physical sciences.
3. To study the influence of the variables Age, Religion, Nativity and their interaction on the scholastic achievement in Physical sciences.
4. To establish a relationship of scholastic achievement with Socio – demographic variables like, Income of the family , Father's Education, Father's Occupation, Mother's Education, Mother's Occupation, Number of children, Birth order, Number of members in the family, Economic position , Separate room for studies, Study hours at Home and works at Home.
5. To study the impact of Study habits on the scholastic achievement of IX class students in physical sciences.
6. To study the impact of self-concepts on the scholastic achievement of IX class students in Physical sciences.
7. To study the impact of personality factors on the scholastic achievement of IX class students in Physical sciences.
8. To predict the scholastic achievement of IX class students in Physical sciences with the help of different sets of variables namely socio-demographic variables, study - habits, self-concepts and personality factors.
9. To predict the scholastic achievement of IX class students in Physical Sciences with the help of all the 51 independent variables in the investigation.
10. To develop mathematical equations for predicting the scholastic achievement of IX class students in Physical sciences.
11. To summarize the findings of present investigation
12. To make appropriate recommendations on the basis of findings of the present investigation.
13. To provide suggestions for further investigation.

Hypotheses to be Tested

On the basis of the above objectives the following hypotheses were formulated for testing:

1. All the IX class students would not have the same scholastic achievement abilities in physical sciences.
2. Educational Divisions, Sex, Caste, and their interactions would not have any significant influence on the scholastic achievement of IX class students in physical sciences
3. Age, Religion, Nativity and their interactions would not have any significant influence on the scholastic achievement of IX class students in physical sciences.
4. Socio-Demographic variables would not have any significant influence on the scholastic achievement of IX class students in physical sciences.
5. Study habits would not have any significant impact on the scholastic achievement of IX class students in physical sciences.
6. Self-concepts would not have any significant impact on the scholastic achievement of IX class students in Physical sciences.
7. Personality factors would not have significant influence on the scholastic achievement of IX class students in physical sciences.
8. It would not be possible to predict the scholastic achievement with the help of different sets of variables namely socio-demographic variables, study habits, self-concepts and personality factors.
9. It would not be possible to predict the scholastic achievement with the help of all the 51 independent variables.
10. It would not be possible to develop mathematical equations for predicting scholastic achievement in physical sciences with the help of different sets of independent variables.
11. None of the independent variables in this investigation turns out to be a significant predictor of scholastic achievement of IX class students in physical sciences.

Variables Included in the Study

On the basis of study of literature, it has been found that the achievement of students in all classes in physical sciences in general and IX class in particular depends on several factors. The investigator has selected the following Psycho-Sociological variables for the present study. Out of total variables,51are independent variables and one is dependent variable. Eighteen were personal and socio-demographic variables for which information was gathered through a personal data sheet.

A. Dependent Variable

The scores obtained by all the subjects (all the students of the sample) in the achievement test, in Physical sciences, constructed and standardized by the investigator has been taken as dependent variable.

B. Independent Variables

The independent variables studied in this investigation are given below.

I. Socio-Demographic Variables (1-18)

The socio-demographic variables included in the present investigation are:

1. Educational Divisions
2. Age
3. Income of the Family
4. Father's Education
5. Father's Occupation
6. Mother's Education
7. Mother's Occupation
8. Number of Children
9. Birth Order
10. Number of members in the family
11. Sex
12. Religion
13. Caste
14. Nativity/Locality
15. Economic position
16. Separate room for study
17. Study Hours at Home
18. Works at Home

II. Study Habits (19-26)

Study Habits questionnaire consisting of seven areas,

19. Home environment
20. Reading and note taking

21. Planning for reading subjects
22. Habits of concentration
23. Preparations for examinations
24. General Habits and attitudes
25. School Environment
26. Study Habits total score

III. Self-Concepts (27-37)

Self-Concept questionnaire consisting of 10 areas.

27. Health and sex Appropriateness
28. Abilities
29. Self-confidence
30. Self-acceptance
31. Worthiness
32. Present, Past, future
33. Beliefs and convictions
34. Feelings of shame and guilt
35. Sociability
36. Emotional Maturity
37. Self-concepts total score

IV. Personality Factors HSPQ (38-51)

In the present investigation High School Students Personality Questionnaire (HSPQ) consisting of 14 personality factors is used. The 14 personality factors are :

38. Factor-A
39. Factor-B
40. Factor-C
41. Factor-D
42. Factor-E
43. Factor-F
44. Factor-G
45. Factor-H
46. Factor-I
47. Factor-J

48. Factor-O
49. Factor-Q_2
50. Factor-Q_3
51. Factor-Q4

Research Tools

1. The investigator has developed Objective Achievement Test (OAT) and standardized to measure the achievement in Physical sciences of IX class students.
2. Study-Habits inventory developed and standardized by Dr. B.V. Patel (1975), is adopted to study the influence of study habits of the pupils on the dependent variable, (Achievement in physical sciences).
3. (Miss) Mukta Rani Rastogi's (1974) self-concept scale is adopted to measure the self-concepts of the students.
4. Cattell's 14 personality factors, Form-A (HSPQ) is adopted to measure the personality traits of the students
5. Personal Data Questionnaire is developed by the investigator with the help of experts in the field of education, to measure the socio demographic variables.

Sample Selected

After the construction, standardization and adoption of all the test tools, the investigator has planned for the selection of the sample for the final study. The Chittoor district is divided into four educational divisions namely, Madanapalle, Puttur, Chittoor and Tirupati. The investigator selected 36 schools, in the four educational divisions, following the stratified random sampling procedure. The sample for pilot study is 370 and the sample for the final study is 1800 students of IX class studying in the academic year 2008-2009.

Collection of Data

The investigator personally visited all the schools selected for the study and explained the heads of the institutions the purpose of collecting the data. The students were given necessary instructions and motivated to respond genuinely. Advance intimation about the visit of the investigator was provided to the Head Master and the students. The students, who attended the schools, on the days of collecting data are considered for the purpose of investigation. All the necessary data was collected with the help of the data gathering instruments and teachers of the concerned schools.

Scoring and Analysis

1. The objective achievement test consists of one hundred multiple choice questions and each correct response is awarded with one mark.
2. The study habits inventory is scored on a five point scale by giving weight-ages 5, 4, 3, 2 and 1 for positive items and 1, 2, 3, 4, and 5 for negativeitems to the five alternatives namely; always, often, some times, rarely and never respectively. The self-concept scale is scored in a similar manner to the five alternatives namely strongly agree, agree, undecided, disagree and strongly disagree.
3. For the 14.PF personality questionnaire, the scoring key prepared by the author is employed.

   The total scores for each area of respective inventories are entered and grand total is obtained by adding all the weightages, on all the statements and marked them on the top right corner of the inventory.
4. The information furnished by the students on socio-demographic variables is numerically coded in order to suit for the computer analysis.

The total scores obtained by each of 1300 students on all the variables were computed. The analysis is carried out on the basis of objectives of the study and hypotheses formulated. by employing appropriate statistical techniques.

To understand the nature of the distribution, descriptive statistics such as Mean, Median, Mode, Range, Quartile Deviation, Standard Deviation, skewness, kurtosis, coefficient of variation and standard error of mean were computed wherever necessary. Frequency distribution tables are prepared for the total sample, for educational divisions, for boys and girls and for different castes..

The inferential Statistical Techniques 't' test and 'F' test are employed to test the different hypotheses. Multiple 'R' is computed for carrying out stepwise regression analysis, for predicting the scholastic achievement with the help of different sets of independent variables. Necessary graphs were also used for presenting the data.

The levels of significance employed with respective symbols are given below:

- Indicates significant at 0.01 level
- indicates significant at 0.05 level
- indicates not significant at 0 05 level

Major Findings of the Study

The statistical analysis of the data reveals the following broad findings of the investigation.

A. Distribution Characteristics of Scholastic Achievements Scores

1. The mean scholastic achievement score of IX class students in physical sciences for the whole group is 35.55. Hence the performance of the students is poor. Median is 33.00 and mode is 27.90. Hence the distribution is not normal. It is more peaked than the normal distribution.
2. The values of skewness and Kurtosis are 0.81 and 3.53 respectively. Hence the distribution of the scholastic achievement scores for the total sample is positively skewed and leptokurtic.
3. It is found that the mean scholastic achievement scores for the pupils of Puttur educational division schools is the highest (43.52) among all the groups viz. (*i*) whole group (*ii*) Madanapalle division schools (*iii*) Puttur division Schools (*iv*) Chittoor division Schools (*v*) Tirupati division schools (*vi*) Girls (*vii*) Boys (*viii*) schedule caste/tribes (*ix*) Backward castes and (*x*) other castes. The mean scholastic achievement score for the students of Madanapalle division schools is the least (31.80), as compared with other groups. The performance of Girls (36.43) is better than that of Boys (34.80). It is also noticed that the performance of B.C. students (36.09) is better than O.C Students (35.58) and S.C/ST (34.46) students. For all the distributions, the value of skewness is positive. Hence all the distributions are positively skewed. The values of kurtosis for the students of puttur division schools (2.06), Chittoor division schools (2.99) and girls (2.65) are less than the normal value (3.00) and hence the distributions are platy kurtic. The value of kurtosis for the remaining groups is more than 3.00 and hence the distributions are lepto kurtic. The value of kurtosis for the students of Tirupati division schools (5.76) is the highest among all the groups and the distribution is highly leptokurtic. For the remaing groups, the values of kurtosis are slightly greater than the normal value (3.00) and hence the distributions are slightly leftokurtic.

B. Factorial Designs

4. There is a significant influence of main effects namely, Educational divisions, Sex and Caste on the scholastic achievement of IX class students in physical sciences at 0.01 level of significance.

5. There is a significant interaction effect of Education Divisions × Caste at 0.01 level on the scholastic achievement of IX class students in Physical sciences.
6. There is no significant interaction effects of Educational Divisions × Sex × Caste at 0.05 level on the scholastic achievement of IX class students in Physical sciences.
7. There is no significant main and interaction effects of Age, Religion and Nativity on the Scholastic Achievement of IX class students in Physical sciences.

C. Influence of Socio-Demographic and Personal Variables

8. Educational Divisions, Annual income and Sex have significant influence at 0.01 level on the Scholastic Achievement of IX class students in Physical sciences.
9. Birth order and Caste have significant influence at 0.05 level on the Scholastic Achievement of IX class students in Physical sciences.
10. Father's Education, Father's Occupation, Mother's Education, Mother's Occupation, Number of children, Total members in the family, Religion, Nativity, Economic position, Separate room for study, Study hours at home and works at home do not have significant influence at 0.05 level on the Scholastic Achievement of IX class students in Physical sciences.

D. Influence of Study Habits

11. All the seven areas of study habits and total score on study habits have significant influence at 0.01 level on the scholastic achievement of IX class students in Physical sciences. It is observed that the students with better study habits achieved significantly better in physical sciences.

E. Influence of Self-Concepts

12. It is found that the computed values of 'F' for the self-concepts namely (*i*) Health and sex appropriateness(SC_1) (*ii*)Abilities (SC_2), (*iii*) Worthiness (SC_5), (*iv*) present-past-future (SC_6), (*v*) Beliefs and convictions (SC_7), (*vi*) Emotional Maturity (SC_{10}) and (*vii*) Self-concepts total score (SC_T), are far greater than the critical value of 'F' (4.60) for 2 and 1797 df at 0.01 level of significance . It is clear from the mean values that who are better in Health and Sex appropriateness, Abilities, Worthiness, Present-Past-Feature, Believes and convictions and total self-concepts are also significantly better in scholastic achievement of IX class students in physical sciences.

13. It is found that the computed values of 'F' for the Self-Concepts namely (*i*) Self confidence (SC_3) and (*ii*) Sociability (SC_9) are greater than the critical value of 'F' (2.99) for 2 and 1797 df at 0.05 level of significance.

14. The areas of self-concepts namely (*i*) Self acceptance (SC_4) and (*ii*) Shame and Guilt (SC_8), do not have significant influence at 0.05 level on the scholastic achievement of IX class students in physical sciences.

F. Influence of Personality Factors (HSPQ)

15. It is found that the computed values of 'F' for the Personality Factors namely (*i*) Factor (B): Less Intelligent vs. More Intelligent; (*ii*) Factor, (D): Phlegmatic vs. Excitable; (*iii*) Factor (E): Obedient, Mild, Conforming, submissive vs. Assertive, Independent, Aggressive, Stubborn, Dominant; (iv) Factor (H): Shy VS. Venturesome (*v*) Factor (I): Though Minded VS. Tense Minded and (*vi*) Factor ($Q_{3)}$: Undisciplined Vs controlled are far greater than the critical value of 'F' (4.60) for 2 and 1797 df at 0.01 level of significance. Hence the above personality factors have significant influence on the scholastic achievement of IX class students in physical sciences.

16. It is found that the computed values of 'F' for the Personality Factors namely; (i) Factor(A): Reserved vs. outgoing and (ii) Factor (F): Sober Vs. Happy-Go-Lucky, Gay Enthusiastic, Impulsively lively are greater than critical value of 'F'(2.99) for 2 and 1797df at 0.05 level of significance. Hence the above personality factors have significant influence on the scholastic achievement of IX class students in physical sciences.

17. It is found that the computed values of 'F' for the Personality Factors namely: (*i*) Factor (C): Emotionally Less Stable vs. Emotionally Stable (*ii*) Factor (G): Moral standards Vs. super ego-strength (*iii*) Factor (J): Vigorous Vs Doubting (*iv*) Factor (O): Placid Vs Apprehensive (*v*) Factor (Q_2): Group dependent Vs self-sufficient and (*vi*) Factor ($Q_{4)}$: Relaxed Vs Tensed are less than the critical value of 'F' (2.99) for 2 and 1797 df at 0.05 level of significance. It is concluded that the above personality factors do not have significant influence on the scholastic achievement of IX class students in physical sciences.

G. Step-Wise Multiple Regression Analysis

18. It is found that the best regression equations for predicting the scholastic achievement in Physical sciences of IX class students are;

    (*i*) With the help of 18 socio-demographic variables

$$ATS = 42.588 - 2.82\ (I) - 0.97\ (ED) - 1.35\ (S) - 1.05\ (F0P) + 0.65\ (BO) - 1.46 (SR) + 0.64 (C) + 1.28\ (FE)$$

The variance explained with the help of the above 8 variables is 2.90 per cent of variance in the dependent variable ATS. Hence it is concluded that ATS test in physical sciences could best be predicted with the help of the above 8 variables among the eighteen (1-18) socio-demographic variables.

(*ii*) With the help of 7 areas of study habits.

$$ATS = 16.630 + 0.17\ (SHT) - 0.54\ (SH_2) + 0.27\ (SH_3) + 0.19\ (SH_7) + 0.16\ (SH_4)$$

The variance explained with the help of the above 5 variables is 7.29 per cent in the dependent variable i.e. scholastic achievement in physical sciences.

(*iii*) With the help of 10 areas of self-concepts

$$ATS = 14.010 + 0.40 (SC_2) + 0.24 (SC_1) - 0.30\ (SC_{10}) + 0.20\ (SC_6) + 0.16\ (SC_5) + 0.20\ (SC_7)$$

The variance explained with the help of the above 6 variables is 6.15 per cent in the dependent variable i.e. scholastic achievement in physical sciences.

(*iv*) With the help of 14 personality factors.

$$ATS = 18.377 + 1.118\ (FB) + 0.400\ (FQ3) + 0.145\ (FH) + 0.338\ (FD) - 0.189\ (FE) + 0.145\ (FF) + 0.127\ (FI)$$

The variance explained with the help of the above 7 variables is 9.90 percent in the dependent variable.

(*v*) With the help of all independent variables in the study

$$ATS = 1.714 + 0.99\ (FB) + 0.33\ (SC_2) + 0.36\ (FQ_3) + 0.36\ (FD) + 0.31\ (FH) + 0.21\ (SHT) - 0.50\ (SH_2) - 2.75\ (I) - 1.03\ (ED)$$

With the help of the above nine variables, it is possible to explain 17.64 per cent of variance in the dependent variable namely scholastic achievement in physical sciences.

It is concluded that the achievement in Physical sciences could be best predicted with the help of (*i*) Personality Factor-B (FB) (*ii*) Abilities (SC_2) (*iii*) Factor Q3 (FQ_3) (*iv*) Factor D (FD) (*v*) Factor H (FH) (*vi*) Study Habits Total score(SHT) (*vii*) Reading and note taking(SH_2) (*viii*) Income of the family (I) (*ix*) Educational division (ED).

19. A model of relationship between independent variables and dependent variables is shown in Fig. 6.1.

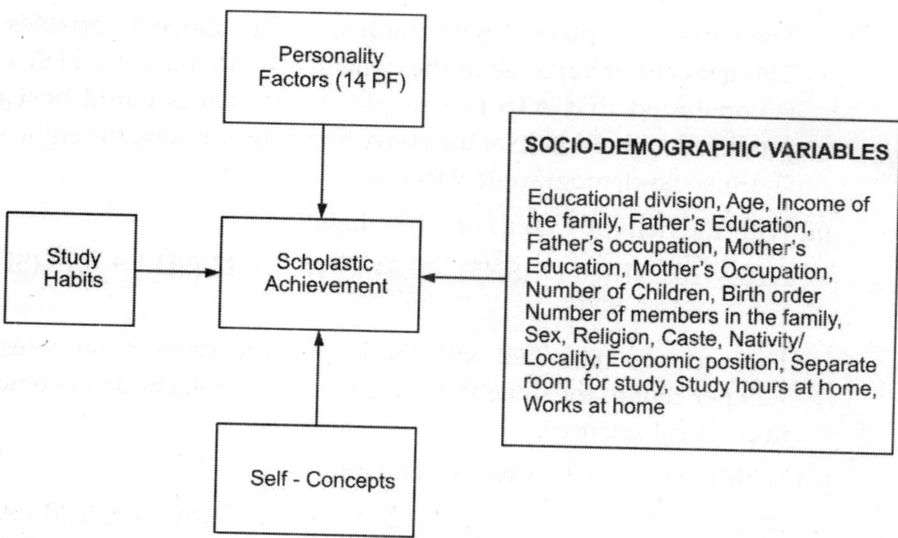

Fig. 6.1 : Model of Relationship between Independent and Dependent Varible

Conculsions

On the basis of the findings in the preceding pages, the following conclusions are drawn:

1. The frequency distributions of the scholastic achievement of IX class students for the whole group is not normal. It is more peaked than the normal distributions.
2. All the IX students do not have the same scholastic achievement abilities.
3. There is a significant influence of Educational divisions, Sex and Caste on the scholastic achievement of IX class students in Physical sciences. Puttur division students, girls and back ward caste students performed significantly better than their respective counterparts.
4. It is concluded that there is significant interaction effect of Educational divisions × Caste, on the scholastic achievement of IX class students in Physical sciences.
5. There is no significant main and interaction effects of Age, Religion and Nativity on the scholastic achievement of IX class students in Physical sciences.
6. Annual income of the family and Birth order have significant influence on the scholastic achievement of IX class students in physical sciences.

The annual income group Rs.25,000 to Rs.50,000 performed significantly better than the other two groups namely below Rs.25,000 and above Rs.50,000 groups of students. Birth order 1 students performed significantly better than the other two groups of students namely birth order 2 and 3 and above.

7. Father's education, Father's occupation, Mother's education, Mother's occupation, Number of children. Total members in the family, Economic position, Separate Room for study, study hours at home and works at home do not have significant influence on the scholastic achievement of IX class students in Physical sciences.
8. All the seven areas of Study Habits Inventory (SHI) and the total score of SHI have significant influence on the scholastic achievement of IX class students in Physical sciences. Better study habits is associated with better scholastic achievement of IX class students in Physical sciences.
9. It is found that the self-concepts namely; (*i*) Health and sex appropriateness (SC_1), (*ii*) Abilities(SC_2), (*iii*) Self-confidence(SC_3), (*iv*) Worthiness (SC_5), (*v*) Present-past-future (SC_6), (*vi*) Beliefs and convictions (SC_7), (*vii*) Sociability (SC_9), (*viii*) Emotional Maturity (SC_{10}) and (*ix*) Self-Concepts total scores, have significant influence on the scholastic achievement of IX class students in Physical sciences. Better Self-concepts are associated with better scholastic achievement in Physical sciences.
10. The personality Factors namely, A, B, D, E, F, H, I, and Q_3 have significant influence on the scholastic achievement of IX class students in Physical sciences. It is concluded that students with personality characteristics namely, (*i*) Out going, (*ii*) More intelligent, (*iii*) Excitable (*iv*) Obedient, Mild, Conforming, Submissive, (*v*) Happy go lucky, Enthusiastic, Lively, (*vi*) Venturesome, (*vii*) Tense minded, and (viii) Controlled have performed significantly better than the students with personality characteristics namely (*i*) Reserved, (*ii*) Less intelligent, (*iii*) Phlegmatic, (*iv*) Assertive, Independent, Aggressive, Stubborn, Dominant, (*v*) Sober, (*vi*) Shy, (*vii*) Though minded and (*viii*) Undisciplined.
11. It is possible to predict the scholastic achievement of IX class students in Physical sciences, with different sets of socio-demographic and psychological variables.
12. It is also possible to predict scholastic achievement of IX class students in Physical sciences with the help of all the 51 independent socio-demographic and psychological variables.

Educational Implications and Recommendations

After analyzing the results of the study carefully, the following implications can be drawn. It is seen from the study that the general performance in Physical sciences of IX class pupils is poor viz below fifty per cent. Physical sciences plays a crucial role in the life of students. To improve the achievement in Physical sciences at IX class level, efficient, dedicated, honest and committed teachers of Physical sciences are to be recruited. Plans are to be made to design more physical sciences activities, as curricular inputs, to eliminate the fear of Physical sciences in children. The knowledge of Physical sciences at secondary level forms the basis for Physical sciences at higher education and hence combined efforts by Physical sciences teachers, parents, educational administrators, inspecting authorities and government, may be made for ensuring the quality of education is Physical sciences for all the children. Special programmes such as providing additional information, encouragement to participate in competitive tests and providing suitable study material, participation in science fairs, quiz programmes, visiting science museum, scientific laboratories, field trips, etc may be taken to safeguard the interests of those students, who want to specialize, in the area of Physical sciences and related branches. The teachers in general should posses the knowledge of results of research findings. They must know which of the psycho-sociological factors that influence the achievement in Physical sciences and act accordingly to improve the achievement in Physical sciences.

On the basis of the results of this investigation, the following recommendations are made:

1. The achievement in Physical sciences of IX class students is very poor in Madanapalle Division, especially in boys that too in SC/ST students, special attention should be paid to improve the achievement in Physical sciences by parents, teachers, managements, administrators and Government.
2. Proper positive attitude towards the subject must be laid down by the concerned teachers. Without positive attitude, it is rather difficult to raise the standards.
3. Fear of the subject, test-anxiety and tension should be removed by proper counseling and guidance by the teachers.
4. Pupils must be made aware of the importance of the subject, uses of the subject in daily life, its correlation with other subjects and thereby interest in the subject must be aroused by the teachers.
5. More importance is to be given for making the concepts in the subject clear, understanding of the formulae and applying the formulae.

6. Sufficient number of oral questions on the subject are to be put and answers may be elicited from the pupils, while teaching.
7. More number of tests, with objective questions namely multiple choice, filling up the blanks, matching type and true or false, are to be conducted.
8. Special training must be given to the students to face different competitive examinations and the students must properly be encouraged to face such examinations.
9. It is observed that the performance of the students belonging to the Madanapalle Division schools is very less. This may be due to the vacant posts of Physical sciences teachers, lack of proper supervision, lack of commitment on the part of the teachers and lack of proper infrastructural facilities in the schools. Parents, teachers, administrators and government have to put up a combined effort to raise the standards in Madanapalle Division schools, there by creating confidence among the parents. More competitive, highly qualified and dedicated teachers are to be recruited for the posts of Physical sciences teachers in this Divisions.
10. It is also observed from this study that the achievement of SC/ST and OC Students is less, when compared with BC Students. Therefore special attention should be paid towards SC/ST and OC students. Extra classes and suitable remedial measures for SC/ST and OC students are to be taken by all the concerned teachers, to raise their achievement levels.
11. It is observed that performance of girls is significantly better than Boys. Healthy and proper competitive spirit may be developed among boys in their academic activities.
12. Middle annual income group performed significantly better than low and high income groups of students, parents and teachers should be taken special care about low and high income groups of students. The parents are advised to supervise the studies of their wards at home.
13. Students may suitably be provided with proper study facilities at home and at school, by the concerned.
14. It is found that all the seven areas of study habits are positively related with the scholastic achievement of pupils. Hence proper study habits may be developed in the pupils for better achievement both at home and at school.
15. The following self-concepts among the pupils may be developed through guidance and counseling for better scholastic achievement

in Physical sciences. (*i*) Health and Sex appropriateness, (*ii*) Abilities (*iii*) Self-Confidence, (*iv*) Worthiness, (*v*) Present-Past-Future, (*vi*) Beliefs and Convictions, (*vii*) Sociability, (*viii*) Emotional Maturity and (*ix*) Self-Concepts Total score.

16. The following personality characteristics may be developed among the IX class pupils, through counseling and guidance for better scholastic achievement in Physical sciences. (*i*) Out going, (*ii*) More-intelligent, (*iii*) Excitable, (*iv*) Obedient, Mild, Controlled, Submissive (*v*) Happy go lucky, Enthusiastic, Lively, (*vi*) Venture some, (*vii*) Tense Minded and (*viii*) Controlled.
17. The investigator, with the present scientific investigation, combined with his vast experience feels that proper commitment on the part of the teacher, handling of the subject, his potentialities and humor, his efforts in developing positive attitude towards the subject, his motivational efforts, his efforts in making the students to realize the importance of the Physical sciences and its usefulness, its relation with other subjects and its practical values in the daily life of human-beings; lowest or highest class of the society and narrating often and often some interesting and important events from the life history of famous physical sciences scientists would help create interest in the subject and thereby improvement in achievement of Physical sciences can be made possible.
18. The combined efforts of teachers and parents in developing good study habits at the early stage of a child, would be fruitful.
19. Further majority of the students have test-anxiety in Physical sciences and hence this anxiety is to be removed by proper guidance and counseling and also by involving scientific activities.
20. Parents must constantly encourage the children towards their education, know their interests and aptitudes and safe guard their interests.

Delimitations of the Study and Suggestions for Further Research

The following delimitations and suggestions are considered for further investigation:

1. The present study is confined only to 1800 students. Future researchers may undertake studies with large samples.
2. This study is confined only to Chittoor District. It may be extended for other districts of Andhra Pradesh and other states of the country.

3. This study is tonfined only to IX class students. It may be extended to other classig, lower or higher viz 6th, 7th, 8th and 10th classes, Intermediate gourse and Degree leve_s.
4. This investigd ion is limited :o Physical sciences subject only. This kind of researt h in different school subjects can be planned to plug the weak areatiin the respective subjects.
5. The tool usedg or measuring the ach_evement in Physical sciences is developed ared standardized by the investigator. Therefore, it is suggested thal standardized tools, for measuring the achievements in different suejects should be developed for repeated use, by different researchers, k/,eping in view, the existing syllabus in school subjects.
6. Only very fevrasocio-demographic variables and psycho-sociological variables are rtsed in the present study. Some other variables like attitude of tea thers towards.the subject, attitude of students towards Physical sciem es, facilities in the school, parental involvement in the education ofnheir children, teachers qualifications and merits, regularity ot students etc may help to know their impact on achievement er Physical sciences.
7. Studies to estienate the influer ce of course content, books available, vailability ofaguide material for teachers, laboratory facilities for Physical sciemes, may be under taken.
8. A longitudinae study may be conducted in order to prove that good scholastic adnievement, in secondary level, will lead to the correspondinglsuccess in higher levels.
9. Studies to estumate the influer ce of medium of instruction may be under taken.
10. Studies relateuitto the 'Commitment of Physical sciences Teachers' may be under takev., keeping in view their teaching style, completion of syllabus on tpme, taking special classes for backward students, conducting œsperiodical tests and evaluating them, maintaining cordial relations with students and parents etc.
11. Studies relater-to the teacher-pupil rat:o may be under taken to know the impact of neis ratio on the achievement in Physical sciences at IX class and higl r levels.
12. The governmgnt is spending huge amounts of money on in-service training progvsmmes of Physical sciences teachers and other subject teachers. Heny e studies may be under taken to know the impact of these in-servigi training programmes on the achievement of students in Physical scisnces at IX class level or other levels.

13. Studies may be conducted to know the impact of higher qualifications of Physical sciences teachers on the achievement in Physical sciences of IX class students.
14. Studies may be conducted to know the various causes for under-achievement in Physical sciences at IX class level, so as to enable school administration to take suitable remedial measures.

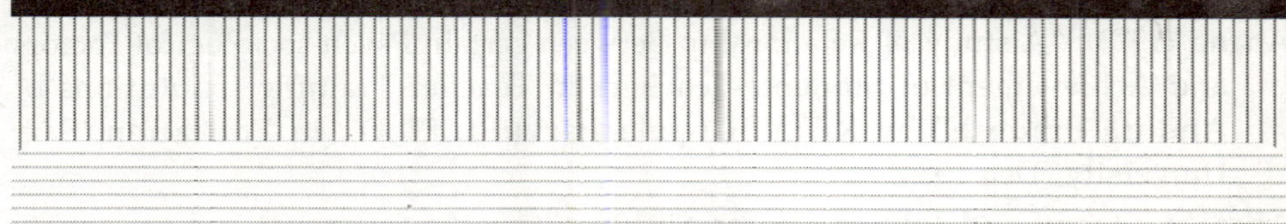

Bibliography

Abiam and Odok Abiam, P.O. and Odok, J.K (2006): "Factors in Students achievement in different branches of secondary school mathematics" *Journal of education and Technology*. (1) 161 - 168.

Aggarwal and Saini (1969): *"Pattern of study Habit and its Relationship with Achievement and Parents economic and educational status"*, *Journal of Educational Research and Extension*, vol. 5. No. 4, April 1969 pp. 1593169.

Aggarwal (1974): *"A study of the correlation of Achievement Motivation"* unpublished Ph.D. Dissertation, Kurukshetra University.

Aggarwal (1990): *Statistical Methods*, a text book, Sterling publishers Pvt. Ltd., New Delhi-16, pp.131-139.

Agarwal Archana (2002): *"Some correlates of Academic Achievement"*, *Indian Journal of Educational Research*, Vol.21(2): 75-76, Educational Abstracts, pp.47-48.

Ahuliwalia and Shyam (1975): *"A study of Relationship between socio-economic status and academic achievement of high school students"*, *Journal of Educational Research and Extension*, Vol. IX, No.12, No.1, pp. 1-5.

Ahuluwalia and Deo, Shyam(1978): *"Relationship between socio-economic status ande academic achievement of High School students"*, *Trends in education*, Vol. IX, no.1, pp.50-53.

Alam (2001): *"A Comparative study of Academic Achievement, Self-concept and Alienation of Hearing impaired and Normal Students"*, *Educational Abstracts*: Vol. 4, No. 1, Jan 2004, Abstract No: 23, p. 24.

Alam (2001): *"Academic Achievement in relation to socio – economic status"*. Anxiety level and achievement motivation: a comparative status of Muslim and non-Muslim University.

Alexander (1965): *"Relation of environment to intelligence and achievement-A longitudinal study"*, as quoted in Bloom, B.S;" Stability and change in human characteristics" (John: New York), p.113.

All Port (1949): *"Personality-psychological interpretation"*. A Text Book, London-Constable and Co.

All Port (1961): *Pattern and Growth in Personality*. John Wiley.

Anand (1973): "A study of Relationship Between certain Psych-sociological Factors and Achievement of Students-Teachers in Teacher Training Institutions of Andhra Pradesh" by R.V.V. Gopalacharyulu: Ph.D., in Education, S.V. University, Dec 1983.

Anca Munteanu and Iuliana Coatea (2010) : *"School achievement and personality dynamics in adolescence"* Department of Psychology, west University of Timisoara, Timisoara, 300220, Romania, available online May 2010.

Anice James (2005): *A Text Book, Teaching of Mathematics,* p. 21, p.23.

Anice James and Marice (2004): *"Achievement in Science as Related to Scientific Aptitude and Scientific Attitude Among XI Standard Students in Tamil Nadu", Journal of Educational Research and Extension,* Vol. 41, No. 2 April- June 2004, pp. 13-16

Annakodi (2008): *"Study of Scientific Attitude of pupils of class XI and Their Achievement in Science". Miracle of Teaching* - A quartly Journal - January - February, March - April, 2008, Vol.VIII, No.1, Published by Asian Academy of Education and Culture, pp. 39-41.

Anuradha johi (1990): *"Teaching elements of science to class IX students of Madhya Pradesh State: Evolvement of an instructional strategy", Indian Education Review,* Vol. 25, No.1, pp. 56-62.

Anuradha and Bharathi (2002): *"Effect of TV viewing on elementary school children's academic achievement", Perspectives in Education,* Vol.2, No.2, July 2002, abstract No. 183, pp. 50-51.

Archana and Monasharma (2002): From *"Study Habits of Intermediate Students in Relation to Certain Psycho-Sociological Factors"*, by Rajni (2004) Ph.D., Thesis, SVU, Tirupati, p. 53.

Arockiadosis (2005): *"Study Habits and academic performance of college students", Experiments in Education,* Vol. 33, No. 33, pp. 77-79.

Aruna (1981): *"A study of the Factors influencing the achievement of standard VIII students Belonging To scheduled and scheduled Tribes Whose medium of instruction is Kannada"* Ph.D., in Education: Mysore University.

Aruna (1984): "Study habits of 9th class pupils" un publisher M.Ed dissertation, S.V. University Tirupati.

Asha Bhatnagar (1980): *"A study of some Factors Affecting student Involvement in studies" Journal of Education Research,* Vol. 15, No. 3, pp. 70-75.

Asudulla khan, Sudha, Mrs Lalitha Tirth (1982): *"Scholastic Achievement as a Function of Aspiration, Religion and socio-economic status" Journal of Education and Psychology,* Vol. 39, No. 4, Jan 1982, pp. 218-223.

Ayishabi and Moly Kuruvilla (1998): *"Achievement Motivation of secondary School children of working and Non working Mothers of Kerala". Experiments in Education* Vol. 26, No. 12, Dec 1998, pp. 203-205.

Baharudin (2009): *"Relationship with Father and Mother, Self – Esteem and Academic Achievement amongst College Students" Amirican Journal of Scientific Research* ISSN 1450 – 223XISSUE 6, pp. 86-94.

Bal (1988): *"The Effect of Mother's Employment on Achievement Motivation of Adolescents," Journal of Personality and Clinical Studies"*, Vol. 4, No.1, pp. 81-84.

Balasubramanian and Feroze (1966): *"A Comparative Study of the Academic Achievement in Mathematics of Urban and Rural Students of Standard X in the High Schools of Coimbatore", Journal of Educational Research and Extension,* Vol. 3, No.1, p. 25.

Basantia and Mukhopadyaya (2001): *"Effect of Environmental Factors on Achievement: a study on Rural Students", The Educational Review,* Vol.44, No. 11, Nov. 2001, pp. 201-204.

Bernstein (1968): *"Some Sociological Determinants of Perception – An enquiry in to sub cultural Differences" British Journal of Sociology,* Vol. 9, p. 159.

Best (1959): *"Research in Education"* Prentice-Hall Inc Englewood Cliff, USA-31.

Best (1977): *"Research in Education"*, A Test Book, Prentice-Hall of India, New Delhi.

Bhujendra Nath Panda (1991): *"Academic Achievement and selected Demographic Factors-A study on Urban- Rural High School Adolescents" Journal of Education and Psychology;* Vol. 49, No. 1-2, April-July 1991, pp. 49-54.

Biswas, Prabir Kumar (2001): *"Learning Strategies and Academic Performance: A Study of the Successful Distance Learners of PG DDE Programme of IGNOU", Indian Journal of Open Learning,* Vol.10, No. 2, pp. 211-220.

Borbora and Rupa Das (2002): *"Influence of Parental Literacy on the Academic Achievement of children Belonging to the Backward classes: A study of Kamrup District". Journal of Indian Education,* vol.27(1), 59-65 from *Indian Educational Abstracts* vol. 2. No.2, July 2002 Abstract No. 141; pp. 13-14.

Britannica Word Language Dictionary (1961) *A Dictionary,* Funk & Wagnall's Company, New York: Vol. 2, p. 1126

Bose and Joshi (2004): *"Effect of Involvement of Parents in the education of children: An exploration", Educational Abstracts:* Vol 5, No: 1 and 2, Jan and July 2005, 88 Abstract No. 111, p. 87.

Brown and Dubois (1964): *"Study Habits and attitudes, college experience and college success" Personal and Guidance Journal* Vol. 43, pp. 287-292.

Brown and Holtzman. (1955): *"A study of attitude question for Predictor Academic success." Journal of education Psychology,* Vol. 46, pp. 75-84.

Brownell (1945): *"When is arithmetic meaningful". Journal of Education Research,* 38, 481-98.

Brownell (1947): *"The place of meaning in the teaching of arithmetic". Elementary School Journal,* 47, 256-65.

Burnet (1951): *"Study Skills and chancellor Training – A, Two way Teaching programme". California Journal of Educational Research.* Vol. 2, pp. 18-21.

Cattell (1950): *"The main personality factors in questionnaire, Self estimated material", Journal of Social Psychology,* Vol. 31, p. 3-38.

Cattell and Eber H.W (1962): *Manual for 16PF Test,* IPAT, Champaign, Illinois, USA.

Cattell Saley and Sweeney (1966): *"What can parents and Motivation Source Trait Measurements Add to the prediction of School Achievement", British Journal of Educational Psychology,* Vol. 45, pp. 280-295.

Cattell (1969): *Hand book for Junior Senior High School Personality Questionnaire:* Ellinois, Institute of Personality and Ability Testing.

Cattell (1970): *Theories of Personality,* John Wiley & Sons, Inc (2nd ed), p. 386.

Chadha and Sunanda Chandana (1990): *"Creativity, intelligence and Scholastic achievement – A Residential study" Indian Educational Review Quarterly,* Vol. 25, No. 3, July-1990, pp. 81-85.

Chakrabarthi Bhupal Prasad (2002): *"Experiments in using comprehension Type Tests with Multiple choice Type Items In Primary Mathematics". Vigyan Shikshak,* Vol. 46(3), 5-9. *Indian Educational Abstracts,* p. 33-34.

Chakrabarthi Sharmistha (2002): A critical study of Family Problems faced by the Learners, Socio-Economic status Physical facilities Available in Literacy centres, organizational and Instructional Aspect as Literacy Programme and their Relation with Literacy Achievement of Female Learners in West Bengal" Research Project, University of Culcutta; NCERT, (ERIC Funded) from *Indian Educational Abstracts*: Vol. 2, No. 2, July 2002. Abstract No. 28, p. 3.

Chandran & Lim (2010): *Factors associated with poor academic achievement among urban primary school children in Malaysia,* Dept of Optometry, Faculty of Allied Health Sciences, University. Malaysia.

Chatterjee et.al. (1971): *Effect of Certain Socio-economic Factors on the Scholastic Achievement of the School Children,* Psychometric Reach and Srvice Unit, Indian Statistical Institute, Calcutta.

Chauhan and Smg (1982): *"An Investigation into the study Habits of 10 to 12 years of children with regard to their parental Profession". Indian education Review NCERT.* New Delhi, Vol. 22, No. 1, pp. 92-96.

Chel, Madan Mohan (1990): "Diagnosis and remediation of under achievement in compulsory mathematics of Mathematic examination in west Bengal". Ph.D Thesis in education, University of Calcutta, India.

Chitra Tyagarajan: (1983): *"Psycho socio Educational factors of schedule caste students in higher secondary school". Journal of Education Research and Extension* Vol. 30, Vo-2, p. 61 – 67.

Chopra and Kanna (1980): "A study of some non intellectual correlates of academic achievement" Litt in education Lucknow University.

Chopra (1982): "A study of organizational climate in school in Relation to job satisfaction of Teachers and students Achievement". Ph.D in Education Agra University. Third survey of Research in education (1987): *Abstract No. 1133,* pp. 796-797.

Christmann, Edvin, Badgett and John (2001): *"A Four-Year Analytic Comparison of Eleventh Grade Academic Achievement in the Slippery Rock Area High School and District Pupil Expenditures"*. A report presented to the Slippery Rock School District's Board of Directors and the Pennsylvania Department of Education Division. *Technical Report, ERIC*, Vol. 36, No. 1, Jan. 2001, ED 443824, p.171.

Cloncie Wilson (2009): *"The relation among parents factors and academic achievement of American Urban youth"*. http://does.rnw.edu/fed:fn/9.

Cobb, et al. (1991): *"Assessment of a problem centred second-grade mathematics project"*, Journal for Research in Mathematics Education", 22, pp. 3-29.

Corlos & Rodrgvez (2009): *"The impact of academic self concept, expertations and the choice of learning strategy on academic achievement" Higher education Research & Development*, Vol. 28, Issue. 5 Pages : 523 – 539.

Corter (1955): *"Development of a Diagnostic scoring scheme for a study method test". California Journal of educational Research* Vol. 6 pp. 26-32.

Cury R2 (1962): *"The Effect of the Socio Economic status on the school achievement of 6th class children". British Journal of Educational Psychology*. 46- 49.

Dash (2002): *"Trends and problems of Higher Education of Scheduled Tribes in Orissa"* D.Litt in Education, Ukal University, from *Indian Educational Abstracts*. Vol.2. No.2: July 2002 Abstract No: 142, pp. 14-16

Dave and Dave (1971): *Socio-economic environment as related to the non verbal intelligence of rank and failed students*. Regional College of Education, Mysore.

Davidson Seaton and Simpson (1998): *Chambers concise 20th century Dictionary*, Allied publishers Pvt. Ltd., pp. 336, 889

Davidson (1985): *Small group cooperative learning in mathematics in R. Slavin (Ed) "Learning to co-operate – cooperating to learn*, pp. (211-30), NY: Plenum.

Deb and Gravel (1990): *"Relationship between study habits and Academic Achievement of under Graduate Home Science Final year students" Journal of Educational Research*, Vol. 25, No. 3, pp. 71-74.

Della Thompson (1996) (Ed): *The concise Oxford Dictionary of Current English*. Ninth Edition, Oxford University Press; p. 1235.

Derek Rowntree (1981): *A Dictionary of Education*. Haper & Raw Publishers London, pp. 16, 41, 65, 75, 89, 126, 214, 236, 244.

Desai (1979): *Under achievement syndrome among high ability High school boys"*. In M.B. Buch(ed), Second survey of Research in Education, Baroda, p. 579.

Devi and Mayuri (2000): *"The Effects of family and school on the Achievement of Residential School Children", Educational Abstracts*: Vol. 4. No. 2, July 2004: p.35; *Abstract* No: 154

Dhalakia (1980): *"Effects of observers and feed back upon changing the classroom Performance of Public Teachers"* Ph.D. in Education, M.S University, Baroda, in Third Survey & Research in Education (1987). *Abstract No: 1138*, p. 799.

Dhall Gautam, Avtar, Ram and Sankar (2000): *"Effect of u)0ng Remedial Materials in Mathematics on Achievement of Slow Learners", Educatiorn! Abstracts*: Vol. 2, No.1, Jan 2002, p. 70; Abstract No. 97.

Diener (1960): *"Similarities and differences Between over achieting and under Achieving students". Personal Guidance Journal*, Vol. 38, No. 5, pp. l. 96-400.

Dowson, Martin Mclnerney, Dennis, (1999): *"Age, Gender, C 'ltural and Socio-economic Differences in Students Academic Motivation, Cognition ancoAchievement", ERIC*, Vol. 34, No.6, June 1999, ED 427016, p.166.

Drapper and Smit (1981): *Applied Regression Analysis*, A tent book, Second Edition, John Wiely and Sons, New York.

Dubey (1982): *"Persistence, Sex Difference and Educational perf rmance", Asian Journal of Psychology and Education*, Vol. 9, No. 3.

Dubey and Mishra (1977): *"Determinants of Academic Success ccaong Rural Girls", Journal of Psychological Researches*, Vol. 41, Nos.1 and 2, pp. 46.153.

Dubey and Mishra (1999): *"Psycho-Social Determinants of Deademic Success in Rural Boys", Prospectives in Education* Vol. 15, No.3, July 1999 pp: 157-164.

Edwards (1969): *Techniques of Attitude Scale construction.* A teot book Vikas, Feffer and Simmons Pvt. Ltd., Bombay.

Elegbeleye and Akoda (2001): *"Psychological Implications of single and Double patenting background on Nigerian Adolescent's Academic Performancer. Journal of Social Science*, Vol. 5, No. 1 and 2, pp. 11-20.

Ellekka Kumar (2001): *"Achievement motivation of Higher Setiondary students and their achievement in Physics", Journal of Educational Research ario Extension*, Vol. 38, No.1

Ekanadha and Sunanda Chandana (1990): *"Creativity, i):telligence and scholastic achievement-A residential study"*, Indian Educational Ri view Quarterly, Vol 25, No. 3, July 1990, pp. 81-85.

Entwistle (1997): *"Personality and achievement" British Journalt"f Educational Psychology*, 39, pp. 5763.

Farquhar (1963): *A comparative study of Motivational Factors ivnderlying Achievement of Eleventh Grade High school studies.* Columbia Universitır Team Library p. 44

Fayegh yoosefi & Rumaya Juhari (2010): *"The relationship betie een gender, age depression and academic achievement"* Dept. of human developrnent and family studies University Putra Malaysia, Malaysia.

Fisher (1950): *Statistical Methods for Research Workers*, A text book, Hafner Publishing Co., New York.

Ford Dawson (1970): "An Analytical study of the Effects of Maternal Employment of some sex Denials In Pre-adolescence and of Resicential Mobility on self Actualization-Achievement in a Sample of Adoarscents", Dissertation Abstracts International, Vol. 3, p. 924.

Fraser (1959): *Home environment and school London,* UniversLcy of London Ltd.

Gakhar (1982): *"A Study of Acquisition of Mathematical concepts among 8th Grader of different types of schools experiments in education"*, Vol.II, No.9, pp. 164-167.

Gakhar and Assema (2004): *"Social stress, Locality and Gender Affecting Academic Achievement and Reasoning Ability"*, *Journal of Educational Research and Extension*, Vol. 41, No. 4, Oct-Dec. 2004, p. 60-66

Garrett (1973): *Statistics in Psychology and Education.* A test book Valiks, Feffer and Simous Pvt. Ltd; Bombay, India pp: 213-215, 337-370.

George Chitra (1992): *"A study of family Relations Socio –Economic status intelligence and adjustment of failed high school students"*. Ph.D, Education, Hemavathi Nandon, Bahuguna Garhwal University.

Gilson, Judith (1999): *"Single Gender Education versus Co-education for Girls: A study of Mathematics Achievement and Attitude Towards Mathematics of Middle – School students": ERIC*, Vol. 34, No. 9, Sep. 1999 ED 430011, p. 56.

Girija Bhadra and Ameerjan (1975): *"The Relationship of study Habits with study skills, academic Achievement Motivation and Academic Achievement"*, *Journal of Educational Psychology*, Vol. 33, No.1, pp. 47-53.

Gnanasundaratharasu and Vincent De Pauls (2002): *"Effectiveness of video Assisted Instruction in Teaching and Learning Social Science at Primary Level" Experiments in Education*; Vol. 30, No. 5. May 2002, pp. 98-101.

Gnanaguru suresh (2008): *"Under achievement B.Ed students in relation to their home environment attitude towards teaching"*. *Edutracks* : Vol. 7, No. 12 Neelkamal Publications Pvt. Ltd. Koti Hyderabad. Aug 2008 pp. 20

Goel, Swami Pyari (2002): *"Feeling of Security, Family Attachment and values of Adolescents Girls in Relation to their Educational Achievement"* Indian Journal of Psychometry and Education, Vol. 33(1), 25-28. Indian Educational Abstract, p. 51.

Golden and will (1978): *"A profile of high and low achievers is Mathematics among 6th grade students" District. Abst. Int.* Vol. 38(8), p. 4639

Golden (1941): *"Study Habits Inventory score and scholarship"*. *J. of Applied Psychology*, Vol.25, pp. 101-107.

Good (ed) (1941): Dictionary of Education, (2nd ad) McGraw-Hill. Newyork.

Gopal Rao (1956): *"A study of sum factors related to scholastic achievement"*, Ph.D thesis University of Delhi.

Gopala Charyulu (1984): "A study of Relationship Between certain Psycho-sociogical Factors and Achievement of student Teachers Training Institutes of Andhra Pradesh", Ph.D Thesis in education; SVU in Fourth survey of research in education (1991), Abstract No: 1069, p. 940.

Gorden, (1941): *"Study Habit Inventory Scores and Scholarship"*, *Journal of Applied* Psychology, Vol.25, pp. 101-107.

Gordan Darlene (1998): *"The Relationship among Academic Achievement self-concept, Academic Achievement and persistence with self Attribution, Study Habits and perceived school Environment"*. *Dissertation Abstracts Inter-national*, Vol. 58, No.12, p. 26.

Gorden and Will (1978): *"A profile of high and low achievers in Mathematics among 6th grade students" Dissr. Abst. Int.* Vol. 38(8), p. 4639A.

Gorden (1941): *"Study Habits Inventory Scores and Scholarship". Journal of Applied Psychology,* Vol.25, pp. 101-107.

Goswamy, Minakshi (2002): *"Achievement Motivation and Anxiety Among children of working and Non working Mothers studying in Secondary Schools of Shillong". Journal of All India Association for Educational Research.* Vol. 12. (1 & 2) 25-28 from Indian Educational Abstracts Vol. 2 No. 2 July 2002. *Abstract No*: 187, pp. 54-55.

Govinda Reddy (2002): *"Influence of certain psycho-sociological Factors on scholastic Achievement of DIET students"*; Ph.D Thesis, S.V.U. Tirupati.

GuilFord (1950): *Fundamental statistics in psychology and Education:* International Student Edition, New York, McGraw Hill.

Guilford (1954): *Psychometric methods* A text book, Mc Graw-Hill Publishing Company-New York, pp: 47, 373, 37, 4, 378, 417

Gupta (1983): *"A study of personality characteristics of Ninth Grade over and under Achieving Boys and Girls at Different levels of Achievement Motivation"*. Ph.D Thesis Punjab University.

Gupta (1968): *"Intelligence, Economic status, sex and Academic success" Journal of Educational Research and Extension* Vol. 5, No. 2.

Gupta (1974): *Statistical Methods* A text book, Sultan Chand and Sons, New Delhi.

Guravaiah (2004): *"Study Habits of Residential and non-Residential pupils of Xth class in Relation to certain Psycho-sociological Factors"* Ph.D in education, SVU Tirupati.

Har Govinda Gupta (1968): *"A study of the Relationship Between some environmental Factors and Academic Achievement", Journal of Educational Research and Extension.* Vol. 5, No. 1, July 1968, pp. 17-23.

Harbans Singh (1989): *"An Investigation in to the study habits of scheduled caste Adolescent in Relation to their sex and Achievement Motivation" Journal of Education and Psychology;* Vol. 47, No.1-2 April-July 1989; pp. 21-25.

Hari Krishna (1992): "A study of Academic achievement of the students of Higher Secondary stage in relation to achievement motivation and Socio-Economic status", M.Phil, Annamalai - University.

Head, John (1981): *"Personality and learning of Mathematics". Educational Studies in Mathematics,* p. 339-350.

Hijazi and Naqvi (2006): *"Factors affective students performance. A case of private colleges" Bangladesh E-Journal of Sociology,* Vol. 3, No. 1, 2006

Husen (1967): *"International study of achievement in mathematics"*, Vol.2, NY: Wiley.

In Tse Ka and Wat kins (1994): *"Doing Living and study Habits and Academic Achievement of secondary school students in Hong Kong" Perpetual and Motor Skills,* Vol. 79, No.1, pp. 231-234.

Jagannadhan (1983): "The Effect of certain socio-psychological Factors of Academic Achievement of children studying in class V to VII" Ph.D Thesis in education, SVU, pp. 212-216.

Jagannadhan (1986): *"Socio-Economic Status and Academic Achievement": Journal of Educational Research and Extension,* Vol. 22, No. 3, pp. 141-149

Jammur (1958): *"Study Habits and Achievement" Psychological Studies,* Vol.3, No. 1, pp. 37-42.

Jammur (1964): *Achievement and some background factors psychological studies.* 10, pp. 239-243.

Jammur. (1971): *"Study Habits and some back ground factors".* Psychological studies, Vol. 17, No. 2, p. 14-18.

Jayachandrarama Naidu (1998): *"A Comparative Study of Academic Achievement of Formal and Non-Formal Education", Indian Educational Review,* Vol. 33, No. 1, Jan 1998, pp.152-158.

John Bellingham (2004): *Academic s Dictionary of Education.* Academic (India) Publishers, New Delhi, p. 2, 4, 20, 83, 228 252, 260, 261, 265, 269, 333.

John Bellingham (2004): *Academics' Dictionary of Education, Academic (India)* Publishers New Delhi, pp. 2, 4, 20, 21, 213.

Junani and Redzuan (2010): *"The Relationship between gender, age, depression and academic achievement"* Current Research in Psychology 6(1) 61-66, issue 1949 - 0178.

Jyoti Rathore (2000): *"A study of Scholastic Achievement of children studying at Primary level in Environmental studies with special Reference to MLL and Development of remedial Teaching strategies", Journal & Educational Research and Extension* Vol. 37, No. 4, Oct - Dec. 2000, pp. 9-13.

Kagade (2002): *"A Critical Study of Some Personality Factors of Students of Classes VIII, IX of pimpri Chinchwad Area",* Ph.D in Education(1997), University of Pune; from *Indian Educational Abstracts,* Vol. 2, No. 2, July 2002, Abstract No. 189, pp. 55-56.

Karl and Pyari (2004): *"Family climate and Income as determinants of educational Achievement", Educational Abstracts:* Vol. 4, No. 2, July 2004, p. 38 Abstract No. 159

Kennedy (1975): "Influence of certain psycho-sociological Factors on scholastic Achievement of DIET students" Ph.D Thesis by Govinda Reddy. V (2002) S.V.U: p. 74.

Khalid, Mohd Nasin (1997): *"Factors affecting Mathematics achievements in Malasian Schools", Dissertation Abstracts International,* Vol. 58, No. 7, p. 34-49.

Khan (2005): *"Scholastic achievement of Higher secondary students in science stream" Journal of social sciences,* Vol. 1, No. 2, 2005, pp. 84 - 87.

Khanna..(1980): "A study of Relationship Between students of Socio-Economic Back ground and their Academic Achievement at Junior Level", Ph.D in Education, Kanpur University.

Kneankwo and Kemjakon (2003): *"Relationship between anxiety and academic achievement of secondary school students in Anambra state of Nigeria" Experiments in Education* Vol. 3, No. 9, Sep - 2003, pp. 172 - 177.

Kobal - Palcic - Darya Musek and Janek (1999): *"Self concept and "Academic Achievement of central and western European Groups of Adolescents", ERIC* Vol. 35, No. 4, Oct - Dec 1998, pp. 29-35.

Kothari (D.1) et al., (1964-66): *The Education and National Development, Ministry of Education,* Government of India: New Delhi.

Koteswara and Ramachandra Reddy (1998): *"Impact of 14 personality factors on reading achievement of high school students in A.P." Journal of Educational Research and Extension,* Vol No. 4, Oct-Dec. 1998, pp. 29-35.

Krishna Moorthy and Rao (1969): *"A comparative Investigation of study Habits of Sub-Urban and urban children in some high school incompatible". Journal of Education Research and Extension,* Vol. 6, No. I, pp. 32-41.

Kulbir Sidhu (1995): *Teaching of Mathematics,* A Text Book, Sterling Publishers Pvt. Ltd., L-10-Green Park extension, New Delhi, p. 1-2.

Kumar and Anita (2004): *"Effectiveness of self-learning Module in Mathematics in Relation to class-room environment", Educational Abstracts;* Vol.4, No, 2, July 2004, p. 51. Abstract No. 180.

Kumara Swamy (1992): *"A study of certain Factors Related to achievement of Adult learners".* Ph.D in Adult Education, SVU., pp. 335-338.

Lakshmi Devi (2004): *"Vidya Jyoti (DIET Calendar):* Bukkapatnam: DIET Hand Book, p. 42-43.

Lal Singh (1984): *"Effect of socio-economic Status on the Academic Achievement of XI Grade Students", Journal of Education and Psychology.* Vol 42. No: 4 Jan 1984. pp. 223-228

Lalithamma (1975): *"Some factors affecting achievement of secondary school pupils in mathematics", Second Survey of Educational Research,* No. 2, p. 349.

Lalithanhawla (1983): *"An investigation into the causes of failures in science and Mathematics in high school certificate examination in Mizolam, Aizwal";* Northeastern Hill University campus, unpublished M.Ed Dissertation.

Lavanya (2000): *"A study of Personality development and study skills for Scholastic Achievement" Journal of Psychological Researches,* Vol.44, No.1, pp. 47-58.

Laxmidhar Behera and Sushanta Kumar Roul (2004): *"Trainees performance of B.Ed in Relation to their Gender, Academic Back Ground and Type of Institution". The Educational Review:* Vol. 47, No. 11, Nov. 2004, pp. 206-211.

Lidhoo and Khan (1990): *"Bright under Achievers Among the Socially Backward counselling and Remedial measures", Indian Journal of clinical Psychology.* Vol.17, pp. 28-32.

Lincoln Hall (1969): *"Selective variables in Achievement of Junior college students" Journal of Educational Research,* 63, 2. pp. 61-63.

Mac Aulay, Dolina (1990): *"Classroom Environment: A Literature review" Educational Psychology,* Vol. 10, No. 3, pp. 239-253.

Mandankar (2004): *"Relationship Between Adjustment Problems and Academic Achievement of Students Studying in Morarji Desai Residential Schools of Karnataka", Experiments in Education*, Vol. 32, No. 5, May, 2004.

Madhu Raj (1996) (Ed): *Encyelopaedic Dictionary of psychology and Education*, Anmol publications Pvt. Ltd. New Delhi Vol. 1, No. 3, pp. 8, 210, 211, 1482.

Majolribanks (1982): *Family Environment and Children's Academic Achievement". Sex and Social Group Difference, Psychological Abstracts*, 68(1), 2096. Quest in Education, Vol. XXVIII, No. 4, October 2004, pp. 22-33. A quarterly Journal, Published by Vajubai Patel and Dr.Kamal A. Patnakar.

Malvinder Ahuja (2006): *"Parental Involvement and academic achievement across various SES levels", Recent Researches in Education and Psychology*, Vol. II, No. 3, p. 84-93.

Manas Ranjan Panigrahi (2005): *"Academic Achievement in Relation to Intelligence And Socio-economic Status of High School Students", Edu tracks*, October-2005, Vol. 5, No. 2, pp. 26-30, Publisher: Suresh Chandra Sarma Koti, Hyderabad.

Manchala (2007): *"Achievement of B.Ed Students"* published Ph.D Thesis in Education S.V. University Tirupati, pp. 50-52, 66-74 270.

Mangal (2002): *Statistics in Psychology and Education*, A Text book of second edition, Prentice Hall of India Pvt. Ltd., New York.

Manoranjan Panda (2002): *"Analysis of Relationship between Academic Achievement and school Interventions of Class IX students". Journal & Educational Research and Extension* Vol. 37, No. 4, Oct – Dec. 2000 pp. 1-8.

Manoranjan Panda (2005): *"Correlation between Academic Achievement and Intelligence of Class IX Students" Edu Tracks*, September 2005, Vol. 5, No. 1 Published by Suresh Chandra Sarma Neel Kamal Publications, Pvt. Ltd., Koti, Hyderabad, pp. 36-38.

Marcon, Rebecca (1999): *"Demographic and Educational Influences on Academic Motivation, Competence and Achievement in Minority urban students". ERIC*. Vol.34, No.9, Sep., 1999, Ed 430061, p. 162

Marentic pozarahik (1974): *"Study Habits and Attitudes towards learning as a factor of scholastic achievement" Psychological Abstracts*; Vol – 51, No.12, p. 480.

Marrow and Williamson (1961): *"Family relationship of school children, Child Development"*, 32, 501-521. *Quest in Education*, Vol.XXVIII, No. 4, October, 2004. A Quarterly Journal Published by Vajubhai and Dr. Kamal Patnakar.

Martin (1995): "Achievement of B.Ed students": A Ph.D Thesis by Dr. C. Manchala, SVU., Tirupati, p. 103.

Mary Esther St (1945): "An Analysis of Study Habits and catholic high school students". *Catholic Education*, London, pp. 542-549.

Mary and Eswara Prasad (1997): *"A study of academic achievement in relation to selected personality variables of tribal adolescents". Experiments in Education* Vol. 25, Nos. 7 & 8 July and August 1997, pp. 155-161.

Martinsen & Swanberg (2010) : *"Personality approaches to learning and achievement" Educational Psychology,* Vol : 30 Issue. 1 passes : 75 - 88.

Meena siwath (2008): *"Impact of Home Environment on the scholastic achievement of children". Journal of Human ecology Haryana India* 23(1): 75 – 77.

Mehara (1992): *"Level of School Performance of Backward and Non Backward Rajasthani Higher Secondary Boys", Journal of Psychological Researches,* Vol. 36, No. 2, pp. 64-67.

Mehera (2004): *"A study on the Achievement at the Secondary Level and Some of its Determinants" Educational Abstracts*: Vol. 5, No. 1 and 2, January and July 2005, pp.10-11.

Mennon (1973): From *"A study of relationship Between Certain Psycho-Sociological Factors and Achievement of Students- Teachers in Teacher Training Institutes of Andhra Pradesh"* by R.V.V. Gopala charyulu; Ph.D in Education S.V.U 1983; pp. 69-70.

Mishra et al (1960)*: "An Investigation into the influence of Home Environment on the School Achievement", Journal of Educational and Vocational Guidance, 7, 72-76, Quest In Education,* Vol.XXVIII, No. 4, October, 2004. A Quarterly Journal Published by Vajubai and Dr. Kamal Patnakar.

Mohmood Allam (2009) : *"Academic achievement in relation to creativity and achievement motivation a correlation study" Edutracks,* Neel Kamal Publications, Koti, Hyd. Vol. 8, No. 9, p. 31-33

Mohammad Khayyer and Philip. DeLacey (2005): *"Prediction of academic achievement from some demographic, family background and locus of control variables"*, from internet www.uw.edn.AU: A study from Australia.

Mohanty (2002): *"School type psychological differentiation and academic achievement" Psychological Studies* 45 (2) 100 – 102.

Molia (1999): *"A study of the effectiveness of Inductive Thinking Model of Retentional Indices in Mathematics of class VIII", Educational Abstracts*: Vol 2, No.1 Jan 2002, p. 35, Abstract No: 47

Moula (2010): *"A study of the relationship between academic achievement motivation and home environment among standard eight pupils" Educational Research and Review,* Egerton University, Nyahururu, Kenya Vol. 5, pp. 213 – 217

Mukta Rani Rastogi (1975): *Manual for self concept scale,* published in Agra Psychological Research; Tiwari Kothi Balagani, Agra: 282004, India.

Nagaraju (2001): *"Study Habits of high school pupils in Relation to certain Psycho-sociological Factors".* Ph.D in education, SVU Tirupati.

Nair (1974): *"Impact of Certain Sociological Factors on Teaching Ability in the Classroom",* NCERT Financed Project, Government Training College, Trivandrum, India.

Nalini & Ganesha Bhatta (2009): *"Study habits and students achievement in relation to some influencing Factors" Edutracks* Neel Kamal Publication, Koti, Hyd, Vol. 2, p. 26 - 28

Narayana Koteswara and Rama Chandra Reddy: B. (1998): *"A study of reading Achievement in Relation to Demographic variables": Experiments in Education,* Vol. 26, No.11, Nov. 1998, pp. 180-200

Naresh Kumar Gupta (2002): *"Need to Boost Primary Pupils' Achievement"* – A Strategy of Education for All, *Indian Educational Review*, Vol. 38. No=1, Jan 2002, pp. 115-138.

Natesan and Susila (2000): *"Personality Factors and Achievement in Environmental science of V standard students", Experiments in Education* Vol. 28, No. 12, Dec. 2000, pp. 188-192

National Policy and Education (1986): "Ministry of Human resource development", New Delhi, Government of India Dept of Education.

Naveen Kumar Reddy. (2003): *"An Investigation into study Habits of Secondary School Children"* M.Ed Dissertation, SVU, Tirupati, p. 48.

NCERT (2008): *"Mather's Education is important than Father's Education – A mid term National Survey"*. Published in *"The Hindu"*, Chennai Edition, October 2008, p. 5.

Neetha George, Anitha Ravindran (2005): *"Academic Achievement in Relation to Time Perception and Coping Styles" Journal of Community Guidance & Research*, Vol. 22, No. 1, March 2005, pp. 55-65.

Noorjehan & Wajiha (2009): *"Factors affecting academic achievement of 9th standard students in mathematics" Edutracks*, Neel Kamal Publications Koti, Hyd. Vol. 8, No. 7.

Nolton (1959): *"The Relationship of study habits and other measure of achievements of 9th grade general science". Experiments in Education*, Vol.27 pp. 211-217.

Nwankwo and Kemjika (2003): *"Relationship Between Test Anxiety and Academic Achievement of Secondary School Students in Anambra State of Nigeria", Experiments in Education*, Vol. 31, No. 9, Sep. 2003, pp.172-177.

On Tsk Ka and Wat Kins (1994): *"Doing Living and Study Habits and Academic Achievement of Secondary School Students in Hong Kong", Perpectual and Motor Skills*, Vol. 79, No. 1, pp. 231-234.

Padmanabhan Nayar and Visveswaran. (1966): *"A Comparative Study the Achievement in General Science of Urban and Rural Students Studying in X class in the High Schools in Coimbatore District", Journal of Educational research and Extension*, Vol. 2, No. 3, p. 20.

Panchalingappa (2004): *"Study Habits, Family Climate, Adjustment and Academic Achievement of Children of Devadasis", Quest in Education, Quarterly Journal*, Vol. 28, No. 4, Oct. 2004, pp. 22-23

Panchalingappa, Shahpur Nagappa (1995): *"An Investigation into the causes of under achievement in secondary school Mathematics", Educational Abstracts*. Vol. 2, No. 1, Jan 2002. p. 37, Abstract No. 50

Panchanathan and Shanmuga Ganesan (1992): *"The Effect of Psychological Stress on Academic Achievement", Journal & Community Guidance and Research*, Vol. 9, No. 2.

Panchanadhan (1999): *"Psuchologist and autoconnecting on the academic achievement of University students". Journal of the Indian Academy of Applied Psychology*, Vol. 25, No. 1-2, pp. 143 & 146.

Pande (1978): *"Interest, aptitude and personality factors as predictors of school achievement" Indian Educational Review* Vol. 13, No. 3, pp. 45 – 47.

Panda (2000): *"Astrology of Factors affecting pupils" Achievement in primary schools of Orissa"* Research Project, Regional Institute of Education, Bhubaneswar; (NCERT; ERIC Funded)

Panda (2000): *"Interest aptitude and personality features as predictors of school achievements" Indian Education Review*, vol. 1, no. 3, pp: 45 – 47.

Panda (2002 a): *"A study of Factors Affecting Pupils Achievement in primary schools of Orissa"*. Research project. RIE, Bhubaneswar, (N C E R T, ERIC funded): *Indian Educational Abstracts*: Vol. 2, No. 2, July 2002, Abstract No: 185, pp. 52-53

Panday and Faiz Ahmad (2008): *"Significance of Difference Between Male an Female Adolescents on Academic Motivation, Intelligence and Socio-economic Status"*, Abstract: *Journal of community Guidance & Research*, March 2008, Vol. 25, No. 1, pp. 34-39.

Patel (1975): *"Study Habits Inventory"*, Ludiana: Psychological Laboratory.

Patel (1981): *"The impact of study Habits of Intellectually Backward pupils upon their academic Achievement". The Progress of Education*, Vol. 56, No. 2, pp.33-37.

Patel (1996): *"Study Habits of Pupils and it's impact upon their Academic Achievement", Indian Educational Abstracts*; Vol 3, Number 1, Jan 2003, Abstract No. 73, p. 57.

Pathak (2007): *MER1 Journal of Education*, Vol.II, Number, II, October, 2007, p.45, Printed and published by Lalit Aggarwal, 53-54. Institutional Area (Opp. D Block), Janakpuri, New Delhi-58.

Pattison and Grive (1984): *"Do spatial skills contribute to sex differences in different types of mathematical problems"; Journal of Educational Psychology*, 76, p. 678-689.

Pavithran and Feroze (1965): *"Influence of socio-economic Factors on the scholastic achievement of Tenth standard of Pathanamthitta educational District" Journal of Educational Research*: Vol. 1, No. 4, pp. 6-12.

Periaswamy (2005): *"Impact of Using Fraction Disc in Teaching of Addition and Subtraction of simple proper Fractions with Same Denominators", Edutracks*, A Monthly Scanner of Trends in Education, Vol. 4, No. 5, Jan. 2005, pp. 23-26.

Philias Olatunde (2010) : *"Students Self Concept and Mathematics achievement in some secondary schools in Southwestern Nigeria". European Journal of Social Sciences.* Vol. 13, No. 1.

Prabha (2004): *"Effect of Direct Instruction on IX Standard Students Achievement in Science", The Educational Review*, Vol. 47, No. 2, Feb. 2004, pp. 28-23.

Prabhu Swamy (2010): *"Social science Achievements among D.Ed trainees : influence of institutions and Locality" Asian Journal of Development Matters* Vol. 4 Issue. 1 Issun 0973 – 9637.

Prakash (2003): *"Temperament and Memory as Determinants of Mathematics of Achievement of Intermediate Students" Educational Abstracts*, Vol.3, Number 2; July 2003, pp. 50-51.

Prakash. (2000): *"A study of Mathematical creativity and Achievement of Elementary school students in Relation to problem solving Ability, Anxiety and Socio-Demographic Variables"*, Ph.D. in Education, Punjab University, Chandigarh.

Premalath sarma (1986): *"Study Habits and Academic achievement Among Rural Girls" Journal of Educational Research and Extension*, Vol. 22, No. 4, pp. 220-224.

Quraishi and Bhat (1986): *"Academic Achievement in Relation to socio economic status, Age and sex" Indian Journal of Psychometric and Education*, Vol. 7, No. 1 and 2, pp. 57-66.

Radhamohan (1998): *"Academic Achievement and certain selected variables: A suggested discriminate Function model" Prospectives in Education*, Vol. 14. No:3 PP. 161-171.

Rahaman (2003): *"A study of Achievement in Mathematics of Eighth Grade Students of Different Ethnic Groups of Nepal", Educational Abstracts:* Vol. 5, No. 1 and 2, Jan and July 2005, p. 35. Abstract No. 41

Rajani (2004): *"Study Habits of inter mediate students in relation to certain Psycho-sociological factors"*. Ph.D in Education, SVU, Tirupati.

Rajendra Mistra (1980): *"A study of attitude towards mathematics of secondary school students"*. (Thesis submitted to Patna University (1978), *Indian Educational Review*, pp. 91-94.

Rajput (1985): *"Academic Achievement as a Function of Some Personality Variables and Socio-economic Factors"*, Ph.D. in Psychology, Gujarat University.

Rama murthy (1993): *"Developing good study habits"* – Hand book Tirupati Sri Venkateswara press.

Ramakumar (1969): *"Self concept and academic University in school subject of prospective"* University entrance Ph.D thesis, Kerala.

Rama Rao and Sinha (1993): *"Female Education and Achievement in Higher Education". Journal of Higher Education*, Vol. 16, No. 2, spring 1993, pp. 293-302.

Ramana Sood (1990): *"A Study of Academic Achievement of Pre-Engineering Students in Relation to Socio-Economic Status", Journal of Educational Research and Extension*, Vol. 26, No. 4, April 1990, pp. 223-230.

Ramana Sood and Dalvinder Kumar (2007): *"Academic Achievement of First Generation Generation learners and Subsequent Generation Learners M.E.R.I, Journal of Education* Vol. II, Number II. October (2007) Editor Pathak. pp. 45-49.

Rama Swamy (1990): *"Study Habits and Academic Achievement Experiments in Education"*; Vol. 18, No.10, pp. 225-259.

Rangaswamy and Visveswaran (1977): *"A comparative study of Academic Achievement of High school sports Men and other students in Coimbatore District", Journal of Educational Research and Extension:* Vol. 13, No: 4, pp. 239-240

Rao (1965): *"A Study of Some Factors Related to Scholastic Achievement"*, Ph.D. Thesis, Delhi University.

Rao (1983): *"A study of some factors related to scholastic achievement"*, Ph.D thesis Delhi University.

Ravindra Basavaiah and Basti (2000): *"Gender Difference in Mathematical Abilities", Educational Abstracts*: Vol. 4, No. 1, Jan. 2004: p. 61, Abstract No: 61.

Rawat and Leela (1995): *"A study of the effect of parental absence on Adjustment, study Habits and academic Development of students of high school classes."* Ph.D in Education, Hemavathi Nandan Bahuguna Garhwal University.

Raymond (1977): *"The Relationship between socio Economic status and academic achievement". Dissertation abstracts international* Vol.37 PP 5067A.

Reddy and Jeevanantham (2004): *"A Study on school effectiveness Factors (Physical, Curricular and Administrative Factors) and their contribution towards enhanced Learning Achievement at Primary Stage" Educational Abstracts*: Vol. 5, No. 1 and 2, Jan and July 2005, p. 8-9: Abstract No. 6.

Regnerus, Mark (2000): *"Shaping school success: Religions Socialization and Educational out comes in Metro Politan Public Schools". Journal for Scientific Study of Religion* Vol. 39, pp. 363-370. From Internet www. Youth and, religion org/Publications.

Richard and Virginia (1967): *"The Relation ship of knowledge and usages of study skill Techniques to academic performance". Journal of Educational Research* Vol. 61, No. 2, pp. 78-80.

Roach (1979): *"Effects of conceptual style Preference, Related cognitive variables and sex on Achievement in Mathematics" British Journal of Educational Psychology*, Vol. 49, pp. 79-82.

Robbie and Fraser (1993): *"Achievement of B.Ed Students"* From the Ph.D Thesis by Dr. C. Manchala (2007) Discovery Publishing House, Delhi, p.103.

Rose and Elizbeth (2001): *"A Longitudanal Study of the Course of Academic Achievement of Urban and Minority gifted and Generl Education Students", ERIC*, Vol. 36, No. 9, Sep. 2001, ED 452 338, p.194.

Ross and Stanley (1955): *"Measurements in to days school"* Prentice-Hall Inc, 70; Newyork P -141.

Rossi. (1950): *"Social Factors in Academic Achievement - a Brief Review"*- as Quoted in educational, Economy and Society, the Free Press-New York Collien- Mac Millan Ltd p. 47.

Ruth Leef (1992): *"Development of Study skills pocket to improve Grades of IX and X students" ERIC*, Vol. 281, No. 3, p. 137.

S.N. Pondey and Md Faiz Ahmad (2008): *"Significance of Difference between Male and Female Adolescents on Academic performance, Achievement motivation and Socio-Economic status", Abstract: Journal of Community Guidance & Research*: ISSN: 09701346, March 2008; Vol. 25, No. 1, pp. 34-39.

Saakshi: daily news paper, Telugu: June I (2008), *"Girls are also great in Mathematics"* p. 31.

Saini (1968): *"A Study of Socio-economic Levels of parents and School Achievement of Their Children"*, M.Ed. Dissertation, Kurukshetra University.

Salim Kumar (1998): *"Impact of Select Factors on Academic Achievement" Experiments in Education*. Vol. 26, No.1, Nov. 1998, pp. 194-197.

Salvin (1990): *"Student team Learning in mathematics"* Boston: Allyn & Bacon. pp. 69-102.

Samuel and Rao (1967): *"An Investigation of study Habit of the Pre-university colleges students in Coimbatore". Journal of Educational Research and Extension,* Vol. 5, No. 4, pp. 18-28.

Sam Willam Bassey and Joshua (2009): *"Gender differences and Mathematics achievement of Rural senior secondary students in cross River state. Nigeria"* Cross River University of Technology Nigeria.

Sanandaj & Jouhari (2010) : *"The effects of Family income on test anxiety and academic achievement among Irranian High school students" Asian Social Sciences,* Vol. 6, No. 6, pp. 1-5

Sarma (1984): *Academic Achievement of School Students vis-à-vis. Their Parents Education. Indian Journal Psychology,* Vol. 59, pp. 33-40.

Satyanandam (1969): *A study of Socio-Economic Status and Academic Achievements.* Govt College of Education, Kurnool; AP. State: India.

Saxena (2001): *"Self-concept as function of socio economic and cultural setting in First Divisionary of High School Students". Indian Journal of Educational Research* Vol. 20, No. 2, pp. 53-58.

Secondary Education Commission (1952 – 53): It is also known as mudaliar.

Selvam and Sundara Valli (2002): *"An Empirical Study of Problems of Higher Secondary Students and their Achievement" Resent Researchers in Educational Psychology,* Vol. 7, No. 324, pp. 102-104.

Sensarma (2004): *"Mathematics Achievement, Predictive Power of different class room Inter Action Variables"* Quest in Education, Vol.XXVIII, No. 2, April 2004, pp.33-44, A *Quarterly Journal,* Published by Vasubai Patel and Dr. Kamal A-Patnakar.

Shakiba – Nejad, Hadi Yell in and David (1983): *"Socio-Economic status, Academic Achievement and Teacher Response" ERIC* Vol.18, No:11. ED.231754, p. 177.

Shamsuddeen (1996): *"The Influence of Socio – Economic Factors on teachers carrier the Primary teacher"* Vol. 2, No. 1, pp. 6-7

Sharma (1976): *"Battery of Tests for the Delta Class in General Science and Mathematics",* Ph.D, Udaipur University.

Sharama (1977): *"The effect of different Techniques of feed back upon the attainment of Teaching skills Related to stimulus variation, Reinforcement, silence and non-verbal cues in the student Teachers".* Unpublished Doctoral Thesis, M.S. University of Baroda.

Sharma and Bhargava (1980): *"Academic Achievement and Prolonged Deprivation" Journal & Education and Psychology,* Vol. 37, p.4.

Sharma, Nidhi (2002): *"A study of the Effect of Parental Involvement and aspirations and Academic Achievement of + 2 Students". Indian Educational Abstracts,* Vol. 3, No: 1, Jan 2003, Abstract No. 78, p. 61

Shukla (1981): *"A comparative study of personality characteristics of innovative and non innovative teachers and their pupils creativity"* Ph.D, Edn, Allahabad University, p. 4

Shukla (1982): *Kothari Commission Report*, Published by Prakash Kendra, Railway crossing, Sitapur Road, Lucknow-226007, p. 61.

Sidney Siegel (1956): *Non Parametric Statistics for Behavioural Sciences,* A text book of McGraw Hill Book Co., Inc, New York.

Sing (1993): *"Academic Achievement motivation of the SC and upper caste Boys"* Paper Presented at 8th Science Congress, Goa.

Sing (2002): *"Encyclopedic Dictionary of Education"* Vol. 1, pp. 11, 132, 215, 219, 243, 283, 478, 526.

Sinha (1966): *"A Psychological Analysis of Some Factors Associated with Success and Failure in University Examination-intelligence, Anxiety and Adjustment of Academic Achievers and Non- achievers" Psychological Studies,* Vol.11, No. 2, pp. 69-88.

Sinha (1972): From, *"Study Habits of High School Pupils in Relation to Certain Psycho-sociological Factors"*, by M.T.V.Nagaraju, 2001,Unpublished, Ph.D Thesis, S.V.U, Tirupati.

Slemmer, Gerald (1997): *"The impact of a Tutorial policy on the Academic Achievement of Extra Curricular Participants", Dissertation Abstracts International,* Vol. 58, No. 3, Sep. 1997, DA9724497.

Smith (1961): *Personality and adjustments,* Newyork McGraw-Hill.

Smith, Paul (1966): *"Personality of students Whose Fathers are Professional and Non-Professional Workers", California Journal of Research,* Vol.17, No.1, Jan.1966; pp. 22-25.

Sood (1999): *"A study of creativity, Problem solving Ability and personality characteristics as correlates of Mathematical Achievement of students of Residential and Non-Residential schools"* Ph.D in Education, Punjab, University; Chandigarh.

Soundaravalli (2001): *"Effect of various problems of Std. XII Students on Their Academic Achievement", The Educational Review,* Vol. 107, No. 1, Jan. 2001, pp. 12-13.

Sundaravalli (2002): *"An Empirical study of problems of Higher Secondary Students and their Achievement", Recent Researchers in Educational Psychology,* Vol. 7, No. 324, pp. 102-104.

Srivastava (1967): *"An Investigation into the Factors Related to Educational Under Achievement"*, Ph.D Thesis, Patna University.

SriVastava Sigh and Thakur (1980): *"Examination Anxiety and Academic Achievement as a function of socio Economic Status" Psychological Studies* 25, 2, pp. 108-110.

Srinivasan and Arivudayappan: (2004): *"Interest and Achievement of Eighth Standard Pupils in Social Sciences in Nilgiri District" Experiments in Education,* Vol. 32, No. 1, Jan 2004, pp. 8-12.

Stella and Purushotham (1993): *"Study Habits of under Achievers", Journal of Educational Research and Extension,* Vol. 29, No. 4, pp. 206-214.

Subramanyam and Sreenivasa Rao (2008): *"Academic Achievement and Emotional Intelligence of Secondary School Children". Journal of Community Guidance and Research* 2008. Vol. 25, No. 2, pp. 224-228.

Sudamma (1973): *"A study of the Effect of Library use on Academic Achievement of Post graduate students"* Ph.D. Thesis, MSU, Baroda.

Sudha and Sinha (1980): *"Effect of school system on the competence of secondary school students", Indian Educational Review*, January, pp. 62-77.

Sukhia Mehrotra and Mehrotra (1980): *Elements of Educational Research.* A text book, Allied publishers, Bombay India, pp. 101-102.

Sumangala (1998): *"Effect of tutoring at home on achievement in Mathematics of secondary school pupils", Experiments in Education*, September, Vol. 26, No. 9, pp. 155-158.

Sundararajan and Dhandapani (1991): *"Attitude of higher secondary students of Pondichery Territory towards the study of mathematics and their achievement in it". Experiments in Education*, Vol. XIV, No.9, September, pp. 249 – 260.

Suneel Sumar Sing, Shaheen Malik and Sing (2003): *"Achievement difference in class II students in Maths, with regard to Area, Gender and social grounds during B.A.S and M.A.S in Gonda District". The Educational Review*, March, Vol. 46, No. 3, pp. 55-57.

Suneetha and Mayuri (2002): *"A study on Age and Gender Differences on Factors Affecting High Academic Achievement"*, Journal of community Guidance and Research, Vol.18 (2); 197-208-from *Indian Educational Abstracts*, Vol. 2, July 2002, Abstract No. 199. p. 64

Taneja (1991): *Dictionary of Education*, Anmol Publications New Delhi, pp. 3, 4, 224.

Tenibiaje Joseph (2009): *"Influence of family size and family Birth order on academic performance of adolescents in higher institution". Pakisthan Journal of Social Sciences*, volume 6 Issue 3, pp. 110-114.

Thivari (1980): *"The effect of anxiety and aspiration on academic achievement of adolescent bys and girls" Asian Journal of Psychology and Education*, Vol. 6 No. 1

Thomas (2005): *"Comparing theories of Child development"*. California Thomson and Wadworth.

Thomas & Robert (2006): *"Inter relationships among student's study activities, self concept of academic ability and achievement as a function of characteristics of high school biology courses" Applied Cognitive Psychology*, Vol.7, issue 6. pp. 499- 532.

Thorndike (1952): From *"A study of Academic achievement of pre-engineering students in Relation to socio-economic status"* by Ramana Sood, *Journal of Educational Research and Extension*, Vol. 26, No. 4, April 1990, pp. 223-230.

Tiwari (1982): *"Study Habits and Scholastic Performnce at Three Levels of Education"*, Unpublished Ph.D Thesis, BHU,Varanasi.

Tuli (1980): *"Study Habits as Correlates of Achievement in Mathematics", Journal of Educational Psychology*, Vol. 38, No 3, pp. 141-148.

Tuilford (1950): *Fundamental Statistics in Psychology and Education.* International Student Studies Edition, New York McGraw-Hill.

Umadevi (2009): *Relationship between Emotional Intelligence, Achievement motivation and academic achievement.* Edutracks Neel Kamal Publications, Koti, Hyd Vol. 8, No. 12, p. 31-35.

Upadya (2003): *"Effect of Constructivism on mathematics Achievement of Grade students in Nepal", Educational Abstracts*: Vol. 4, No. 1, Jan 2004, Abstract No. 27, p. 28.

Vamadevappa (2002): *"An Investigation in to Factors causing under achievement in Biology among pre-university students"*. Ph.D in education, Kuvempu university; from *Indian Educational Abstracts* Vol. 2, No. 2 July 2002, Abstract. 175, p. 43.

Vamadevappa (2005): "An Investigation into Factors counseling under achievement in Biological among pre-University Ph.D."

Varghese (1995): *"School facilities and Learner achievement: Towards a Methodology of Analysing School Facilities in India". Perspectives in Education*, Vol. 11(2), 97-108, *Indian Educational Abstracts*: p. 29-30.

Varma (1996): *"Test Anxiety and study Habits; A study of the main and interaction Effects on Academic Achievement" Journal of Applied Psychology*, Vol. 33, No. 2, pp. 55-61.

Vasantha Ram Kumar (1969): *"Self-concept and Achievement on school subject of prospective university entrance"*. Ph.D Thesis, Kerala University

Venkataiah (1980): *"A study of achievement of students of different Socio – Economic status", Journal of the Institute of Education Research*, Vol. 4, No. 3 pp. 42-45

Venkataiah and Jayachandrama Naidu. (1990): *"Who are better non-starters in non formal education centres in India". Educational Review Quarterly*, Vol. 25, No. 3, July 1990, pp. 32-39.

Verma and Kumar (1999): *"A correlation study between study habits and Achievement in different school courses", Educational Abstracts*: Vol. 3, No. 2 July 2003, p. 82, Abstract No. 206.

Verma and Gupta (1990): *"Influence of home Environment on children's Scholastic Achievement". Journal of Education & Psychology*; Vol. 47. No. 3-4 Oct-Jan 1989-90, pp. 159-164.

Vijay Kumar Sethi (1990): *"Personality Patterns of High Achieving and low Achieving students in professional courses" Indian Educational Review Quarterly*, Vol. 25, No. 1, Jan 1990, pp. 92-94

Vijaya Lakshmi and Hemalatha Natesan (1992): *"Factors Influencing Academic Achievement"*, Research High lights *Journal of Avanashilingam Institute of Home Science and Higher education for women, Quarterly*, Vol. 2, No. 1, Jan 1992, pp. 62-67.

Viswanathan Nair Pand Bindu (1998): *"Association Between certain Demographic variables and Discrepant Achievement in six school projects of secondary pupils" Experiments in Education* vol. 26, No. 7, pp. 13-20.

Vyas (1982): *"Relationship of selected factors with Teaching success of prospective teachers of Rajasthan"* Ph.D. in Education, Rajasthan University, from fourth Survey of Research in Education: Abstract No. 1239, p. 854.

Walberg &Paik (1997): *"Home Environments for Learning"*, In Walberg, & Heartel, (Ed,) Psychological and Educational Practice, Berkeley, Mccutchan Publishing, pp. 365-368.

Walf Richard (1996): *"Family Learning Environments and Students outcomes": A follow-up-study"* Journal of Negro Education; Vol. 64, No. 3, pp. 354-359.

Wash Burne (1959): *"Socio-Economic status, urbanism and Academic performance in college", Journal of Educational Research* (APA), 93, 4, pp 130-137.

Watkins Haltie And Astilla (1984): *"Approaches to study by Filipino students- A longitudinal Investigation" The British Journal of Educational Psychology.*

Webster's' New Dictionary and Treasures (1995): *"A Dictionary"* Promotional Sales book, Inc; Printed in U.S.A, pp. 337- 421.

Winner (1971): *"Statistical Principles in Experimental Design"*, New York, McGraw-Hill.

Wiseman Stephans (1964): *"Education and Environment"* University Press: Manchester. p. 89

Wiseman (1967): *"The Manchester survey in children and other primary schools"*: The plowder Report: Vol. 2, London: Her Majesty's' Stationary office, p. 90.

Wood (1999): *"Creating a context for argument in mathematics class", Journal for Research in Mathematics Education*: 30, pp. 171-91.

Woodruf (1940): *"Study Habits of Intermediate students in Relation to certain psycho-sociological Factory"* by Rajani Nov.2004 Unpublished Ph.D Thesis, Dept of Education, SVU, Tirupati, p. 47.

Wrenn (1933): *Study Habits Inventory,* Stanford University press, California.

Wrenn and Hamber (1941): *"Study Habits Associated with High and low scholarship". J. Edu. Psy*, Vol. 32, No. 8, pp. 611-615.

Yate (1965): *"Statistics in Education and Psychology"*, New York. The MacMillon.

Yeh-Hsiang Yeng (1991): *"Achievement in History as Related to Academic achievement Motivation"*. By Krishna Moorthy, *Experiments in Education*, Vol. 28, No.3, March 2000, pp. 47-52.

Young, Deirdra (1999): *"Self-esteem in rural schools. Dreams and Aspirations" ERIC*, Vol. 34, No. 9, Sep. 1999. Ed. 429789, p. 117.

Index

S